Sex and Age
as
Principles of
Social Differentiation

Association of Social Anthropologists

A Series of Monographs

A.S.A. MONOGRAPH 17

Sex and Age as Principles of Social Differentiation

Edited by

J. S. LA FONTAINE

Department of Anthropology
London School of Economics
England

1978

ACADEMIC PRESS

London · New York · San Francisco

A Subsidiary of Harcourt Brace Jovanovich, Publishers

ACADEMIC PRESS INC. (LONDON) LTD.
24/28 Oval Road,
London NW1

United States Edition published by
ACADEMIC PRESS INC.
111 Fifth Avenue
New York, New York 10003

Library of Congress Catalog Card Number: 78–54535
ISBN: 0–12–433050–9

Printed in Great Britain by
Whitstable Litho Ltd., Whitstable, Kent.

PREFACE

The papers presented here represent six out of eight papers delivered at the Conference of the Association of Social Anthropologists at Swansea in April 1977. The local convener was Dr. J. Loudon to whom I am indebted for taking all the organisation off my hands and so allowing me to concentrate on inviting contributions, finding discussants and chairmen of sessions. This conference differed slightly from those of earlier years; in order to obtain as full a discussion as possible I limited the numbers of papers and each was presented in a single seminar with a more extended discussion led by a discussant. The papers were not circulated in advance although a summary was available to all participants. For this reason, the papers had to be limited to what could be read in an hour. That the format turned out to be as much of a success as it did is largely due to the efforts of participants, discussants and chairmen to whom I offer my thanks. Papers were amended in the light of the discussions so that the versions presented here differ slightly from the originals and unhappily not all of them could be included. The Introduction is based on the summary I presented as the closing session.

My aim in bringing together what appeared at first sight to be rather different topics was to focus in a general way on the nature of principles of ascription. Much of the recent literature on women in society has done this but from a limited point of view. The frank avowal of an intention to change the place of women in society which is made by several authors in this field does not alter the inherent bias in their work, salutary though this has been in drawing attention to neglected areas of investigation. As an East Africanist, I was also aware of the rather narrow regional focus in which comparative discussion of age-systems was viewed, partly through the reluctance of others to master the very complex ethnography involved. I had had the opportunity to participate in a conference on such systems held in Manchester the previous year and realised how much of general theoretical value risked being lost to a wider anthropological audience. I hoped that the inclusion of similar material in the conference would stimulate interest in what are only more complex developments of a common principle of organisation. Particular thanks are due here to Dr. Paul Baxter whose general command of the topic is unrivalled. To me the comparison of these two principles of social differentiation has proved most rewarding. There are many questions raised which have still to be answered. A similar approach to problems of kinship ascription for example, as one participant suggested, might well be rewarding. I hope that the publication of these articles may stimulate others to follow up their ideas.

I have had a great deal of help in preparing this volume. Gill Short has retyped two chapters and sections of others and several people, including Mrs. Hilda Jarrett, have typed many sections more than once. To Dr. Anne Akeroyd who did much of the final editing I offer my thanks. Academic Press have been the most tolerant and helpful of publishers. Finally, to the contributors, who have borne much impertinent advice, high-handed editing and delays on my part, I am happy to acknowledge a particular debt of gratitude.

London   Jean La Fontaine
March 1978

CONTENTS

INTRODUCTION

J.S. LA FONTAINE

The main premiss underlying much of the recent and extensive
literature on the social and symbolic significance of the division
between the sexes is that differences in physiology (natural differences) are universally transformed into cultural inequality. The
'universal asymmetry of the sexes' is seen as a means by which
women are classified as inferior and excluded from the exercise of
power in society. Earlier writers such as Durkheim, Linton and
Lowie associated the sexual division with divisions based on
differences of age as social universals, but the two principles have
not been discussed within the same framework for many years. As a
result the theoretical contexts in which each has been considered
differ very considerably, although age differentiation is as much a
cultural transformation of a process of human physiology, ageing,
as sex differences are a transformation of the physiological process
of reproduction. Both social principles select significant features of
these processes in order to characterise oppositions, to which may
be attributed a whole range of characteristics not inherent in the
initial dyadic contrast. Thus among the Laymi of Bolivia male and
female may be associated with different crops and domestic
animals, with valley and mountain, hot and cold (O. Harris, this
volume) or, in Pirá-Paraná society with hunting and agriculture,
meat and manioc, public affairs and domestic life (C. Hugh-Jones,
this volume). The association of opposed pairs of concepts with
male and female is usually presented as evidence of further cultural
underlining of the 'natural' inequality of men and women but as
Harris's paper shows, this is not always the case. Among the Laymi
of Bolivia male and female symbols together form a model of
unity which serves as an ideal for domestic organisation but which
accounts for only part of the actual behaviour of Laymi men and
women.

It thus seems important to distinguish between concepts of male

and female which use male and female as material symbols to
represent more abstract qualities and the expected behaviour in male
and female roles. Wallman (1976) has distinguished between sex class,
the basic dichotomisation of human behaviour and sex roles. She
points out that in any society the relation between sexual identity
and the allocation of social roles is complex; some roles may only be
undertaken by persons of the appropriate sex but others, though
classified as male or female roles, may be assumed by members of the
other sex without necessarily changing the sex-linking of the role. An
example of the former type is the role of mother, that of the latter,
breadwinner for the domestic group, which is a male role that is
being assumed nowadays by increasing numbers of women. Yet
other roles may change associations, becoming associated with the
other sex or losing any link with the division into sex classes.
Symbolic elaboration of sexual differences is associated with what
Wallman calls sex class, male and female, although in many societies
certain roles seem to epitomise that division.

This distinction has long been made in the work of anthropologists
concerned with age-differentiation. The classification of men as
'Warriors' (moran)[1] and 'Elders' and the association of the two
classes with fighting and domestic life respectively does not mean
that men not classified as warriors do not fight (see below p. 173)
and the extent to which marriage is a privilege reserved for the class
of elders is related to the internal dynamics of such systems and is
not universal. Among the Arusha (Gulliver 1963) men marry and
establish their families before or after the promotion of their class
to elder status; the timing depends on individual circumstances such
as wealth and position in the natal domestic group. Thus the description of the classes as those of elders and of warriors refers, not to a
prescriptive rule allocating the occupations of individual men, but to
a general division of life into stages and a system ranking such stages.

In discussing differentiation by sex or age, we are thus faced, first
with a conceptual model which establishes distinctions based on the
perception of significant 'natural' differences. Symbolic elaboration
may associate these distinctions and the oppositions they create with
other concepts of varying degrees of abstraction from the natural
and social environment. The clusters of contrasted qualities are
accorded the status of intrinsic ineluctable 'facts of life' by association
with what are asserted to be natural differences. That these are, on
the contrary, 'facts of culture' has been established beyond question.
The controversy surrounding the beliefs of the Trobriand Islanders
and certain Australian Aboriginal groups has indicated that there is no

universal interpretation of the nature of human reproduction. Barnes has clearly shown (1973) that, in England, beliefs in the male part in conception predated any reliable knowledge of the physiology involved and were indeed a stimulus to research in that field. So the biological features which are seen to determine sexual differences may vary from culture to culture. In this country some specialists in geriatric medicine would argue that the idea that senility is the result of the breaking down of the brain in old age is a folk myth that brings about the behaviour it purports to explain.[2] There is no biological determinant of old age as such. Cross-cultural studies of child-bearing have shown quite considerable variations in the behaviour expected at different ages; in all societies individuals mature at different rates. Such variations in what are significant 'natural differences' make it clear that we are dealing with principles of social differentiation, that is with the classification of human beings.

The classification of human beings differs from the classification of animals or plants in that it constrains the behaviour of those who are classified. Members of a society identify themselves and others in terms of the distinctions and act in relation to these identifications. The behaviour of individual men and women is moulded by the ideas of what men and women 'are' and how they 'ought' to behave. However, the relation between the classification of persons, the general features of behaviour which the classifications appear to entail and the allocation of social roles is by no means as clear and simple as has sometimes been assumed.

Differentiation by age is not only a social mechanism which resembles sexual differentiation in the manner in which it is constructed, the two principles co-exist in all societies. As Radcliffe-Brown long ago pointed out, distinctions of sex and generation form the basis of systems of kinship terminology. Many systems also rank siblings according to birth order or relative age (see the significance of this latter principle among the Laymi discussed below). Generation and birth order are two of the ways in which age serves as a principle of differentiation and ranking, just as emphasis on male or female kin receives complex recognition in kinship systems (R. Abrahams, this volume). However, the different theoretical perspectives with which the two principles have been analysed depend, in large part, on ignoring one in favour of the other. This approach might be justified as a heuristic device were it not for the fact that the two principles are, in some cases, logically interconnected.

Among the Hadza of Tanzania where a collective opposition between male and female has been alleged (Bloch 1977) to be the sole form of hierarchy, the transition to adult status is, for both sexes, the subject of initiation rites, so that one can say that the identification of adults as men and women depends on the ritual recognition of their change of status from immature to mature. If sexual function in the reproductive process is the criterion for defining male and female, rather than anatomical differences, then maturity is logically entailed. Uninitiated Hadza boys, like women, are excluded from the ritual eating of 'god's meat' which is the focus of male ceremonies emphasising the opposition of the sexes. The relationship between the sexes depends on the existence of a ritualised distinction between mature and immature.

In this volume, Schildkrout's paper shows how the characteristic Hausa pattern of male/female relations in Kano cannot be maintained without the existence of a class of persons, children (or servants in the case of the wealthy) who are exempt from the rules establishing strict spatial segregations which reflects sex differentiation in this urban, Moslem society. However, Hausa children do not form a sexually undifferentiated category. While age is the primary source of ranking among children, they are classed as male and female and taught behaviour appropriate to their sex. Thus male and female as identities are independent of age, but the transition to adult status modifies the significance of the distinction by relating it to adult sexuality. Moreover, while relations between adult men and women are generally conceptualised as unequal, the principle may be modified by age or rank in particular social contexts. While in general men are superior to women, an older woman may expect deference from a younger kinsman as well as younger kinswomen and from male inferiors or servants.

Similarly, age distinctions have often been considered in isolation from the sexual divisions with which they are articulated. An extreme case is presented by the treatment of the most elaborate form of age differentiation, the age-set systems of eastern Africa. Until recently the fact that such systems depend on an asymmetry between the sexes was mentioned briefly if at all, yet, as Almagor clearly demonstrates (this volume) for Dassanetch society relationships between the age-divisions in male society are maintained and expressed by the exchange of women. In this context it is significant that the most important rite de passage of the male life-cycle, *dimi*, requires for its celebration the existence of a daughter growing up to be some other man's wife. Even those societies which show a less elaborate form of age-differentiation or merely a simple distinction between immature and mature, marked by initiation, can be seen to combine it with sex differentiation. Thus, to date, the primacy of distinctions based on age or sex in any ethnographic context would seem to reflect in large measure the interest of the anthropologist, for the question of their interrelation and relative weighting is ignored.

Yet the interdependence of these two principles is clearly demonstrated in Sansom's article. The people with whom he is concerned are Australian aborigines, drawn from a wide variety of linguistic and cultural backgrounds, whose common language is a form of English. They have their base in a squatter camp in Darwin from which they travel to work and live on stock-farms or in other similar urban settlements within a large territory in northern Australia. The members of 'mobs' or camp groups are structured by four terms: ol' fellow, young fellow, marrit woman (pensioner) and girl. The four classes so designated are clearly combinations of age and sex classifications, with the decisive boundary between old and young being drawn by publicly recognised cohabitation, that is in their terms 'marriage'. When a marriage breaks up, the respective partners change status; a married woman becomes a girl, no matter what her age or the number of children she has had. A man becomes a young fellow;[3] elderly unmarried men may be accorded the epithet old, though not the honorific connotations of the title masterful man. Sansom shows how the economic and demographic shifts in the camp require periodic redefinitions of marital status in order to maintain a distribution of resources and preserve social order. Power and authority rest in the hands of one or two old men and their female allies, wives and kinswomen who are pensioners, possessors of a regular income from child allowances as well as from their husbands. Sansom's conclusions indicate the priority of sexual differentiation over age-ranking.

It is not easy to compare anthropological findings on age-differentiated systems and on sexual differentiation because they have developed different theoretical concerns. There seem to be two strands in recent writing on sexual differentiation; an analysis of the symbolism associated with male and female, usually but not always in ritual contexts, and an exploration of the degree to which women in any particular society have positions of authority or effective power. These two features are usually distinguished, for it is generally recognised that women may have informal influence and control of resources in societies where they are 'officially' excluded from legitimate office. Age-differentiation has not been much considered in symbolic terms although its relation to the allocation of power and authority has been a central issue. However, the approaches to each topic have developed without insights gained in the other so that convening the conference on which this book is based seemed justified in terms of promoting communication. However, I think that anthropologists stand to gain theoretically from the juxtaposition of a variety of approaches to these issues, as I hope the following discussion will serve to indicate even if I raise questions which are left unanswered.

In part, the discussion of sexual differentiation has suffered from the attempt to redress what has been seen as a male bias in anthropology. Thus Ardener (1972: 136) has written of: 'a real imbalance. We are, for practical purposes in a male world. The study of women is on a level little higher than the study of the ducks and fowls they commonly own'. The study of sexual differentiation has often been confused with the study of women with the result that perceptions of the inferiority of women have coloured both discussions of the symbolism of sexual differentiation (only women are perceived as defined in 'biological' terms) and the relationship between such symbolism and the allocation of social roles (all men are seen as dominating all women).

It is by now well established that male and female are important symbols in many, if not all, societies. In this book, the significance of this pair of contrasted categories is shown in a small-scale society based on slash and burn agriculture, the Pirá-Paraná of Colombia (C. Hugh-Jones) a peasant community in Bolivia (O. Harris) and the urban society of Hausa in Kano, Nigeria (E. Schildkrout). At the conference on which the articles were first presented James Woodburn gave a stimulating account of the varying significance of distinctions between the sexes in hunting and gathering societies. In these articles and the large literature that has accumulated, male and female have been shown to be associated with the most important ideas and activities in social life. Ardener (1972) has shown how the distinction between the village and 'the wild' is associated with male and female qualities among the Bakwerri of the Cameroons, Rosaldo (1974) has convincingly demonstrated the implications of association of male and female with hunting agriculture, the two main economic pursuits of the Ilongot and other examples are easy to find. In this volume Hugh-Jones, in an intricate analysis, shows the very complex interweaving of the associations which male and female assume in this particular society where the residential units are composed of men who share common descent and a common language and women who come from other descent groups and speak other, different languages. Among the Laymi of Bolivia, features of the environment and key domestic buildings are classified as male and female, while among the urban Hausa the very common association of women with the domestic sphere and men with the 'outside world' takes on an added dimension of significance from the institution of purdah which confines respectable adult women to their houses most of the time.

The initial stimulus for this type of analysis came, as Ardener has pointed out (Ardener 1972: 141) from Levi-Strauss. However, it has its roots in an earlier Comtian tradition which conceived society as consisting of the imposition of distinctions on a relatively unordered world. The bounded categories constructed in this way are ideas which relate to distinctions at a number of levels, between persons, groups and offices but also in more abstract fashion between abstract ideas and qualities such as 'nature' and 'culture' and those I have listed above. Levi-Strauss has pointed to the distinction between sisters and wives as the basis for all social life, creating, in this distinction, the necessity to exchange women which forms the basis of structures of kinship. Later in his work on myth he has stressed as primary the division between nature and culture, which is fundamental to human thought. In a paper on the female life-crisis rituals of the Gisu, I attempted to use this approach to show that, for the Gisu, women's reproductive powers, and women themselves as sisters and wives, could be represented as the 'nature' over which men strove to exert control in the ritual of a patrilineal society.

However useful that approach might have been in understanding Gisu ritual, it is limited by the fact that, as Levi-Strauss himself has pointed out (1967: 12), both pairs of opposites are concepts within a culture, not analytical distinctions. It seems more useful to approach an understanding of sexual differentiation by considering first the logical implications of the division between the sexes as an elementary structure, that is as a model with implications in a number of conceptual and behavioural contexts.

The features of human biology which are essential to sexual differentiation are physiological differences. The opposition rests on a perception of the specialised reproductive functions of the sexes and their essential complementarity. The sexual division of labour reinforces this concept of interdependence just as the association with biological functions makes the social allocation of tasks appear ineluctable. However, the 'biological' facts are a selection from the natural process and their formulation into a cultural concept ignores others which are significant. There is no biological demonstration of the physical link between father and child; paternity is thus a purely social construct.[4] Further, the attachment of women to their children is related to the physiology of suckling, a fact which often receives cultural recognition. No such attachment necessarily binds men to their children, or indeed to women beyond the period of sexual attraction. From this we must conclude that the joint care of off-spring and social responsibility for them is social in nature and must be more firmly imposed on the male than the female. Where children have a socio-economic value, paternity may be sought after but recent work (Macfarlane 1978, Woodburn conference ms) has made it clear that this situation is by no means universal. Later I shall try and indicate how the allocation of authority is another mechanism whereby men are attached to domestic groups, yet associated with wider concerns. Here I merely wish to underline the fundamentally social or cultural nature of the idea of 'natural differences', an idea which entails the notion of specialisation and the division of labour.

As Mauss pointed out over fifty years ago (Mauss 1926), the social division of labour implies exchange. Exchange creates and maintains a social relationship. Thus the conceptualisation of sexual differences as specialisation, entailing mutually necessary functions in economic life as well as in reproduction, establishes mutual interdependence. The concept of *chachawarmi* discussed by O. Harris in this volume illustrates this very well. This Laymi term is composed of the terms for man (*chacha*) and woman (*warmi*). It refers primarily to the household but by extension to other opposed concepts such as kitchen/storeroom, high and low zones and Laymi society as a whole; it also implies a unity which is productive. Each element of a pair is inadequate alone but no hierarchy as such is implied. Inequality, competition and conflict are symbolised by the relations between older and younger brother, although some com-plementarity also enters into this concept for while the elder brother is senior, the younger brother inherits land and must distribute shares among his siblings. Complementarity between man and woman however, being based on differences, precludes competition. This model of egalitarian unity does not, as Harris argues, explain the incidence of violence, when men may beat their wives, however well it represents the constitution of a household and the different rights and duties of spouses. It does, however, emphasise the point I wish to make here: that sexual differentiation implies the mutual depen-dence of specialisation.

The Barasana discussed by C. Hugh-Jones represent adult relations between the sexes as mutual interdependence which structures the daily round of activities, distinguishing day from night, morning from afternoon and domestic from public. She also notes that pepper which transforms male and female products into food and drink, also incorporates strangers into the community and is a symbol for the conjunction of the sexes in sexual intercourse. The structural relationship underlying these metaphors is similar to that represented by *chachawarmi* and it is rendered explicit in the initiation ritual of a boy whose first social act as a mature adult is to establish an exchange relationship with a 'sister', representing the future exchange which will establish his marriage.

If the male/female dyad represents a model of the necessary conjunction of opposites or of exchange, it may also serve as a model for inequality and I would accept that it often does. However, it is clearly a mistake to argue from the relations of spouses to an interpretation of symbolism as though these particular domestic roles were identical with the categorical relations of male and female, for men and women are related in ways other than the conjugal bond. This is interestingly brought out by the case of the Hadza, described by Woodburn, among whom the conjugal tie is fragile and easily broken by either husband or wife but the opposition of the sexes is a powerful social force. Thus it is clear that the relation between the complex symbolism associated with sexual differentiation and other aspects of social life is more subtle and complex than the teleological argument from conjugal roles would imply.

Further, it is worth considering the neglected half of this dyad, for in the recent literature men are seen as freed from the confines of the domestic group and less hampered by an identity which derives from male physiology. Yet the use of biology to legitimise socially derived expectations of temperament, behaviour and character, as well as roles, must apply to both sexes, as indeed Mead's work emphasised (Mead 1950).

In most of the recent literature it is accepted that women are defined as bearers of children (Rosaldo and Lamphere 1974: 6, 8; Ortner 1974: 73). The possibility that men are equally defined by their reproductive capacity is not usually considered. Yet in many, if not most, societies they are recognised as begetters of children; even among the matrilineal Bemba girls are taught in their initiation rites to honour husbands who will give them children. Male potency is the conceptual counterpart of female pregnancy and receives symbolic emphasis in ritual contexts in many societies, e.g. among the Ndembu (Turner 1967: 65). Among the Maasai of Kenya it is believed that young girls should have sexual intercourse for this will develop their reproductive powers, cause their breasts to swell and the menses begin (Llewelyn-Davies: in press). In this formulation there is a parallel with pregnancy, also the result of male potency.

Alternatively, it is accepted that the physical strength of men is connected with their universal association with weapons, with hunting and killing (Woodburn, conference paper). This, as Woodburn pointed out at the conference, gives men the monopoly of the means of physical coercion. There is also a clear symbolic association between spears, arrows and guns and the phallus; hence hunting is somehow 'appropriate' for men. (It is also clear that hunting is socially defined as an activity; when women kill small game it is not 'hunting'.) Moreover success in these pursuits is uncertain, as is male potency. It thus comes as no surprise to learn that various sexual taboos are commonly linked with hunting and warfare and that the success and honour of men may be seen as threatened by the sexuality of women. Yet little attention has been paid to the problem of linking male identity as defined by biological characteristics with the assignment of social roles to men.

Sansom's article in this volume gives us interesting insights into one such set of links. The organisation of the urban aboriginal mob depends on the allocation of resources among cooking units but also on protection for its members and particularly its women. The role of Masterful Man, or leader, depends on its incumbent being able to organise a defensive force of fighting men for this purpose. Sansom discusses the case of an older man who was unable to provide this protection, for the fighting men of his group refused to cooperate, so that men from other groups were able to threaten and assault the women with impunity. The senior women of the mob, those with secure financial resources which were important to the leader, went to him and forced him to relinquish the young wife, who was the cause of the disaffection of the young men. For the leader it was the choice between his private interests, the marriage and his position in the group; the marriage broke up. The role of men as both attackers and defenders of women is also a significant element in Laymi society (Harris, this volume); in this society a woman may be defended by her brother against the beatings administered by her husband, against which she may not defend herself.[5] Other Laymi women may sympathise but unlike Hadza women they will not go to the aid of a woman who is beaten. The strength of men is thus manifest in their power to beat women or defend them from such attacks but that this is a cultural expectation rather than an inherent male quality can be seen from its varying incidence: Harris states that not all men beat their wives and some are prone to this behaviour more often than others.

The symbolism of age-differentiation has barely been discussed, in spite of the remark of Southall's, quoted by Baxter and Almagor: that 'age-organisations are particularly compatible with elaborate symbolic identifications' (1970: 32). Analyses of initiation have usually entailed an examination of the social roles from which the immature are excluded and to which initiates may be admitted but age classes have not often been discussed in terms similar to those in which the symbolic elaboration of sexual differentiation has been so fruitfully analysed. In discussing the rituals in which Samburu moran are dominated by the elders, Spencer has drawn a contrast between the stereotypes of moran and elder which shows some parallels with the kind of oppositions which often appear in discussions of the symbolic associations of male/female divisions (Spencer 1965, 1973). Thus the elders are said to be imbued with respect (*nkanyit*), which moran lack. Moran, by contrast, are said to be beautiful, strong and attractive to women; they are brave and fierce, while elders are wise and prudent. Moran express their easily aroused feelings in aggressive behaviour while elders curb theirs and seek to settle disputes not in fighting but by negotiation. Moran are associated with the bush outside domestic life, elders with the homesteads. Thus qualities of character, the division into an ordered social sphere and the wildness of nature as well as expected modes of behaviour are all linked to this division of adult manhood into two classes, in a manner similar to that by which the two classes of male and female are contrasted (and including some of the same characteristics differently attributed).

There is less information about the stereotype of boyhood in these systems but in fact the Samburu/Maasai system distinguishes three main classes of males: boys, moran and elders, ordered in a progressive sequence of increasing social prestige. Boys are uncircumcised, may not have sexual relations and do not carry spears. Moran are circumcised, carry spears, may have mistresses among unmarried girls, but may not marry. The effect of such categorisation is to distinguish between adulthood as the presence or absence of sexual activities (Boys/Moran) and full social responsibility as head of a domestic group (Moran/Elders). The hierarchy of classes also embodies the precept that sexual activity and family responsibility or the procreation of children are distinct aspects of life. It is worth noting as well that it is marriage which gives a man the right of dominance for the relationship of Samburu lovers is one of equality; men may be twenty years older than their wives but are closer in age to the girls who are their mistresses, so that age is also significant in the more unequal relation.

In discussing Gisu initiation (La Fontaine 1977) I indicated that youth and age are presented in the ritual as symbols of the opposed qualities of physical strength or force and the authority of wisdom. I argued that male initiation rites among the Gisu are as much a dramatic performance demonstrating the superiority of traditional wisdom and authority over youth and physical powers as they are the means of conferring adult status on young men. The Gisu ritual enacts the transformation of boy into man and in so doing demonstrates the effectiveness of the ritual powers of the elders. The successful outcome is seen partly as the result of the organised co-operation of the community directed by the elders and particularly as the result of their ritual knowledge. The boys who are initiated by the ritual both experience and express the underlying principles of age-differentiation: that life is an ordered series of stages, that experience confers authority and demands respect, that traditional knowledge is the basis of the elders power. Two further points are of relevance to this discussion: first, that immaturity and maturity are ranked stages in the life-cycle. Their relationship is thus one of intrinsic hierarchy, not complementarity. Secondly, boys are equated with women and men with the role of husband, that is initiation confers domestic authority on men.[6] Gisu initiation rituals thus link the principles of age and sex differentiation in a manner that establishes men as both superior to, and legitimately exercising authority over, women. Gisu recognise this when they claim that circumcision endows men with the power to command women.

Inequality is intrinsic to a system of age differentiation, that is a system in which differences of age are made socially significant by formal marking. All societies seem to break up the life-cycle into a series of stages rather than considering it as an undifferentiated flow. Terms for different points on the life-span indicate, not only observed regularities in human development but also theories about their significance for social behaviour. In her article in this volume, Schildkrout indicates how the Hausa expect different degrees of social consciousness at different stages of childhood, with associated expectations about behaviour. What is more important for Hausa children however and in Hausa society generally is relative age-ranking; similarly among the Laymi inequality and hierarchy are represented in terms for older and younger brothers. Neither age-grading nor ranking by relative age generalise the principle of age differentiation into a system of classification by age, although in both age-differences indicate inequality.[7]

Where all individuals are classified by their position in an ordered series of age-based classes, there is an elementary structure which is comparable to that established by sexual differentiation. The simplest system is one that is constituted by two classes: child and adult, immature and mature, but some societies show a much more elaborated set of divisions as the last two articles in this volume demonstrate. The common fact in all such differentiating systems is that the boundaries are marked by ritual and that the classes thus constituted are associated with contrasted sets of behaviour and moral qualities. One effect of such structuring as Baxter and Almagor point out (p. 164) is to order time into a series of jerks, as each cohort of individuals moves through the system. Another, which has been extensively discussed, is to create a hierarchy from a 'natural' process.

The elementary structure of age-differentiation is the articulation of relations of inequality and equality. Equality is defined as membership of the same class, inequality as membership of different classes; some elaborated systems, such as that of the Arusha of Tanzania (Gulliver 1963) link alternate classes but they are united by opposition to the intervening class, not identified as equals. The ranking has wide connotations for social behaviour; inequality not only implies authority and respect but differentiated privileges, which may extend from rights to marriage, to shares in sacrificial beasts to minute details of elaborate hair-dressing as among the Turkana. Equality is marked not only by informality but an insistence on sharing, including in some East African systems the sharing of the sexual favours of an age-mate's wife. This should be interpreted as Baxter and Almagor point out (p. 174) as a suspension of rules of adultery, preventing the possibility of conflict over women among equals who are defined as united in intimacy. In addition an element of opposition is inherent in relations of inequality: elders and moran, junior and senior within a wider class are defined as opposed as well as unequal. Adultery in such a society thus becomes a challenging offense against a senior, rather than against the exclusive rights a married man has in the sexual services of his wife.

A further characteristic of this structure is that it entails the progress of sets of individuals through the stages defined by it. By contrast with the elementary structure established by sexual differentiation the relation between age classes is constituted, not by complementarity and exchange, but by the assumption that individuals are transients through the system; no single individual or cohort of individuals is *permanently* classified by it. Cohorts, sets, or classes are constituted as permanent units by the rituals which either establish the units or transfer individuals into pre-established units; age-mates remain age-mates all their lives. However, cohorts of individuals move through the various positions designated by the total system; indeed time is a necessary element in this structure. The boundaries between classes are maintained by the very ritual which transfers individuals from one class to the next and the transition itself relates classes to one another in an ordered sequence. Ranking is also intrinsic to the system as the difference between classes is seen as upward movement. As Baxter and Almagor put it (this volume): 'Age-systems are a device to make the cruel *descent through life to decay* appear as if it were an *ascent* to a superior, because senior, condition'. My emphases indicate the contrast between what may be the general Western view of at least the latter half of life and the view established by age-set systems. Such systems establish a hierarchy of authority with the most senior roles being those with ritual powers.

The ordered progression to elderhood seems to offer authority to all men who live long enough. However, Baxter and Almagor argue that to discuss age-set systems as though they were political systems, that is systems by which power is allocated, is to misunderstand them. Almagor's article in this volume shows in one society the truth of the general assertion, made in conjunction with Baxter, that age-differentiation of itself is not the means by which resources are controlled or allocated, nor is elderhood an office with recognised powers of command over others. The formal equality of age-mates masks the fact that they compete with one another for power and influence. Political power is acquired by the skilful use of resources, rights over women and property, to create social ties and exercise influence in situations of conflict. Such rights are distributed through the kinship system; age-sets control no resources. In effect, the 'power of the elders' is a myth for it is individual elders who acquire power, not the elders as a collectivity who govern. Similarly, the 'power of men' is a myth for men do not exercise power collectively over women; some men exercise power over some women and some over other men. Masculine identity is of itself no guarantee of power. Abrahams' article in this volume indicates the range of variation in the jural relations between men and women even within broadly comparable systems. Kinship is one means by which the rights of women and of men are allocated and it can be affected by other variables, such as ascribed rank within a system of stratification; the nature and distribution of economic resources also fundamentally affect the final pattern of behaviour which the observer sees.

Systems of age-differentiation imply that authority is the natural concomitant of age, that all men will achieve the highest position in the fullness of time. There is thus some truth in the characterisation of these systems as egalitarian, for age as a principle of social differentiation, unlike sex, does not permanently exclude any individual from office. Yet the actualities of life: demographic fluctuation, the uneven distribution of resources, floods and droughts, the illness and death of men, women children and cattle are such that the formal system represented in the elementary structure of age-classes remains an ideal. The political reality is competition for scarce resources. What then, is the connection between a classification of men by age which seems to allocate political duties: fighting, dispute settlement and control of ritual but which does not establish political offices nor determine who shall fill them? It would be oversimplistic to interpret this disjunction merely as a 'mystifying ideology' which hides the realities of political and economic life from the understanding of the actors. Such a formulation does not explain the apparent disjunction; it merely describes it.

The formal system of authority limits competition and controls behaviour. The formalities of age-differentiation define the range of political competitors. In a simple system like that of the Gisu, initiation is the only qualification demanded to enter political affairs; only the uninitiated (and women) are excluded from the political arena. Systems of a more complex nature may delay the entry of young men into political competition both with their seniors and their age-mates, for a considerable period. Such complex systems also have the effect of retiring older men from continued political activities by associating the highest authority with the dispersal of property, the means of creating politically effective alliances. The right to compete for pre-eminence is thus conferred on a narrower cohort of middle-aged men.

The idiom of formal equality and inequality places a premium on preserving the solidarity of equals and thus constrains the behaviour of competitors, keeping rivalry within bounds. Elders who have been fiercely competitive as moran, for honour and cattle in raids and for the approval and favours of girls, are still as competitive but must maintain the moderate and judicious behaviour of seniors lest their prestige suffer in the eyes of those who are now moran. They cannot therefore seem to ignore the ideals of solidarity and equality with which the young men are being urged to comply. Age-differentiation then establishes the legitimate aspirations and behaviour of segments of the male population and therefore creates a framework for the political organisation as such.

Marriage is a key feature in age-differentiated systems, relating the

formal system of authority with the means by which command of
resources is achieved. Moreover the right to marry defines a man as
eligible to be considered as a potential affine;[8] where affinity is a
major source of ties which can be utilised for economic and political
support, such legitimation is of the utmost practical significance.
Marriage does not necessarily entail economic independence as is
made clear by the case of the Tallensi, where a man remains a jural
minor until his father's death. However premortem devolution of
property at marriage is commonly associated with age-differentiated
systems. Initiation confers on the Gisu man the right to establish a
household, that is to land and the cattle for bridewealth from his
father. Spencer's statement that it is a 'deep-rooted Samburu ideal
that each man should have his own herd and ultimately be able to
manage independently' (Spencer 1965: 12) is generalised by Baxter
and Almagor to all East African pastoralists. Such a desired state of
affairs begins with marriage. This is not surprising for, in any society
in which the control and management of resources is located in
households, and political influence depends on the manipulation
of resources, management of such a household is the basis of a man's
political capital.

We return then to a consideration of the domestic group, the area
in which sex and age-differentiation intersect. Even in societies which
do not formalise age differences, marriage is the mark of the socially
adult. Among the Hausa, marriage is the sign that a man has established
himself economically and is therefore independent. Indeed in most
societies, male adult status, headship of a household and an independent role in public affairs are closely associated. Headship of a
domestic unit is clearly of the same nature as any other position of
authority, although the unit within which it is exercised is not a
permanent corporation. It presents an interesting contrast to the age
set or class, which Baxter and Almagor argue, cannot act politically
for it lacks resources and effective organisation, while a household
possesses both these characteristics. The permanent association of
male and female in the domestic group is based on the exchange
relationship intrinsic to the division of labour, which includes management of its resources, including labour. The locus of power within the
household can vary quite widely, from the male dominated, author-
itarian household which seems characteristic of East African pastoral
societies to the partnership of Laymi peasants; domestic *authority*,
however is male.[9]

A household head is identified with his household in so far as his
status as an adult man depends on his role.[10] Where this is so, as

among many of the societies discussed in this volume a man's interests coincide very closely with those of his household although they are not identical. Among the Laymi the expenditure on public ritual, including drinking in which men indulge, is for them a public duty, while their wives who are the managers of the domestic economy complain of the drain on resources; for the Barasana couple the obligation to provide meat for communal meals must be balanced against the private interests of members of the household. The disapproval incurred by couples who retain too much for their own consumption is a measure of the strength of such private concerns. Sansom documents a society where public interests have occasioned the dissolution of marriages, sacrificed to the requirements of wider social order and the management of group resources. In all these situations a man must balance the immediate interests of the domestic group against the longer-term security to be gained from exchanges and alliances outside it. It was long ago pointed out by Stenning (1958) and reiterated since (Harris, this volume) that the long-term survival of the household depends on such organisational ties, so like any political leader a household head is concerned with external relations.

The contributions in this book make it clear that the effect of social differentiation by sex and age is to create a social order beyond the household. Age-differentiation places domestic authority at the bottom of a hierarchy of authority to which all men may aspire, while the behaviour of men and their prestige among their equals depends on their achievement. Such achievement is inherent in the definition of: first, the ideal of the moran who enriches himself at his enemy's expense by raiding, then the elder whose large herds, ordered household and strong alliances show his respect for tradition and finally the elder whose achievement is the experience of longevity and the knowledge of ritual. In all these classes, defined by age, a man is lured to compete to show his fulfilment of the role to which his age entitles him. Hugh-Jones' brilliant demonstration of the effect of sexual differentiation among the Barasana shows how the public sphere is created by the sexual division of labour and the divisions of time and space associated with it. In this society, a typical day ends with the men sitting together in an ordered circle, chewing coca, while at the other end of the communal dwelling the women and children retire into the family compartments to sleep. Coca-chewing is a purely associational activity for individuals defined as equals by their sex and lineage membership but ranked by age and kinship status. The exclusion of women and children is a necessary element in the symbolic subordination of domestic interests to communal solidarity, for when they are present, as they are for communal meals, domestic divisions appear in the group which sits by household groups.

Pirá-Paraná ritual is an extended version of male sociability, as Hugh-Jones demonstrates; both celebrate the superior powers of men manifest in their lesser need of sleep and food and their knowledge of traditional ritual. The assembly is made to seem superior to the household unit by the fact of its being composed of heads of households, whose presence is legitimised by this fact. Masculine assemblies of a non-instrumental kind occur in most of the societies we have discussed in this volume[11] and in each case they represent, in the assembly of men, the material embodiment of a social order which transcends the domestic and hence individual interests of men and women.

The two principles of social differentiation that are the subject of analysis in this volume show many features in common. They are both constructed of selected elements drawn from the processes of human physiology and as formal systems have certain logical properties. These differ in that sexual differentiationis based on the unity of conjoined opposites,[12] while differentiation by age creates a hierarchy out of ordered divisions of the human life-span. Both principles exercise direct constraints on human behaviour in that they present clusters of attributes which by association with the 'natural' origin of the differentiating structure are ascribed to individuals. Indirectly, they define authority, associating it with ritual, knowledge and experience, properties ascribed to a certain class in each set of classes. Distinctions between domestic and public life, between spheres of competition and the goals for which there is competition are defined by the cross-cutting divisions between the sexes and between old and young. I have also argued that both the conjugal tie and hence the domestic group, and the wider social sphere are the creation of these two principles which associate in a single unity the self-interest and responsibilities of the individuals who are defined by them. Any such system must also be related to the material world in which it must operate but here I have concentrated on an analysis of the conceptual apparatus with which societies order their world and create a social order.

Footnotes

1. The term 'moran' which is the Maasai word for those who are adult but not yet elders, is sufficiently well-known for me to use it from now on without translation; moreover warrior is imprecise for it emphasises only one aspect of the role associated with the class.
2. Dr. Roger Naylor: private communication.

3. Men in this category are referred to and addressed by their personal names.
4. A blood test can only indicate that a man did *not* father a particular child, it cannot indicate paternity.
5. It seems that in other contexts, such as the ritual battle between moieties, girls (and perhaps women?) fight each other. For a woman to defend herself against her husband would therefore imply that they were identical and thus rivals, opposed rather than joined as partners.
6. Note that this equation is a matter of ideal ordering: a few Gisu youths may marry before initiation (which entails extra expense for the ritual purification after the operation) and many will not marry until some time after the ritual conferment of the right to domestic authority.
7. I exclude from consideration here the classification by generation, which occurs together with some East African age-set systems, like that of the Dassanetch (Almagor, this volume) for this classificatory principle is, to my mind based on principles other than age. It is in effect patri-filial linking and the classes based on it contain men of a wide age-range. (Cf. Baxter and Almagor, this volume.) It resembles age systems proper in many ways, including the fact that it ranks classes in a hierarchy.
8. Among the Gisu it is the sons of wealthy men who marry before initiation; they are thus highly eligible in other terms. Gisu told me that, traditionally, no girl would wish to sleep with an uncircumcised youth, so that the sons of important men were initiated early so that they were then free to marry.
9. It seems difficult to argue that there is a domestic group at all among the Hadza, although there are stable conjugal relations. Certainly there seems to be no role of household head so that the Hadza prove an exception to this rule as to so many.
10. Abrahams, this volume, notes the relatively high proportion of elderly un-married men among the Gonja, where status ascription by birth is significant.
11. It is perhaps not coincidental that male violence directed against women appears to follow such male gatherings, in which the significant identity that is being strengthened is male power. Rape is also commonly threatened against women who seek to discover male ritual secrets.
12. Among the Barasana, pepper, the symbol of this conjunction, is called by a term which means renewal and hence, one might suppose, life itself.

References

Ardener, E. (1972). Belief and the Problem of Women, *in* "The Interpretation of Ritual: Essays in Honour of A.I. Richards" (ed. J.S. La Fontaine). Tavistock, London.

Barnes, J.A. (1973). Genetrix : Genitor :: Nature : Culture? *in* "The Character of Kinship" (ed. J. Goody). Cambridge University Press, Cambridge.

Bloch, M.E.F. (1977). The Past and the Present in the Present, *Man*, Vol. 12, No. 2.

Gulliver, P. (1963). Social Control in an African Society. Routledge & Kegan Paul, London.

Levi-Strauss, C. (1949). The Elementary Structures of Kinship (2nd edition 1967, English edition 1969). Eyre & Spottiswode, London.

Llewelyn-Davies, M. (in press). Two Contexts of Solidarity among pastoral Maasai women, *in* "Women United, Women Divided: cross-cultural Perspectives on Female Solidarity" (ed. P. Caplan and J. Bujra).

Macfarlane, A. (1978). Modes of Reproduction. The Malinowski Memorial Lecture delivered at the London School of Economics, 6 February 1978.

Mauss, M. (1925). The Gift (translated I. Cunnison), Cohen and West, London.

Mead, M. (1950). Male and Female. Penguin Books, Harmondsworth, England.

Ortner, S. (1974). Is Female to Male as Nature is to Culture? *in* "Woman Culture and Society" (eds. M.Z. Rosaldo and L. Lamphere). Stanford University Press, Stanford, California.

Rosaldo, M.Z. (1975). Man the Hunter and Woman, *in* "The Interpretation of Symbolism" (ed. R. Willis). A.S.A. Studies **2**, Malaby Press, London.

Rosaldo, M.Z. and Lamphere, L. (eds.). (1974) Woman Culture and Society, Stanford University Press, Stanford, California.

Stenning, D.J. (1958). Household Viability among the Pastoral Fulani, *in* "The Developmental Cycle in Domestic Groups" (ed. J. Goody). Cambridge Papers in Social Anthropology, No. **1**, Cambridge University Press, Cambridge.

Turner, V. (1966). Colour Classification in Ndembu Ritual, *in* "Anthropological Approaches to the Study of Religion" (ed. M. Banton). A.S.A. Monographs **3**.

Wallman, S. (1976). Difference, Differentiation, Discrimination, *New Community: Journal of the Community Relations Commission*, Vol. **V**, No. 1–2.

COMPLEMENTARITY AND CONFLICT:
AN ANDEAN VIEW OF WOMEN AND MEN[1]

OLIVIA HARRIS

Introduction

The analysis of binary conceptual systems frequently includes man
and woman as a paradigm of categorical opposition. In many cultures
the use of man and woman to think with seems to be part of a ranking
system in which women are consistently placed on the less valued or
inferior side of the opposition. Thus various writers have suggested
that woman is to man as nature is to culture;[2] many others have
drawn attention to the way the right and left hands are used to
express gender differences, where in the words of Evans Pritchard,
'a slight organic asymmetry is made the symbol of absolute moral
polarity' (1973).

In the case I wish to discuss, such absolute polarity is absent:
categorical opposition is founded in representation of the unity of
such opposites, and gender ranking is complex and related to context,
not consistently weighted on one side. In traditional Andean culture
the complementary unity of the conjugal bond is reiterated in a way
that leaves submerged the categorical opposition between woman
and man.[3] It has a further significance in that the model of conjugality is used in the definition of gender roles. One criticism that
can be levelled at much of the literature on women that has appeared
in recent years is that it over-emphasises the conjugal relationship to
the exclusion of many other roles played by both women and men,
many other relationships in which they are involved. But the identification of the category 'woman', which is in essence a biological
and not a social one, with the roles of wife and mother is not
accidental. In many cultures just such an identification is made, while
categories of maleness are less closely tied to the roles of husband and
father (cf. Edholm, Harris & Young 1977).

One of my themes then, is the limitations of gender definitions
which are closely identified with conjugal roles. However, I shall start
by outlining the use of the concept *chachawarmi* by the Laymis –

the ethnic group whose culture I studied.[4] In Aymara, the first language of the Laymis, the terms for man or husband (*chacha*) and woman or wife (*warmi*) can also be combined as a single substantive — *chachawarmi* — and refer to the conjugal pair as a unit.[5] *Chachawarmi*, man-and-woman, represents symbolically many of the fundamental relationships of Andean society, but it also has a direct social referent in the peasant household which is the basic unit of the traditional Andean economy. Again, the ideas of complementarity and unity, implicit in the Laymi model of conjugality, in certain respects provide a model of Laymi society as a whole. This level of representation is founded in the social and economic organization of the household.

However, while such a representation is a compelling one, and is moreover, a normative statement of how the conjugal relationship should be, or should appear to be, my argument is that we cannot understand fully the relationship between Laymi men and women in terms of the concept of *chachawarmi*. There are important features of the gender relationship which it cannot account for, which derive from the contradiction between a social organization which creates units out of individuals of each sex, and gender definitions at a societal level, which transcend the conjugal unit.

I. The Laymis

The Laymis are one of a number of ethnic groups of the North of Potosi, Bolivia, and with a population of about 7,000, they are one of the larger groups of the region. The North of Potosi came under Spanish colonial rule along with the rest of the Andes, in the early 1530's, after only a few decades of domination by the Incas; today it is the site of one of the largest mining complexes in the Andes. In colonial times the population of this area was a source of compulsory labour, especially for the silver mines of Potosi, and agriculture or livestock-herding was never commercialised enough to destroy the traditional economy. Today the Laymis sell a part of their agricultural and livestock surplus in the nearby mining complex, but rarely work in the mines, or even in the mining towns.[6] Various products vital for Laymi subsistence have to be obtained by exchange, and in many cases the exchange is along traditional routes with other ethnic groups, rather than via the market. Thus while the Laymi economy could not in any way be termed self-subsistent, neither is it dominated by market relations. Since the abolition of the land tax in 1953 dues to the State have taken the form of work on the roads for 3 days each year, and the partial maintenance of rural schoolteachers.

The basic staples – tubers, maize, certain cereals and beans, are all produced within the ethnic group, and their requirements for meat and wool are largely met by their own herds of llamas and sheep. While a few individuals in any locality hold the titles land is not alienable in most cases and they are also obliged to distribute usufruct rights amongst all other house-holders, so that all have sufficient parcels for subsistence in the different micro-climates of this mountainous environment. At present there is little evidence of individual accumulation by some households at the expense of others, nor of those households who 'borrow' land having to sell their labour. Ultimately, to be resident in a Laymi locality means to have access to sufficient land for subsistence; correlated to this is the obligation of each household to sponsor one of the *fiestas* that mark the agricultural calender, to provide men who will fight in defence of Laymi land, and stand their turn in the ritual and political offices. The only exceptions to this are a couple of traders who have set up shops in the big Laymi village nearest to the mines, the *mestizo* administrators of a few small mines, and the rural schoolteachers who struggle in isolation for half the year to teach Laymi children the basics of 'civilization' – the three Rs and the National Anthem.

The boundaries of the Laymis as a group are clearly marked, both socially and territorially. Their style of dress is distinctive; in artistic expression – both in music and in weaving – they differ systematically from their neighbours. They are a largely endogamous group and have an internal system of rotating political and religious authorities. Their territory, divided into two separate areas, has clear boundaries, and is identified as Laymi land. Even though there are obviously differences in wealth and in access to land, within the group there is no systematic social differentiation, or even hierarchy of sub-groups. As such, the Laymis provide a good case in which to examine sex as a principle of social differentiation, in a group untrammelled by other cross-cutting forms of stratification.

The fact that their territory is in two discrete blocs is no historical accident, but relates directly to the ecological configuration of the Andes, and the way this ecology has been exploited by Andean peoples. As in any alpine environment there is a huge variation in ecology and therefore in the possibilities for agriculture and livestock over even a small area. In the case of the Laymis, one half of their territory is in the high, treeless zone, the *suni*, at an altitude of 11,000 – 15,000 ft, where varieties of tubers, together with some wheat, oats and beans are grown, and llamas and sheep are herded. The other half of Laymi territory lies several days walk away, where the eastern cordillera of the Andes is broken by deep river gorges, that cut their way down towards the Amazon basin. Here in the *likina* at an altitude of 7,000 – 9,000 ft, a radically different ecology produces maize, squashes, peppers, and various cereals. It is also the main source of wood.

As the indigenous Andean economy has been characterised, the products of both ecological zones are staples for every household. Access to them has been maintained historically, and still to a certain extent today, by kinship links, rather than by the development of markets or a class of long-distance traders. (Murra 1975 pp. 59–115.) In the case of the Laymis there is documentary evidence from 1592 that the larger political grouping in which they were part had both *suni* and *likina* lands in the areas that they do today, even though the extent of these territories has been partly reduced by the intrusion of outside landowners into the area.

II. Chachawarmi as a concept

It seems likely from the sources available that the Incas on conquest of new territories brought the conquered peoples under their conceptual, as well as their political sway. Whether or not we should explain the common features in symbolic structures throughout the former Inca domain in this way, or whether we should rather see it as the result of a more gradual process of diffusion, it is certainly remarkable how pervasive is the symbol of *chachawarmi*, of man-and-woman. Silverblatt (n.d.) suggests that some of its meaning may derive from the androgynous nature of the pre-Columbian Chanca creator deity – Viracocha – whose worship was taken over by the Incas. Today the Laymis do not identify such a deity but a linking of male and female is explicit in much of their cosmology. Thus not only are the sun and moon – central to the Inca cult – regarded as male and female, but also there are male and female forms of lightning the Pachamama – the fertile earth – is female and her male counterpart is the mountain-tops. Various sacred stones, and places on the mountainside where lightning has struck are seen as the guardians of human society, and these are sexually paired. Platt (1976) gives an extended analysis of the importance of male and female as a symbolic matrix for the neighbouring ethnic group of Macha.

The concept of *chachawarmi* extends much further than the attribution of gender characteristics to supernatural guardians. For example, the main staples, maize and potatoes, are respectively male and female, as are the two main forms of livestock – llamas and sheep. In all ritual, too, the *chachawarmi* pair is necessarily present, as a human married couple. Unmarried ritual sponsors must find a partner of the opposite sex to accompany them. At various points during an elaborate ritual the *chachawarmi* pair stand together, the woman on the left, the man on the right, each with two drinking cups, a larger one in the right hand and a smaller in the left, and pour libations for the ongoing fertility of themselves and the community. These libations in turn are frequently addressed to *chachawarmi* pairs — the tutelary deities mentioned above, and male and female ancestors. Thus in ritual, the unity of man and woman is repeated in many contexts.

This idea of unity is well-illustrated by the use of hands, which, as Needham and others have shown, following Hertz (Needham 1973), have been used in many cultures as symbols of sex-difference. While Laymis concepts follow the common pattern of equating male with right and female with left, in general a propitious ritual act in Laymi terms must be performed with *both* hands. Thus, for example, formal libations must be poured by both hands — successively from the right-hand and then from the left-hand drinking bowl. Ritual obeisance involves kissing both hands of the recipient; and food and coca[7] must *always* be received in both hands. Here we have an illustration of the specificity of the *chachawarmi* concept, and one that differentiates it from much of the literature on 'complementary opposition', where we are presented only with a series of recurrent antitheses.

Ritual continually celebrates the importance of the marital pair, and locates in this unit the well-being of the entire community. The biological roles of the sexes in reproducing the human species are brought to represent the reproduction of the whole social fabric, that is, not only the reproduction of human beings, but also the well-being of the community the fertility of the soil, and of animals. Further, the Laymis conceive of themselves as a group in terms of the fertile *chachawarmi* couple. For example, as mentioned above, their territory is divided: in the highland *suni*, with its extremes of temperature, land must lie fallow for at least six years after three years under cultivation, while the temperate lower *likina* zone produces more abundantly, and in greater variety. However, the products of both zones are essential for the subsistence of the household, and thus the two zones are perceived as being in a relation of complementary unity, even though they are separated by several days' walk and the territory of other ethnic groups. The lower *likina* zone is thought to be stronger; there crops are produced each year without rotation, and in great variety. It is correspondingly said to be male because of its 'strength', in comparison with the highland *suni*, where the land is 'weaker' and needs to rest before it can be productive. This is seen as the female zone. A metonymical relationship is thus asserted between the conjugal pair as *chachawarmi*, and the divided Laymi territory.

Another similar relationship is posited between *likina* and *suni* zones, and between the two buildings of which every Laymi household is composed, that is, a kitchen and a storehouse. In Laymi cosmology the kitchen is the female house and the storehouse the male, in the same way as the *likina* zone, being more productive, is said to be the storehouse from which food is taken to the *suni* to be processed and consumed. Here we find a composite analogy on the one hand of the *chachawarmi* couple to the household – to the buildings which form the concrete spatial location of the household – and on the other hand of both the household and the conjugal pair to the two distinctive zones of Laymi territory (see figure).

LAYMIS

(Low zone) *Likina*   *Suni* (High zone)

Storehouse   Kitchen

(Man) *Chacha*   *Warmi* (Woman)

Chachawarmi
(household)

The perceived identification between the Laymis as a group, and the individual household.

I shall return to the centrality of the household in Laymi thought and organisation. First however it remains to elaborate on the relationship between man and woman as it is conceived in the *chachawarmi* dyad. Let us first look at the relationship between *likina* and *suni*. As I explored Laymi concepts, it seemed illogical that the higher zone should be conceived as female; firstly I thought I could detect a direct analogy between the opposition up:down and male: female, on the basis of the association between the male mountain peaks and the female productive earth that lay below; secondly the high *suni* region seemed to be the locus of political power for the group as a whole. Indeed the neighbouring ethnic group of Macha make an explicit connection between the political dominance and greater fertility of the higher and lower ecological zones respectively, and with the corresponding association of the high zone with male, and the low zone with female. (Platt 1976.)

The paradoxical nature of the Laymis's reversal of this analogy lies in the fact that formal politics both within the group and in its dealings with outsiders are entirely in the hands of men. Political offices rotate amongst male householders, and the two main authorities of the Laymis, known as *segundas mayores*, traditionally lived in the *suni* during their term of office. But the explanation the Laymis offer for this configuration of relationships is that the *likina* is the 'stronger' region in productive terms, and that the weaker *suni* dominates the *likina* just as within the household the weaker woman has the controlling voice over her stronger husband.[8]

However, 'control' should be understood as managerial rather than coercive. As the Laymis perceive it, the high zone does not dominate the lower zone, but merely provides the locus of political authority. Similarly within the *chachawarmi* model any predominance is seen as highly relative, and to be understood in the context of overall mutuality in the relationship. It is reminiscent of Marcel Granet's outline of complementary opposition in Chinese symbolism: 'Never do we find absolute oppositions: a left-hander is not sinister and neither is a right-hander. A multitude of rules show the left and the right as predominating alternately' (1973) (see also Willis 1967 for a similar approach).

Two more points will illustrate what I have already said. Firstly the association that is often made in ethnography between women and nature, men and culture is derogatory both to nature and to women, and is often associated with beliefs about the polluting dangers of menstruation and childbirth. It is thus significant that in the Laymi case menstruation, far from being seen as polluting, is held to be the period at which a woman is most fertile. In no sense that I could discover was menstruation seen as polluting and dangerous, or as implying women were closer to nature. Similarly there are few beliefs associating childbirth with states of ritual danger or pollution.[9]

A second illustration of this argument can be taken from ideas about the deaths of unmarried men and women. It is considered extremely unfortunate to die without having been married, and the corpse has to be interred with a symbolic companion for the after-life: a hen for a man and a cock for a woman. Unmarried people are thought to have a far harder journey to the land of the dead. They can travel only at night, which is an activity that Laymis consider unfit for human beings, and do not do if they can avoid it. The road unmarried souls must go is over the thorn bushes, while those of married people travel on paths, and by day. In this belief there is a clear opposition between nature and culture: married souls are cultural, travelling on culturally recognised paths, and by day like human beings. Unmarried souls on the other hand remain outside the sphere of culture, travelling by night, like animals and witches.

If we have here the social correlates of the nature-culture opposition for the Laymis, it suggests that male-and-female together is identified with culture in this opposition. It is the fruitful cooperation of woman and man as a unity that produces culture, and this is counterposed to an unmarried person as non-cultural; culture is based on duality, and contrasted with what has remained single when it should be paired.[9]

III. The Laymi Household

a) The household as a social unit.
The conceptual insistence on the *chachawarmi* couple is matched to some extent in household organization. In fact, one of the lexical references in Aymara to what we identify as a 'household' is *chachawarmi*.[10] Many of the characteristics of the concept *chachawarmi* derive from the economic relationship of wife and husband within the household.

The final rituals of marriage in the Andes takes place after a couple have been living together virilocally for probably several years. The initial concubinage is the result of courtship between the two, in which their parents play no formal role. Until the final rituals take place, either party is free to end the liaison. However, after the marriage rituals no separation is possible, and the only two cases of permanent separation that I heard about were of people who had to leave the Laymi community as a result. Since it is also usually after the marriage rituals that a new household is set up, it follows that the only natural breakup of the household unit is through death.

Kinship structures over the whole Andean region are predominantly bilateral (cf. Lambert 1977). There is little differentiation between sibling and affine of the same generation as ego; each household has a unique set of relationships with other like units, and uses kin-ties both on the male and female sides alike.

However, while lineality is not emphasised among the Laymis, the 'bilaterality' of their kinship rules is in fact biassed towards males both in inheritance forms and residence practices. Land is held in large units by a few people who allot parcels to their agnatic kin; the majority of Laymis have access to land through agnatic links and consequently form a corporate agnatic group in certain contexts. As a result marriage is usually virilocal, unless a woman inherits in the absence of male heirs.[11]

Thus, while in formal terms kinship relations are based on cognatic principles, in practice agnatic links are of major significance at a local level. In any hamlet, there is likely to be a core of agnatically-related men, whose wives will be outsiders, related to each other primarily through the mediation of their menfolk.

b) The household as an economic unit.
An analysis of the household as an economic unit reveals, I think, the same type of discrepancy. While I hope to show the limitations of the *chachawarmi* model both as a symbol and as a principle of social organization, it is nonetheless true that the economic relations between a woman and her husband correspond, at least formally, to the outline in section I of *chachawarmi* as a concept. In the allocation of labour, we find the principles of egalitarianism and complementarity which were suggested above. Agriculture is carried out equally by all: at seed-time and harvest husband and wife should work together. The absence of one partner is thought to bring bad luck.[12] Livestock herding is divided on the basis of sex and age so that women and children herd sheep and goats, which need to be taken daily to pasture, while men make the longer but less frequent journey up to the mountain-tops to mind their llamas. While members of each sex can and do herd the animals allotted to the other from time to time, this division of labour in practice corresponds to a sexual division in the ownership of animals: on the principle that 'ownership' derives fundamentally from labour-input, women tend to own the sheep and goats and men the llamas.

Thus in the productive tasks which are of primary importance for subsistence, the principles both of unity and complementarity are found. The product of the household's joint labour in agriculture is seen as belonging to the whole household, and is reflected in inheritance patterns. In herding, where there is a division of tasks, ownership, control and inheritance derives largely from labour-input but the household has use of the livestock of all its members.

However, there are also cases of a stricter division of labour based on sexual differences. For example in ploughing, a team of bulls is generally used, and Laymis believe that only a man should drive the team,[13] while the placing of the seed in the ground should be done by a woman. Thus the technical division of labour in sowing demands the participation of both man and woman, i.e. of the *chachawarmi* pair.

A second example is weaving – the most important craft production carried out by the Laymis. Most of their need for cloth and clothing is today met by their own labour and their own wool, and the weaving of the region is justly renowned for its fineness and artistry, in the best tradition of this notable Andean art-form. Men weave long lengths of a fine, usually plain, cloth on an upright loom; from this they sew most of the basic items of clothing: dresses, trousers, skirts, jackets, cummerbunds. Women use a horizontal or backstrap loom and weave a more durable, heavier cloth which is often highly ornamented, and which serves for the ubiquitous carrying cloths – the *awayu* – ponchos, blankets, sacks, bags and belts. Neither sex knows how to do the weaving of the other and each possesses their own weaving implements. It is this unbreakable division of labour in weaving that is given as one of the most urgent reasons for marriage.

Much has been written on supposed physiological bases of the sexual division of labour; more convincingly, Judith Brown has suggested that one of the universally predominant criteria in the sexual division of labour is the requirement for women's tasks to be compatible not so much with child-bearing and suckling, as with child raising. (Brown 1970.) Many features of the Laymi sexual division of labour confirm this thesis, e.g. in that women's tasks do not take them far from home, and often require less concentration than those of men. But where such pragmatic determinants may be said to apply, such as in the allocation of herding tasks, the division of labour is informal and flexible: either sex can do the herding of the other when the occasion arises. What is termed 'domestic work' is another example of the same principle: is it women's task to cook, fetch water, keep the house tidy, wash clothes; but men can and do perform all these tasks if a woman is ill, absent, or busy doing something else.

This functional division of labour must be distinguished from the strict rules governing the cases of ploughing/sowing and weaving. Here the sexual division of labour is strict and reinforced either by ritual sanctions (the threat of infertility in the case of ploughing and sowing) or by supposed ignorance of the necessary skill (in the case of weaving). In weaving there is no technical division of labour – each individual produces alone, and the final product, cloth, is the same for both sexes. Both sexes need the cloth produced by the other, and in theory at least, comparable amounts of time are spent by both sexes on the production of cloth.[14]

A discussion of the principles of labour allocation does not of itself indicate relative intensity of labour-inputs. As many have pointed out, women do a double shift: not only do they participate equally with men in production in many societies but on top of this they have a whole series of domestic duties that are not shared by men. This is the case for the Laymis too though it seemed to me the degree of inequality in labour-input between men and women was highly variable. However, women's double load means that they ultimately control consumption, through their particular role as cooks. In Laymi terms this is the reason why women are dominant within the conjugal pair, as I described above. Though Laymis see all major decisions in the household economy as being taken jointly by all adult members, they also recognise that the woman is in a better position to make certain decisions: she can calculate how much of each of the staples will be needed for subsistence in the coming year, how much can be sold, and how much must be kept for seed. Again with their daily herding activity women are in a good position to make the vital decisions about the livestock of the household: which animals should be slaughtered, which shorn, which are the good breeders, and which should be sold.

There is another sense in which women have a controlling capacity within the household, within the *chachawarmi* pair, even though I never heard it used as an example by Laymis themselves. This was to do with family size. The Laymis consciously control their population, and talk scornfully of neighbouring groups who, as they see it, 'breed like animals'. They consider it important to maintain a fairly stable land-labour ratio. Of course, family size is a crucial factor in the degree to which women's lives are weighed down by the burdens of childbirth, lactation and childraising, and it is significant that control of family size depends ultimately on the decision of the mother. In addition the mother controls the labour of her children, and small boys do the same tasks, both herding and domestic, as girls.

Whether one interprets these data as showing a domestic economy effectively controlled by women, or one in which a woman has an equal voice with her husband in economic decision, it squares ill with

the model of the patriarchal peasant family familiar in classic writings
on the peasantry which has recently been revived on the basis of the
world ethnographic sample by Michaelson and Goldschmidt (1971).
If there are elements of Laymi social relations that should be termed
'patriarchal' these are not located primarily in the household as a unit.

Within the household, socio-economic organization fits the
representation of *chachawarmi*. Each household has independent
access to land: it initiates an independent agricultural labour process
and in general consumes jointly the common product. The division
of labour rarely requires the participation of more than two people,
and these are usually socially required to be male and female. In
the case of livestock-rearing and weaving the wool that is derived
from it, the social division of labour again ensures the mutual cooperation of a man and a woman. In terms of domestic decisions the
woman ultimately has the deciding voice, at least as the Laymis perceive it. The bilateral kinship system again gives comparable weight
to ties traced through both H and W, and the absence of strong
lineal principles and ongoing corporate kin-groups gives the household a certain identity and autonomy with respect to other similar
units. Of particular significance is the rule forbidding divorce. The
economic rationality of forbidding long-term conjugal separation is
in complete harmony with household organisation and its symbolic
representation. Just as in the symbolic sphere *chachawarmi* is a complementary unity, so in society the union of woman and man is not
allowed to be broken.

IV.   Limitations in the household model of Laymi Society.

It is commonplace in peasant studies to call the household the 'basic
unit' of the society and the economy, (e.g. Wolf (1966) and Shanin
(1972)). In the work of writers such as Chayanov (1966) and Sahlins
(1974) the household is seen essentially as a self-regulating system,
meeting all its own subsistence needs, and virtually autonomous from
other similar 'basic units'. However, such a position concentrates on
the individual enterprise, to the exclusion of the social conditions
which guarantee the continued reproduction of the enterprise in a
particular form. To see the individual household as self-sufficient is
a heuristic device. In practice, a multitude of different types of
exchange relationships, of goods and services, tie together separate
households, and the two separate ecological zones, and the Laymis
themselves to the wider economy. In most instances it is the household that is the unit of exchange, but Laymi society cannot be understood simply as an agglomeration of household units.

The economic relations between households are of a different order from the pooling that occurs within a household, but it seems to me mistaken to deduce from the *form* of inter-household exchange, where accounts are kept and notions of equivalence are used, that the household is a self-contained production unit. In practice economic advances and restitutions are often made on a long-term basis, and the kinship ideology which underwrites cooperation between households suggests that in some senses at least the wider kinship group is an important economic unit.

The conditions of existence of the household in political and ritual dimensions are also reproduced at a wider social level, for example the conditions that guarantee access   to means of labour, natural resources and to mechanisms for exchange and cooperation. Such political conditions both entail an internal system of law-enforcement and of decision-making, and the organization of relations with outsiders, both for cooperation and defence. It is clear that certain political conditions depend on state structures at a higher level than the Laymis as an ethnic group, but the intrusion of Bolivian law has only been partial.

Ritual too is essential for the reproduction of the conditions of existence. The protection of the ancestors and the tutelary deities must be ensured through the mediation of sacrifice, of offerings, vigils and ceremonies, in order to reproduce the ritual well-being and the continuing fertility of the community. It remains to be examined to what degree the household – the conjugal pair – operates as a unit at this level of communal activity. Women are in fact notable by their absence: only men attend the community assemblies and work-parties for each locality. Only men stand their turn as authorities either at the local level, or that of the Laymis as a whole. Most assemblies and political activities take place early in the morning or in the evening: at these times women are sitting in front of the cooking fire preparing a meal. Similarly for warfare and for communal labour women's major role is to prepare food for the men. Thus the same activity which in the domestic sphere gives women a controlling voice over the household economy is a reason for their exclusion from most other collective activities. The major way that women participate in collective activity is by cooking and fetching water.

This at first sight seems to contradict the pattern described above that ritual requires the presence of both sexes. However, an essential component of ritual is drinking, and pouring libations to the guardians of the community; in this the presence of males far outweighs that of females. For example, in my calculations men may spend at least thirty days per year in full-time ritual drinking, while women spend perhaps two or three. Drinking takes place generally in the courtyard of the ritual sponsors, and a table separates the group of men from the group of women. Much of the time there will be ten to fifteen men sharing the cups of cane alcohol and of *chicha* – the beer made from maize or barley. But there are seldom more than two or three women, generally older, post-menopausal women, accompanying the female sponsor.

Drunkenness is *de rigueur* for men in fiestas; however it is rare for a woman, especially a young woman, to succumb. The ritual wellbeing of the community can only be assured if most of the men reach an advanced stage of intoxication, but at the same time the men do their best to ensure that their women remain sober. They argue that women cannot be trusted – if they get drunk they will be led astray, they will forget about their children, they will fail to carry out their domestic duties. This is one reason for the small participation of women in lengthy ritual drinking: another is their daily domestic and shepherding activities alluded to earlier. A third is their important role in looking after their drunk husbands.

While women half resent their exclusion from festivities, they also dislike drinking much. They complain that the men are extravagant and spend all the savings of the household on alcohol. Drinking is seen as a peculiarly male activity even though women are formally there; drinking and coca-chewing are also the form in which the communal surplus, or ceremonial fund (Wolf 1966) is consumed. As such, in this 'public' sphere of ritual drinking, the egalitarian principles of consumption within the household are abandoned, and the bulk of consumption is specifically limited to men.

V. The Problem of Violence.

There is another aspect of ritual drinking which is also relevant to the analysis of relationships between man and woman. This has to do with the violence that breaks out recurrently when people drink heavily. In the normal course of events, Laymis are mild, polite and delicate in their treatment of others, but when drunk violence flares up easily. Men beat their wives, a few regularly, most men only on rare occasions; nonetheless this violence is the standard complaint of women against men. Many women approved of my unmarried state since I had no husband to beat me. In general it is only after the final marriage rituals are completed that men feel free to beat their wives – at earlier stages in the marriage, a woman can simply leave and go home. But it is interesting that while women sympathise with another woman whose drunken husband has beaten her, rarely will they intervene. There is little apparent solidarity on the part of women to defend each other. They seem to feel that, however hard, this violence is a fact of life, and any defensive measure will only lead to worse violence on a later occasion.

However, when she has a full brother to fight on her behalf a woman will defend herself. It seems to be the women with no full brothers nearby who get beaten more frequently. And it is also in times of festive drinking that a man will attack his sister's husband and revenge the violence inflicted on her. A strong — and aggressive — brother can effectively limit the degree to which his sister suffers at the hands of her husband.

I must reiterate that this violence is almost entirely restricted to periods of ritual drinking. Moreover, I see no reason to suppose that this pattern of mens' violence towards their wives is a special case, a unique characteristic of Laymi culture which requires special explanation as such. On the contrary, recent evidence suggests that conjugal violence is a fairly generalized condition of society (e.g. Hanmer 1977). In any case, my concern here is not to speculate as to its causes, but to relate it to the analysis of the conjugal relationship presented so far.

The explanations given by Laymis for conjugal violence are varied, but rarely phrased in terms of punishing women for specific offences, nor did they seem to be correlated with specific household failure. Rather, a reason frequently given by both men and women for wife-beating was to ensure that women did not abandon their children or their domestic tasks — i.e. that they manage the household economy properly. Violence is thus seen more as a preventative than as a punitive measure. It is thought that without the threat of violence women will forget their domestic duties. (I have heard women express this opinion too, though always about other women.)

Such an explanation, while probably only a partial one, is suggestive. It helps to explain why even those women who have no pressing tasks, such as herding, often sit in their homes rather than join the drinkers, and only go out in the early evening when food is served. It also explains in part why women do not often escape from home when their husband is drunk: if a man arrives home and does not find his wife, the eventual retribution will be worse. It also fits the specificity of violence. A woman is only beaten by her husband: neither her father nor brothers punish her physically. The rare occurrences of rape seem usually directed against either unmarried or widowed women, that is, precisely those women who are not within a conjugal relationship. Within marriage, women are said to control ultimately both their children and the household economy; rather than seeing men as jealous of this control, the reasons given by men and women for the incidence of wife-beating suggest that it is a generalised measure to control women's performance of their household duties.

Insofar as the model of *chachawarmi* used by the Laymis focusses on the unity and unbreakable complementarity of the conjugal pair, the antagonistic features of marriage that I have outlined are not included in the representation. In the logic of Laymi categories, a man and a woman cannot fight each other, since while fighting is accepted as part of their way of life, a contest should always be between equals. Ritual battles known as *tinkus* take place in large *fiestas* when many people are drinking together, and are exhibitions of prowess rather than battles for victory. The principle is that like fights like. Thus a young boy will choose another young boy, and older man an older man and a young woman a young woman. The idea of balance is firmly maintained.

The basis for antagonism in the *tinku* is another cross-cutting dual division of Laymi society which I have not mentioned so far — that of endogamous moieties. Initially I assumed, following Platt (1976) that the two moieties which are spatially represented as right and left in the two main Laymi villages were also conceived as man and woman. However, while the Laymis did not deny this analogy outright, they themselves called the two moieties older and younger brother. Thus in the case of the Laymi moieties, the idea of complementary unity which I have suggested is the dominant idea in *chachawarmi* is replaced by one of antagomistic similarity. The two moieties do not — in theory at least — intermarry, but are pitted against each other as equals in the *tinku*, while the relationship of *chachawarmi* is premissed on a sexual coupling between dissimilar categories, who thus cannot fight each other. For the Laymis, a woman can only fight her husband by means of her full brother who is his equal.

I am arguing then that the conflictual aspects of the conjugal relationship are incompatible with the way it is represented as *chachawarmi*. This incompatibility seemed to be exemplified by the puzzlement which greeted my attempts to include marital violence in discussions of the meaning of *chachawarmi*. For the Laymis such a connection was far-fetched. While all recognised that such violence was an almost inevitable feature of marriage, it appeared to be incompatible with the meaning of *chachawarmi*.

On the other hand, in a different area of discourse conjugal violence was discussed: this was in stereotypes of maleness and femaleness. People's complaints about marriage were often phrased in terms of general statements such as that all men are horrible, violent, (*p"iru chacha, wali nuwiri*) or that all women were lazy (*warmi wali jayra*). While it would be a difficult exercise entirely to separate the qualities ascribed severally to *chacha* – men – and *warmi* – women – from those ascribed to *chachawarmi*, in certain respects gender stereotypes do not derive from the organisation of the household.

In particular, the qualities associated with masculinity are those of strength, daring, and fighting ability. To describe someone as *warmi* on the other hand is often equivalent to calling them a coward. Women are thought to be weak and afraid, vulnerable to ghosts and therefore unable to walk at night. Their 'hearts are not strong enough' to talk to the devils and so it is virtually impossible to become full ritual specialists. In these cases, where maleness is a positive attribute and femaleness a negative one, the gender typing can be applied to a member of the opposite sex. A little girl who does not cry when she is hurt is *chacha* and a little boy who does is *warmi*. These meanings are used by women as well as men.

While the qualities of maleness and femaleness do to some extent coincide with those within the concept *chachawarmi* – for example, the 'strength' of the lower ecological zone, the *likina* is a reason for its being considered the male zone, and the reason for women being thought afraid and vulnerable is their role of childbearing – such attributes have particular consequences in the sphere of collective activity. Men fight in public: whether this be in border feuds, the ritual *tinku*, or settlement of a personal quarrel. The characterisation of women as weak and vulnerable has the explicit consequence of disqualifying them from participation in most collective activity.

Conclusion

It is difficult to pull together the stands of a discussion that has been at once so wide-ranging and so summary. One of my aims, in relating the concept of *chachawarmi*, whose centrality in Andean symbolic systems has struck so many observers, to its institutional context, has been to question the common assumption that the symbolic representation of woman and man can be derived solely from the biological basis to their relationship. The complementary unity that is stressed is closely tied to the economic role of the household, centred on the married couple.

I have argued that this representation of the relationship between women and men is selective in its emphases, and cannot contain within itself the violence which is such a common feature of marriage. I don't wish to suggest that *chachawarmi* is a false representation – a distortion of some underyling reality. It seems to be more a case of real incompatibilities between different levels of social organisation, and real conflicts of interest. In some respects the economic function of the individual household is accumulation, while that of the collectivity is consumption. While at the most general level of analysis collective conspicuous consumption may be a necessary element in the reproduction of the social form, in terms of the individual house-hold it presents a conflict of interests, particularly for the woman, the 'housewife'. She is both ultimately responsible for the provision of the household, such that everything that goes into the ceremonial fund means less for the household fund, and at the same time she is excluded from much of the collective consumption.

Chachawarmi is an organisational, a normative principle, but in representing the whole Laymi society in terms of the relationship between husband and wife in a single household it leaves out of consideration the significance of men and women as social groups. For example it is when men act as a group that the asymmetry of the gender relationship is revealed. In using terms such as 'collectivity' and 'group' I have deliberately left vague what I am talking about. Clearly there are different levels of collectivity and hierarchies of groups, and I certainly would not wish to suggest that women never act collectively, nor that they are entirely excluded from public activity. On the contrary the analysis of *chachawarmi* leads me to suggest that they are both included and excluded. Hence the ambiguity of women's position.

To what degree, then, in the case I have analysed, can it be said that sex is a principle of social differentiation? In all societies, all cultures, the difference between women and men is reiterated and elaborated. The sexual division of labour reinforces this by assigning different tasks to each, sometimes on an apparently arbitrary basis. In the case of *chachawarmi* the lifelong cooperation that is enjoined between a woman and a man is clearly seen as a cooperation between unlike categories. The economic significance of the house-hold is stressed as much by the Laymis as by any analyst of the peasant economy, and at this level of social organisation there is a real measure of equality between the sexes. At the same time, the cultural emphasis on the complementary unity of the married couple conceals the arena where there *is* social differentiation between women and men in strictly practical terms.

Footnotes

1. Thanks to Hermione Harris, Jean La Fontaine, Tristan Platt, James Woodburn, and Kate Young for helpful comments on earlier drafts of this paper.
2. Cf. Ardener (1971) and Ortner (1974).
3. I am grateful to Inge Hardman for focussing my attention on this. Cf. also Isbell (1978) and Platt (1976).
4. Most writing on this Andean concept has had a Quechua focus and the Quechua form – *q''ariwarmi* – is more commonly known.
5. I lived in Laymi territory carrying out fieldwork between 1972 and 1974.
6. Cf. Harris and Albo (1975) and Harris (1976).
7. Coca is a narcotic leaf chewed widely throughout the Andes and much used in ritual.
8. As Laymis say in Aymara – *warmi kamachi*, 'the woman gives the orders'. Cf. also Albo (1973, p. 6) and Fortun (1972, p. 942) where the same point is made for the Altiplano region.
9. See Platt (1976) for an extended discussion of the cultural logic of certain terms which express duality and singleness. (passim).
10. A new household is commonly set up on marriage. (Cf. Albo 1973.) For the Incaic period cf. Murra: 'Thus no-one paid tribute who lacked a wife or land, even if he had a child because he had no formally constituted and enumerated household to back and help him.' (1967, p. 345).
11. Women not only inherit land in the absence of Bs or FBS, but frequently retain right in their agnatic land, which they sometimes use to supplement their spouse's land, and sometimes cultivate on their in order to have a source of personal income.
12. Certain parcels are allotted individually, e.g. to unmarried members for private use. Here the presence of both sexes is not important in harvesting.
13. While this is a common phenomenon cross-culturally, the Laymis admit that in the neighbouring ethnic group to the west, Ch'allapata, women do drive teams of bulls with a plough.
14. Today at least this is beginning to be no longer the case. Bought clothes are replacing items woven by men far more than those of women. Women's weaving on the other hand is finding an increased market among tourists.

References

Albo, X. (1973). Esposos, Suegros y Padrinos. Cuadernos CIPCA, La Paz.
Ardener, E. (1971). Belief and the Problem of Women, *in* "The Interpretation of Ritual" (ed. J. La Fontaine). Tavistock, London.
Brown, J. (1970). A note on the Division of Labour by Sex, *Am.Anth.*, **71 (5)**, 1073–78.
Chayanov, A.V. (1966). The Theory of Peasant Economy (eds. Basile Kerblay, Daniel Thorner and R.E.F. Smith). Homewood, Ill.
Evans-Pritchard, E.E. (1973). Nuer Spear Symbolism, *in* (ed. R. Needham), 1973.
Edholm, E., Harris, O. and Young, K. (1977). Conceptualising Women, *Critique of Anthropology*, **3 (9/10)**, 101–130.

Fortun, J.E. (1972). La Majer Aymara en Bolivia, *America Indigena*, **32(3)**, 935–47.

Granet, K. (1973). Right and Left in China, *in* (ed. R. Needham), 1973.

Hanmer, J. (1977). Violence and the Social Control of Women, Paper presented at the British Sociological Association Annual Meeting, Sheffield, 29 March – 1 April.

Harris, O. (1976). Kinship and the Vertical Economy among the Laymis, *in* "Actes du XLII Cong. Int. des Americanistes" (forthcoming).

Harris, O. and Albo, X. (1975). Monteras y Guardatojos: campesinos y mineros en el norte de Potosi. Cuadernos CIPCA, La Paz.

Isbell, B.J. (1978). To Defend Ourselves: a view through the Andean Kaleidoscope. University Press, Texas.

Lambert, B. (1978). Bilaterality in the Andes, *in* "Andean Kinship and Marriage". Harvard University Press, Cambridge, Mass.

Michaelson, E. and Goldschmidt, W. (1971). Female Roles and Male Dominance among Peasants, *S. West J. Anthrop.*, **27(4)**, 330–352.

Murra, J.V. (1967). On Inca Political Structure, *in* "Comparitive Political Systems" (eds. R. Cohen and J. Middleton). Am.Mus. Sourcebooks in Anth., Natural History Press, New York.

Murra, J.V. (1975). Formaciones Economicas y Politicas del Mundo andino. IEP, Lima.

Needham, R. (ed.). (1973). Right and Left: Essays on Dual Symbolic Classification. University Press, Chicago.

Ortner, S. (1974). Is female to male as nature is to culture? *in* "Woman, Culture, and Society" (eds. M. Rosaldo and L. Lamphere). University Press, Stanford.

Platt, T. (1976). Espejos y Mais: temas de la estructura simbolica andina. Cuadernos CIPCA, La Paz.

Sahlins, M. (1974). Stone Age Economics. Tavistock Publ., London.

Shanin, T. (1972). The Awkward Class. Clarendon Press, Oxford.

Silverblatt, I. (n.d.). The Position of Women in the Inca Empire and the Effect on Women's Status of Spanish Colonialism. Thesis proposal, University of Illinois.

Willis, R. (1967). The Head and the Loins, *Man* (n.S.), **2(4)**, 519–34.

Wolf, E. (1966). Peasants. Prentice Hall Inc., Englewood Cliffs.

FOOD FOR THOUGHT:
PATTERNS OF PRODUCTION AND CONSUMPTION
IN PIRÁ-PARANÁ SOCIETY

C. HUGH-JONES

Pirá-Paraná Society provides rich material on the symbolic significance of the categories male and female in a variety of ritual contexts as well as evidence of the political dominance by men achieved through the familiar means of manipulation of ritual, control of women in marriage and so on. Our convener, Dr. La Fontaine has implied that we have heard quite enough to be going on with about these subjects and has directed us to the less familiar subject of the sexual division of labour and its relationship to the symbolic system. I would like to suggest that this topic may be less overworked for a very good reason – we do not know quite how to set about it. We start with a list of male and female economic tasks, to which ones that are not so directly economic – such as waging war, gossiping or using body paint – may be added or not as the case may be. We then try to show that evidence from ideological systems or ritual practice shows that there is something very 'male' about the male activities and 'female' about the female activities. It is obvious from the outset that there is, because the performance of the various activities is part of the cultural definition of the particular sex in any society, but we try to be a little more sophisticated and to set out correspondances between sex roles in the economic domain and those in sexual reproduction and the building of social groups. Although the demonstrations may be more or less comprehensive or convincing, and may develop from different modes of anthropological explanation, the results are hardly surprising. It would be astonishing if there were not some general consistency in the way a society accommodates, marshalls and utilises the differences between the sexes in different contexts.

I shall try a rather different emphasis here – instead of looking for 'nice fits', I shall explore some aspects of the dynamic operation of a particular socio-economic system. After all, people are producing and consuming all the time whatever else they may be doing and so when we say, for instance, 'women produce manioc while men go hunting' we are reducing complex and time consuming activities which structure social life to a mere sentence — an empty opposition. My first point, then, is that if we want to explore the relations between the sexual division of labour and symbolic systems, we should start with the socio-economic domain to which the phenomenon of the sexual division of labour belongs. Within this domain there is not simply a division of labour but, instead, a set of interwoven processes of production and consumption which are organised in such a way that they separate and bring together the sexes, and also families and larger groups, in an ordered manner. Thus, within the socio-economic domain, relations between individuals and groups have a dynamic character and the regular and repetitive changes that occur within these relations are bound up with the regular and repetitive changes in physical materials, spatial positions and temporal categories which make up the process of production and consumption.

In this paper I discuss these regular patterns of production and consumption and their relation to the roles of the sexes in the reproduction of social groups over time. In particular, I compare the patterns of production and consumption in ordinary secular life with those at life-cycle rituals — events which are directly bound up with the sex roles in the reproduction of social groups. The comparison shows that a) the production and consumption of several basic substances are ordered according to sex-roles in the reproduction of social groups, b) these substances, in turn, are used in such ways that they play a part in the reproduction of social groups, c) this part is particularly evident during ritual when use of the substances is associated directly with change in the reproductive status of individuals but d) patterns of production and consumption on ritual occasions have the same basic structure as secular patterns and may be considered a 'stronger' or 'extended' version of the latter. These points raise questions about the nature of the relationship between those occasions or processes we readily recognise as 'rituals' and ordinary secular processes. My discussion is not so much about the relationship between the sexual division of labour and the 'symbolic system' — by which I suppose Dr La Fontaine meant to refer to the general field of myth, ritual and cosmological belief: instead it is an exploration of the ordering of socio-economic activity as an integral part of a wider symbolic system.[1]

Of course when my conclusions are set out in this way, it is clear that I am replacing 'nice fits' with 'pretty circles' since I claim that socio-economic life is ordered according to sex roles in the building of social groups and then that the products and social relations belonging to the socio-economic domain control this very building process through ritual. In spite of its circularity, this type of analysis has the advantage of making it possible to discuss some aspects of how the reproductive differentiation and economic differentiation between the sexes are articulated through regular patterns of activity. In other words, we can begin to explore how the system works, rather than merely elucidating some of its static structural properties.

In order to bring the socio-economic patterns into high-relief, I have avoided mentioning the numerous references in myth and exegesis to my key substances and their production. Although these references are of the utmost importance in a complete analysis of the sexual division of labour, I hope to show by example that anthropologists stand to lose much by relying on these analytic short cuts.

In this paper I cannot cover more than a small area of production and consumption in a very general way and so I shall concentrate on a few important substances for internal consumption. Most of these are derived from four cultivated plants: bitter manioc (*Manihot utilissima*) and chili peppers (*Capiscum* sp.), cultivated and processed by women, and coca (*Erythroxylon coca*) and yage (*Banisteriopsis caapi* – a hallucinogenic vine), cultivated and processed by men. The other substances I shall lump together in the category 'meat and fish'; these are hunted or fished by men using a variety of techniques. I must make it clear at this point that I am omitting other very important vegetable and animal products in order to make the argument simple (see C. Hugh-Jones: 1977).

The society I describe is found in the Vaupés region of Colombia. I shall be referring to Pirá-paraná society although I worked in a Barasana longhouse and through the Barasana language.[2] The Barasana are one of several exogamous patrilineal descent groups occupying the area adjoining the river Pirá-paraná and its tributaries. Each group has its own separate Eastern Tukanoan language which the members speak irrespective of the languages spoken around them or to them and therefore this is a multi-lingual society.[3] Each exogamous group is said to be derived from an anaconda ancestor who swam up river from the eastern edge of the world. The subdivisions of an exogamous group are arranged hierarchically according to the model of a male sibling group ordered from first-born to last-born. This hierarchical organisation applies at all levels of descent grouping-down to the true sibling group.

Today, longhouses are occupied by local descent groups which are small subdivisions of the wider exogamous groups. A large longhouse population contains about 30 people. It is made up of local descent group men, their children and their in-married wives: it does not include their married sisters for, according to the rules of exogamy and virilocal marriage, these have married away. From the point of view of the local descent group, the married women are always foreign outsiders who speak different languages and yet they are essential for the reproduction of the group and the main burden of female productive activity. Marriage is a pre-condition of the next generation of descent group members and yet it breaks up the solidary sibling groups of the present generation. At the same time as separating them physically into separate family units occupying bounded areas of the house, it separates many of their economic interests since the family is the productive unit for most purposes.

The marriage system is prescriptive, the rule being that one must marry into a category of true and classificatory cross-cousins. This is combined with a rule of sister exchange whereby a man has a right to the true or close classificatory sister of his sister's husband.

The marginal status of women on ritual occasions is consistent with their outsider status during adult married life. Direct participation in communal ritual activity is mainly reserved for men. During rituals the assembled company of initiated men of the host longhouse group and of several guest longhouse groups, make contact with ancestral power by re-enacting the ancestral anaconda journeys in chant form and by using the substances and ornaments associated with mythical, ancestral times. All communal rituals conform to the same basic structure but the motive for the occasion determines the emphasis and content. Common motives are ceremonial food-exchange, celebration of seasonal tree-fruits, initiation of boys and the completion of a new longhouse. In the range of such rituals, two opposed extremes may be identified: one is typified by food-exchange rituals where the relationship between host and guest communities is stressed, women are present throughout and the sacredness of the occasion (indicated by number of ritual prohibitions and prescriptions and the danger of transgression) is minimal. The other is typified by male initiation when women are excluded, the relationship between the male community and the ancestral past is stressed and ritual dangers are at a maximum.[4]

Leaving aside the few occasions when longhouse populations join on communal food-getting expeditions or gather for rituals, the longhouse group is a virtually autonomous economic unit. For productive purposes, as for other social activities, it is divided in two principal ways – according to sex and according to nuclear family units. These

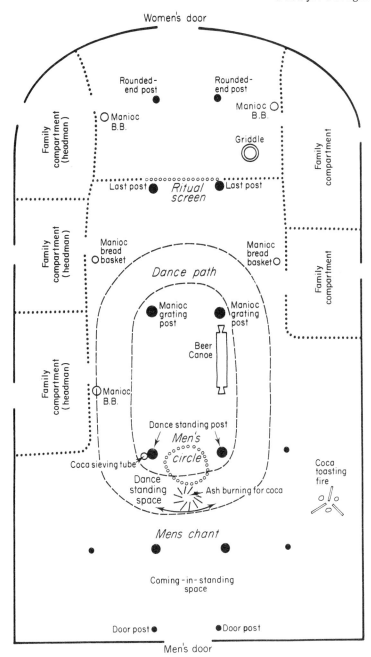

Fig. 1. Groundplan of Longhouse Interior.

Labels within figure:

Women's door

Rounded-end post

Rounded-end post

Manioc B.B.

Manioc B.B.

Griddle

Family compartment (headman)

Family compartment

Last post ● *Ritual screen* ● Last post

Family compartment (headman)

Family compartment

Manioc bread basket

Manioc bread basket

Dance path

Manioc grating post

Manioc grating post

Beer Canoe

Family compartment (headman)

Manioc B.B.

Family compartment

Dance standing post

Men's circle

Coca sieving tube

Dance standing space

Ash burning for coca

Coca toasting fire

Mens chant

Coming-in-standing space

Door post ●   ● Door post

Men's door

(household objects not to scale)

divisions are apparent in the layout of the house itself shown in Fig. 1. It has a male door, the main entrance, at one end and a female door at the opposite, rear end. Each sex performs sex-specific activities in the appropriate end of the house and uses the appropriate door (especially on formal occasions). Clustered along the periphery of the house, towards the female door, are a set of family compartments, each of which has been set up after the marriage of a local descent group man. The compartment space is devoted to private family life – inside, the women cook, food supplies and personal possessions are stored and the husband, wife and children sleep in hammocks slung around the central hearth. Boys leave the compartment at initiation to sleep as a united group in the open middle of the house. This reflects the character of the compartment as a female, child-rearing domain. The collectivity of compartments represent the fragment-ation of the united society of descent-group youths brought about by marriage. Family life contrasts with communal life which takes place in the centre of the house. Here dancing, conversation, communal eating and sharing of productive equipment take place. The two principal social divisions I have described are not wholly independant of one another, either in terms of longhouse space or other aspects of social organisation. I noted that the family compartments are clustered towards the female end and that family life is essentially female in character: conversely communal activity is dominated by men and ordered by the hierarchical relations between local descent group members.[5]

Pira-parana economy is based on shifting cultivation of bitter manioc. Although cultivations are cleared and burnt by men, women complete the rest of manioc production from planting to final cooking. They also cultivate many subsidiary crops including several starchy root crops, peppers and low-growing fruit crops. Men cultivate coca, tobacco and yage as well as some tree-fruits and medicine plants. All hunting and nearly all fishing is done by men who thus supply the bulk of the protein. A wide range of subsidiary foods – frogs, insects, fruits, etc., – may be collected from the forest by either sex, but men tend to collect on a grander scale than women. Clearly my 'meat and fish' category (supra p. 3) does not pretend to be an adequate representation of the non-manioc portion of the Indian diet however meat or fish, eaten with manioc-bread, is regarded as the ideal daily fare, and is available throughout the year in a well-run economy. Between them, hunting and fishing also occupy more male productive time than all other types of food collection put together.

The Meal

First let us turn to consumption and consider the ideal meal. It consists of meat or fish boiled with pepper and eaten with manioc bread by the assembled community. It is followed by a period of relaxation in which men chew coca and smoke cigars. Such meals are held when meat or fish are brought into the longhouse or, if a surplus has been preserved by smoking, it is served when there is felt to be need for a meal. If neither meat nor fish is available, there are many other dishes that can be made but, in general, we can regard these as either seasonal supplements or poorer substitutes for the meat/fish meal. Not all consumption of food is communal, for families invariably reserve some of their protein produce for themselves and eat it within the privacy of their compartment. The proportion of food kept back in this way is a constant source of tension within the community. Since it is families with young, non-productive children who tend to contribute least towards communal meals, food distribution is a concrete manifestation of the principle that marriage and child-rearing separate the interests of the once-solidary group of unattached youths.

Whether a man hunts or fishes alone or joins a male group, the catch is allocated to individual men, who hand it over to females of their family unit — wives, mothers, sisters or daughters according to family composition. The female partner cooks it on the compartment fire by boiling it and adding chilli peppers near the end. Salt is added too but it is of less significance than pepper in Pirá-paraná culture and I do not discuss it further. So firm is the association between communal consumption and boiling with peppers that even meat or fish which has already been thoroughly cooked by smoking is given this treatment before being served to the community.

The woman brings the pot to the centre of the house, together with her basket of manioc bread. The male provider invites the men and the cook invites the women and children to eat. Each female family productive team should provide its manioc basket. These are set in an outer circle around the pot. The eaters squat around the food, tearing off pieces of manioc-bread, dipping them into the peppery juice and picking solid chunks of cooked fish from a banana-leaf platter. It is considered very wrong to eat either fish or juice without manioc-bread. The bread is presented for communal consumption and, between meals, sits in the open part of the house by the entrance to the compartment of the producers (see Fig. 1) where theoretically it is available to all. In spite of this, people should not regularly rely on the supply of other families: they should eat from their family basket and if they do not ill-feeling mounts quickly.

Eventually the eaters announce they have finished and each drinks from the pots of drink placed beyond the meal. Alternatively, women may prepare drinks after the meal and hand them around the dispersed community. These drinks are made of manioc products and fruits – they never contain pepper.

When the meal is over, everyone washes and the men move towards the centre-front of the house, where they hand coca and cigars around amongst themselves. The order in which they are passed from man to man more or less reflects descent group seniority. Eating food and chewing coca are mutually exclusive activities. Men often refuse invitations to eat food on the grounds that they are using coca instead. On the other hand, drink can be taken in combination with coca and is often presented to men specifically during their coca sessions.

After a period of coca chewing, the men disperse to follow their various productive pursuits. They may continue to chew from time to time, particularly if involved in communal activity. A few older women, especially those past the menopause, habitually use coca; sometimes they receive it from their menfolk and sometimes they produce small quantities on their own account. Having passed the portion of their lives devoted to child-bearing and rearing, they are like men in some respects but, significantly, their coca activities are not formalised or ritualised like those of the male community.

The meal sequence shows a clear patterning of events. Peppered protein food is served with manioc bread, while the coca which follows is just for men. As far as our substances are concerned, there are manioc and pepper, cultivated and prepared by women, and protein food, obtained by men, all of which are consumed together by both sexes; then there is coca, produced by men, and consumed by initiated males only. The food and coca are separated by drinks which are compatible with both. In terms of the cultivated plants involved, female manioc and pepper are opposed to male coca. Although the meat or fish is originally supplied by men, the addition of pepper which infuses the cooking flesh and the female control over the cooking fire and cooking process all serve to identify the cooked dish as a female product. We shall see later that the ambiguous character of protein as a male product which becomes part of female meals is consistent with its position in the overall pattern of production. Now it is possible to show that the meal sequence is but a miniature replica of the longer daily cycle which contains it. In the daily cycle we must consider production in greater detail.

The Daily Cycle

The daily cycle is, of course, governed by the sun but, within the framework set by the alternation of day and night, time is structured by the activities of the longhouse community. The most important regular daily productive activities are:—

i) the harvesting and preparation of manioc by women
ii) hunting and fishing by men
iii) the elaboration of the catch into communal meals by women and
iv) the harvesting and preparation of coca by men.

Pepper harvesting and preparation do not come into the regular daily routine because the crop is gathered at intervals and preserved by smoking for gradual use. Pepper is often used as an item of trade for which it is clearly more suitable than perishable manioc and coca products. Of all the crops grown by Pirá-paraná Indians — including all those not mentioned here — manioc and coca are the most closely bound into the daily productive life of the community that cultivates them. It is for these that extensive cultivation sites must be felled and on these that the greatest amount of productive energy is spent.

The manioc production of women is entirely different from men's routine production of protein and coca. The fact that manioc is the staple, the nature of the crop as such and the individual character of women's work all combine to give women less choice over how they spend their time than men. Each female family productive unit, which means a wife and her daughters (if she has any with her) must fetch manioc on most days, so that the family bread-basket is permanently filled. Whereas the family can enjoy protein meals supplied by other families, which leaves the men of the family free to withdraw from protein-production temporarily, there is no equivalent licence to rely temporarily on other's manioc supply. The bread-basket must always be offered even at protein meals supplied by another family and, in addition, the women must keep up with the private consumption of bread by their own family members. Besides being controlled by constant demand, female manioc production is more rigidly structured in time than male activities because it actually takes nearly a whole day to complete. When women co-operate this usually indicates a larger population to feed and so the time is barely cut. The daily rhythm of manioc production dominates the lives of all women and, being the most regular of all productive rhythms, it structures time for the community as a whole.

It is well-known that the processing of bitter-manioc is a long and complex affair, designed to remove poisonous elements (cyanogens) and yield edible cakes, tapioca, etc. Basically the process is one of separating different components of the tubers and then combining and cooking them, using a vast array of basketry and pottery equipment. I shall describe it in its natural stages: the first stage is the harvesting, the second the separation of three components and the third the combining of the solid elements to make bread.[6]

Harvesting

Women leave the house soon after dawn. They spend the morning working in their cultivations, digging up manioc tubers, replanting the sticks, peeling the tubers and then loading them into baskets. The tubers are washed in the river and brought into the house, where they are tipped out into a flat basket. This marks the end of the first stage of the process which is over around midday. The women usually eat from their private family food-supply before continuing.

Separating

Next the tubers are grated up on a board set with quartz chips and the sloppy mash resulting from this is placed on a basketry sieve supported by a tripod stand over a large pot. One or more women pound the mash in the sieve while pouring water over it. The water washes the starch and liquid component out of the mash, so that an opaque, starchy juice drips through into the pot below. The juice is left for the starch to settle out and the three main components of the tubers are now separated: *starch* forms a layer on the bottom of the pot; *juice* rests above the starch and may be decanted off; *fibre*, the coarse part of the root, remains above in the sieve. Starch and fibre are stored away for making bread on another day.

While the starch settles the women leave the house for loads of firewood in order to boil up the decanted juice. The boiling drives off choking, poisonous fumes and when these have subsided the juice is removed from the fire. Cooling is purposefully speeded by taking gourdfuls of juice and pouring them back into the pot from high above. Other women are invited to help the owner of the juice with cooling and this gives them an opportunity to keep a gourdful of drink. When the juice is cool enough to drink it is deposited in the centre-front of the house and the female owner's male partner invites the men of the community to drink. This is the end of the second stage and it roughly coincides with dusk.

The third stage is the recombining of starch and fibre from the

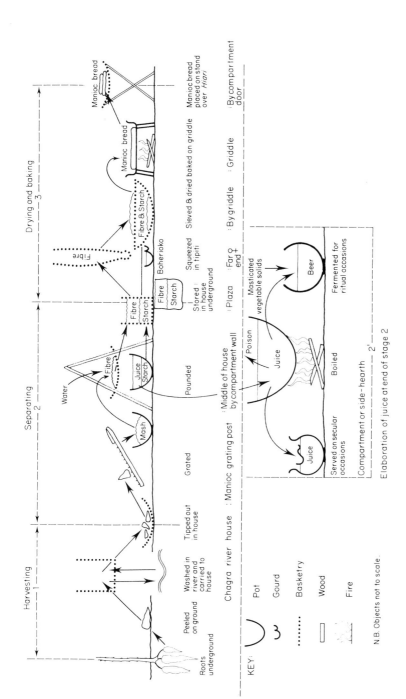

Fig. 2. Manioc Processing.

store. It is important to make a firm distinction between this third stage and the previous two because, between the second and third stages, the solid elements can be stored for days, or even weeks. For maximum preservation the starch and fibre are buried underground outside the female door of the longhouse, but for shorter periods they are packed into baskets or wicker enclosures in the family compartments. For bread-making the fibre is taken from the store and dried by squeezing in a *tipiti*. The *tipiti* is a diagonal-weave basketry cylinder, into which the fibre is fed at the open end. It is hung vertically and stretched downwards by the weight of women sitting on a horizontal pole threaded through the bottom (see Fig. 2). The liquid exuded through the basketry wall is discarded and the partly-dried fibre is tipped out and dried further on a large ceramic griddle. Finally starch is drawn from the store, mixed in with the fibre, and the combination baked on the griddle into a flat round up to 2 in. diameter. Quarters of the finished round are piled into a flat basket kept on a stand by the door to the producer's compartment.

Within this three-stage process no single stage can be broken. The second stage usually follows the first immediately, but it is possible to keep the tubers up to 48 hours before processing them, provided they are unpeeled – after this period they rot. Similarly the raw juice decanted from the starch-pot rots if it is not boiled up immediately. During the ordinary, secular routine, Pirá-paraná Indians like to complete the first two stages each day and also to make fresh bread each day. In this they differ from many Amazonian groups, who either harvest one day and process another, or harvest at intervals and rely on storable cooked manioc products for their staple.

We may summarise the ordinary female routine in terms of two processes which run along-side each other. One is the manioc process which contains a part which is fixed in time and a part which is less so. The fixed part – the first two stages – structures the day neatly, dividing it into a morning spent outside the longhouse and an afternoon in the female end of the house finishing with presentation of the juice at the male end of the house at dusk. The bread-making belongs to a subsequent day and is typically fitted in during the early morning or late afternoon. The second process making up the female routine is the cooking and serving of protein-based meals. The meal serving is confined to the day time, since food is prohibited after dark. Although it is formally initiated by a communal breakfast to which all family units contribute a dish, it shows no other regularity. Therefore protein meal distribution merely shows a contrast between

the day as a whole and the night as a whole.

For men the secular daily routine also includes two processes — hunting and fishing on one hand and coca picking and processing on the other. Alternative activities such as felling trees to prepare new land for cultivation, building or repairing houses and manufacturing material goods are fitted into this two-fold routine as the need arises, generally to the detriment of the supply of protein food. If these non-routine activities are in competition with the male search for food, so also is coca production because it is extremely time-consuming. The most usual pattern is for men to pick and process coca in the after-noon after returning from food-getting expeditions, but there is no particular feature of the process itself that requires this timing. For large quantities of coca, picking must begin in the morning in order to get through the processing in a single day.

The coca process is carried out communally. A group of men pick the leaves and then subsequent tasks of toasting them, pounding them, fetching dried leaves (of *Porouma cecropiaefolia*, the jungle-grape) to provide ash additive and sieving the pounded mixture are usually carried out by different members of the picking group. The processing therefore differentiates the male community and inte-grates it into a functional whole by allocating separate stages of a single process amongst them. The finished product is kept in a round gourd on a stand similar to the one supporting the bread basket but the stand is placed in the centre-front of the house with other items of male equipment.

If we compare the two-fold daily routines for each sex, we find male coca production set against male protein production and female manioc production running alongside female cooking of communal meals. The two basic female tasks are better integrated with one another than the male ones, for cooking is fitted into the old intervals in the manioc routine and the respective products — cooked protein and manioc-bread — are eaten together. By contrast, coca production and protein provision represent alternative uses of male time as well as being directed to alternative types of con-sumption — the meal and the male coca-session. If we look at the male and female routines in relation to one another, male protein production and female cooking are stages in the same process while coca production and manioc production are separate, being all-female and all-male processes respectively. Overall there is one heterosexual productive process and one complementary pair of sexually differentiated processes. This finding corresponds to the use of house space in the course of production. Coca and manioc are produced at the male and female ends of the open part of the house, while protein food is cooked in the family compartment. I mentioned in the discussion of house-space that there is an association between male activity and communal social life and another between female activity and family, or private life. Here we find these associations confirmed for, although manioc is produced outside the family compartment in the public, communal part of the house, it is still produced by female family teams, i.e. within the family social unit. Nevertheless some of the productive equipment is communally used as is that for coca-processing equipment. The final position of the finished product, in the open part of the house but just by the compartment door, once more emphasises the ambiguous social significance of manioc: although a female equivalent of coca in some respects, manioc cannot be a truly communal product precisely because it is under female control.

Returning to the trio of cultivated plants involved in the daily round of production and consumption, we can see that pepper is opposed to both coca and manioc. This is because pepper is a metonymical representative of the cooked protein dish and the production of cooked protein involves both men and women. Pepper not only infuses the meat or fish, so that elements produced by men and women are confounded, but also brings the individuals normally divided by both sex and family membership together to consume a communal meal. It has a further related role in incorporating visitors into the social life of the host longhouse because the standard meal offered to visitors is 'pepper-pot' – a dish of caramelised manioc juice very highly seasoned with pepper. In general pepper would seem to act as an agent of conjunction between the sexes, between the families which are productive units based on the division between the sexes and between whole communities. We shall see this interpretation confirmed in the use of pepper following ritual periods.

While the day as a whole is characterised by meal consumption interspersed by productive activity and brief coca-sessions, it is after dusk that the men's circle gathers and the coca, usually freshly produced that afternoon, comes into full force. All the initiated men of the community sit on stools arranged in a circle towards the centre-front of the house where the coca-gourds and various ritual items are kept. They converse, joke and tell myths while coca is handed from the headman along the line and back (in spite of the circular seating pattern the line has a beginning and end). The least formal men's circles are held when only a small party of residents are present and the most formal when prestigeful visitors are entertained. Towards midnight, the headman disperses the circle by initiating exchange of formal 'goodnights' and shutting the longhouse door until dawn.

The women, who spend the time after dusk in small groups around the men's circle, usually leave for their hammocks well before the men. Their informal chatting and yawning contrasts with the men's formal conversation and wakefulness. The women are also much less strict in observing the prohibition of food after dusk. In general, women are regarded as having little resistance to tiredness and hunger compared with men and in this they are like the children to whom their daily rhythms are geared.

From the description of different consumption activities through the daily cycle, it should be clear that there is a general structure similar to the consumption patterns of the meal sequence (see Figs. 3, 4 and 5). Although men consume coca at intervals during the day, the day time as a whole is a time for eating food, while the first half of the night is given over exclusively to male consumption of coca. For the second half of the night the male community disperses, each withdrawing from social interaction to his hammock, just as each goes off to engage in productive activity after the meal and coca-session are over. For women the social period after dusk is less marked so that the dominant distinction in the female daily cycle is between the day, filled by food consumption and night, filled by sleep and absence of food-consumption. Therefore women abide by the sun's natural cycle while men divide the night into a half which resists the night through heightened social activity and a half in which they sleep along with the women and the majority of natural species. From the point of view of human activity, the change from day to night coincides with two main events: the female offering of fresh manioc juice to the male community and the initiation of full-scale coca-consumption in the men's circle.

The provision of manioc juice is the culmination of the separation stage and, as such, has a fixed position at the end of a day's female work. In a sense, the culmination of coca-production is as significant in the social changeover from day to night as the culmination of the manioc separation stage: this is stated in myth where it is said that the first people got hopelessly muddled in their coca-production before night was created. However, we have seen that for practical purposes the timing of the coca process is not as firmly fixed in the daily timetable as manioc separating. Besides this, coca keeps for several days, so that it is not necessary to produce it quite as regularly as manioc. The role of freshly boiled manioc juice in marking the social change from day to night – a kind of economic dusk which coincides with the solar one – and the role of drink in general in creating the change from food consumption to coca consumption is crucial when we consider another kind of time – the socially manufactured cycle of ritual and secular periods. With this we come to the question of the relationship between secular and ritual life.

The Ritual Cycle

Indians attend communal rituals every few weeks, sometimes as hosts and sometimes as guests. As mentioned before, rituals may be ordered on a scale of 'sacredness' and in the most sacred of all, during which boys are initiated, women are excluded from the main part altogether. Rituals break the normal routine of feeding the community and maintaining the material basis of its existence. The daily rhythms are suspended; food and sleep are forbidden and beer, coca and yage are prescribed. The prohibition on pepper is particularly stressed. As the previous analysis would lead us to predict, women and children observe the prohibition on sleep and food far less strictly than men and do not participate in the ritualised consumption of drugs. A community planning a ritual invites the total populations of a number of other longhouses to attend. The male local descent group members of these guest communities may be classified as either siblings (who share common descent) or affines of the host men. The ritual temporarily unites several communities, who are virtually autonomous producing and consuming units on other occasions, into a wider consuming unit.

Several days of preparation precede the ritual. Some days before the event, a member of the host community travels to the guest longhouse communities and formally invites them to 'drink manioc beer', adding the nature of the ritual to be performed. The invitation speech sets the day by giving the calendar of beer preparation as follows: 'bringing in manioc day', 'pairing-off bringing in manioc day' (for a large attendance), 'beer-working day' and 'beer-drinking day' on which the guests are instructed to arrive. The invitation may also mention coca preparation, although this does not fix the day in the same way as manioc preparation since it may be repeated on consecutive days.

During the preparation period, the ordinary daily pattern of production is done away with – or rather, certain elements are extracted and stretched out. The beer preparation follows the first and second stages of the normal manioc process, but these are extended over two or three days, the tubers being left after the first stage until the next, or next-but-one morning. Once the second stage of separation is begun it must be completed in a day. At the end of this last full day, huge vessels of freshly boiled juice which is to be turned into beer are ready. These are emptied into a wooden canoe-like trough vessel, which has been partly filled with masticated vegetable mash. The bottom of the canoe is heaped around with ashes to retain the heat and the mixture ferments overnight. Before dawn on the following morning, the solids are sieved out and the beer poured back into the canoe from which it is served. It is ready to drink immediately, although its alcoholic content increases with time.

If we turn back to the daily production of manioc juice, we see that the mastication of vegetables, the overnight fermentation and the sieving out of solids occupy the same position between boiling off the poison and drinking the freshly boiled juice as does the cooling process in the daily cycle. Instead of a quick changeover from day to night achieved by quick cooling, the fermentation achieves a drawn out changeover from ritual preparation to consumption during the ritual period proper. The canoe in which fermentation occurs is, of course, a superb transformative vehicle since it is associated with shifts in time and space. In fact the structural equivalence of the manioc juice cooling and manioc beer fermentation, when each is seen as part of a continuous process, perhaps explains why Indians bother to cool manioc juice at all. They are happy to eat boiling hot meat or fish and, in view of this, the purposeful cooling of manioc juice is particularly striking. We shall see that heat is one of the elements purposefully re-introduced after the main ritual period is over.

A general view of economic preparations for the main ritual period shows that only a part of the daily routine of women and a part of the daily routine of men are extended to fill the pre-ritual days. These parts are the first two stages of manioc production and the whole of coca production – the two sequences which, in their different ways effect the social change from day to night. Women's cooking and men's hunting and fishing activities continue over the preparatory period but in a desultory way because nearly all the time and energy is devoted to beer and coca work. In fact, the emphasis on the single-sex activities of manioc production and coca production during the pre-ritual period confirms that the sexual distinctions made in the daily productive cycle are significant. Manioc and coca are destined for ritual consumption while protein food impregnated with pepper is destined for immediate consumption at meals which must stop as soon as ritual proceedings begin. Furthermore, comparison of the daily and ritual cycles serves to classify male sleep. The parallel between the ritual period and the men's circle (Figs. 3 B and C), both of which are marked by prohibition on sleep and food, and prescription of drugs, suggests that the aspect of the male daily routine devoted to protein provision is paired with the part of the night devoted to sleep and the aspect of the routine concerned with coca production is paired with the half of the night devoted to the men's circle. If we remember that sleep and cooking of protein meals are both private activities which take place in the family compartment and thus contrast with coca production and the men's circle which take place in the centre front of the house, we may distinguish two aspects of adult male existence. These are a 'family aspect' manifest in sleep and protein provision and a 'descent-group aspect' manifest in coca production. The 'family aspect' is closely integrated with the female productive cycle.

As for the ritual period itself, it is outside the scope of this paper to describe what goes on except to reiterate the point made at the beginning. The ritual is concerned a) with the creation of a social community composed of several longhouse communities and b) with communication with ancestral events and thus with descent group origins. Now it is possible to consider the plants used during ritual and to note that the manioc beer and yage are specific to ritual and absent in the men's circle. These two make a firm pair for they are served together to the community of participant men: yage, which is an extremely bitter drink, cannot be kept down without a draught of beer immediately afterwards and so it is directly dependent on beer for its hallucinogenic effects. In spite of the pairing of these two substances, beer alone is offered to women and children. It is the yage, reserved for men alone, which is said to show the participants the chants and dances, the ritual activities that reproduce the world of the ancestors. The beer brings whole longhouse communities of men, women and children together in one place, while the yage, which significantly enough is prepared during the ritual itself, provides the ritual context – the state in which communal contact with ancestral times is possible.

The ritual itself may be regarded as a stronger form of the men's circle. While the daily men's circle binds together the men present in the longhouse in an ordered fashion that reflects the ordered structure of patrilineal descent groups, in ritual a wider male community is likewise bound together by the sharing of coca. The united community is then able to participate in the ancestral world by means of yage. Here it is interesting to note that coca and yage are called by the same generic term – *kahi* – and distinguished only as solid and liquid. Thus coca is *bare-kahi*, eating-*kahi*, and yage is *idire-kahi*, drinking-*kahi*. I have shown that in the daily productive cycle, manioc, a female controlled plant, is paired with coca, a male controlled plant. Manioc beer is a substance made from the transformed liquid part of the manioc tuber and is thus related to the daily manioc bread as liquid to solid, in precisely the same way as yage is related to coca. From this point of view ritual could be described as a 'liquid' extension of the daily manioc and coca regime. This is surely an appropriate description for people who believe that, in spatial terms, their present state is related to their ancestral origins by an upstream journey along a great river.[7]

When the ritual is over, the forbidden activities of eating and sleeping are re-established. The most carefully graded resumption of secular time occurs in the treatment of initiates following their initiation – the most sacred ritual of all. These undergo a strict post-ritual seclusion during which direct contact with women is totally forbidden and food intake is limited to manioc bread made of starch alone, together with certain species of ant and termite. The seclusion is ended at a rite of integration, at which pepper is eaten and boiling manioc juice is drunk. After the pepper rite, the initiates take their first meal of male-produced protein consisting of the least harmful species of small fish which have been specially caught in traps made and set by the initiates themselves. After the fish meal, a large dance is held at which the officiating shaman invites young girls to take on his 'renewed ones' (the initiates) as ceremonial trading partners. The re-integration of initiates marked by pepper-shamanism obviously has multiple significance but, nevertheless, there is an underlying unity in all the changes incurred. The initiate eats pepper, a necessary preliminary to his reintroduction to the normal protein foods which are always cooked with pepper. The protein meal which follows marks the initiate's transition from consumer-only to producer-consumer of the products of heterosexual co-operation. At the same time he forms heterosexual trading partnerships in which his own products are exchanged for female products: this exchange of sex-linked artifacts (male basketry for female-produced paint and garters) complements the relation between male protein provision and female cooking upon which the standard communal meal is based. Overall the new adult is a participant in heterosexual productivity instead of a dependant relying on the heterosexual relations of others. It is also significant that initiation is a pre-condition of marriage and must be complete before boys are allowed sexual relations with females, so that physiological, social and economic maturity go hand in hand.

If we return to the seclusion diet, we see that in productive terms the manioc bread made entirely of starch represents the as yet un-matured or 'un-renewed' male initiate's dependance on forbidden females while the pepper, which is an active agent of 'renewal', brings about conjunction of the sexes in closely interdependant relationships. The eating of pepper is the key turning point and so it is appropriate that it should be accompanied by the drinking of hot manioc juice for this re-establishes the secular routine at precisely the point where it was originally broken – the transformation of hot manioc juice into beer. Manioc juice which is not destined for beer is cooled slightly and then offered for the customary drink at dusk.

This treatment of ritual has shown once more that the patterns of production and consumption serve to classify time, bringing the sexes together and separating them on different occasions. But the cursory discussion of events following initiation rituals has shown something more. In the case of the male initiates, these ordered processes of production and consumption are used to control the physical and social growth of individuals. The initiates are separated off from the domain of women and children in which they have spent their early years, and transformed into a state in which they can set up the crucial productive and *reproductive* relations with members of the opposite sex. Productive and reproductive relations are obviously closely allied. In the reproductive process, exogamous marriage and patriliny combine with physiological reproduction to create and dis-perse family units and, at a higher level, longhouse communities which are based on a continuation of this formation and dispersal of families over several generations. It is these self-same units – the family and the longhouse group – with their crucial divisions by sex and age (or generation) that provide the social basis for production and consumption. I now go on to argue that the patterns of production and consumption are ordered according to the processes of reproduction of social units and that this is what makes the substances appropriate for use in rituals, all of which are related to the reproductive process. As I pointed out in the beginning, the argument could be substantiated by use of myth and exegesis, but to attempt this here would be to divert attention away from the division of labour itself.

How does the economic process represent the social order? We have seen that the social order depends upon a solidary unit of male descent group members who exchange their sisters for wives. Just as adult men have two roles as male descent group members and as husbands, adult women have two roles as female descent group members and as wives. But, although women are descent group members as much as their brothers are, they do not form a solidary group in practice for they are dispersed in marriage. Now some of the earlier findings can be pieced together: 1) male production and consumption have a 'descent group aspect' concerned with coca and a 'family aspect' concerned with protein provisions; 2) female production divides into manioc work, parallel but separate from coca production, and cooking which is very obviously a 'family aspect' being bound up with male protein provisions: 3) the entire production of protein meals based on heterosexual relations between family members may be represented by pepper – a female cultivated plant used in contexts which show it to be an agent of conjunction between the sexes. This means that heterosexual family productive relations are thus 'activated' or 'made nourishing' for the community by women's pepper.

I now suggest that pepper represents the wifely status of women while protein provision represents the status of men as husbands. Overall both these family-oriented relationships are classified as female because it is around women's reproductive powers that families are built. This conclusion is consistent with the ability of pepper to incorporate foreign visitors into the community for marriage is also an incorporation of foreigners. Following from this, manioc and coca with their sexually separate chains of production would seem to represent the descent-group status of women and men respectively. The 'descent-group' significance of coca has already been mentioned: with respect to manioc we may remember that in the post-initiation sequence manioc bread (made of starch) and pepper are separated in time.[8] Manioc bread is allowed during seclusion, the period intervening between the initiation rites proper and the re-integration rite. From the point of view of the initiates, manioc is consumed at a time when sexual and other adult, hetero-sexual relations with women are forbidden, while pepper is con-sumed at a time when these relations are newly permitted. Manioc is therefore a gift from prohibited women, while pepper is a gift from permitted women and, as we have seen, the completion of initiation marked by the pepper rite is a necessary preparation for the for-mation of a marriage tie. Manioc may be compared to sexually prohibited sisters and pepper to the wives who replace them.[9] There is an obvious problem with this interpretation as it stands, for at reintegration the pepper does not *replace* manioc in the diet, as wives replace sisters in the social process, it is *added* to manioc. The problem is resolved if, instead of relating manioc to sisters as much, we interpret manioc as a female aspect of descent group structure which is manifest in all women. Women, on marriage, do not lose their descent group identity, rather their separate descent-group identity, which differentiates them socially from their husbands is a necessary feature of marriage. This social separation of husband and wife contrasts with the natural conjunction of the two which results in a child.

Now it is possible to look at male and female aspects of descent group structure in a general way. From one point of view the descent group is autonomous with its stress on patrilineal relations, but from another it depends upon producing sisters in order to get wives and maintain its membership through reproduction. The autonomy of male coca activities, which represent the male aspect of descent group structure, and the dependence of men upon women for manioc products, which represent the female aspect of descent group structure together represent this social aspect of descent group continuity. Protein provision and cooking represent the sexual reproduction of community members which takes place within the socially constructed marital union. The product of this union, the cooked protein dish, stands for the physical child and, as mentioned above, it cannot be consumed without the addition of manioc bread. The child is thus a female product which is only regarded as 'nourishing' for the community provided that it is the product of an exogamous marriage.

The social reproductive process, like the productive process, consists of the separation of men and women and their combining. In the division of labour between the sexes, the separation and combination are not apparent if the tasks of each sex are merely listed – they only emerge when we consider the relations between the entire processes whereby raw materials are turned into substances fit for consumption and then consumed. As the example of the initiation sequence showed, consumption patterns offer a means of controlling individual consumers in terms of the social relations which are manifest in production in a more general way.

This immediately raises questions about the function of ritual for the previous analysis has shown that in socio-economic terms, ritual is simply a large-scale version of the daily round. The initiation ritual itself is parallel to that aspect of daily routine concerned with the separation of the sexes and the ritual of reintegration with its reintroduction of pepper and protein is parallel to the aspect of the daily routine concerned with combination of the sexes in marriage. The qualitative separation between the initiation proper and secular life is introduced by beer and yage but, as we saw, these are really just liquid extensions of manioc and coca so that the qualitative difference can be reduced to a less fundamental one. The events we immediately recognise as 'ritual' occasions actually constitute an expansion of everyday life in which the two paired productive processes (manioc and coca on the one hand and protein provision and cooking on the other) which are normally integrated into a single day, are taken separately, so that one stands for the ancestral state and the other for secular life. If controlled consumption on these ritual occasions is a symbolic manipulation of the role of the consumer in the process of reproduction of social groups, then is not the same true of the every day eating of manioc bread, peppery dishes and coca? The answer must obviously be that it is. In this case the special nature of rituals cannot be derived from the use of symbolic values for everyday things for these everyday things already have symbolic values derived from their association with the social order. Although I cannot attempt a definition of ritual here, it is clear that for Pirá-paraná Indians it is a re-use of products symbolising processes of reproduction of social groups in order to control the same processes of reproduction of social groups by altering the participant individuals.

Finally, I must return to the aspects of symbolism which have remained unexplored. There are many things to be learnt about manioc, coca, meat, fish, beer and yage from analysis of myth, ritual prohibitions and Indian explanations of the nature of these substances. If I had begun with the mythical tapir's wife who wanted to know who had secretly made love to her and said 'who has been stirring my pepper pot?', I could have bypassed a large portion of this paper. I could have written that 'pepper is a female product and myth shows it to be a symbol of female sexuality, QED' and so on with the other female and male products. Of course, in some respects my analysis is less convincing without these extra pieces of information, but I hope at least it shows that the ordering of male and female productive activities is more than simply a 'division of labour'.

Footnotes

1. I am indebted to Jean La Fontaine and Terry Turner for their comments on the original draft of this paper. These comments have been extremely useful in preparing this version.

2. The Barasana are on the south western limit of the Vaupes culture area and possess most of the cultural elements described for other Vaupes groups. They are rather less similar to the Cubeo (Goldman 1963) and Desana (Reichel-Domatoff 1971, 1975) than they are to the Tatuyo (Bidou 1972), their immediate neighbours to the North, and the Bara (Jackson 1977), their immediate neighbours to the East. The Bara and Tatuyo are the principal groups with whom the Barasana exchange women. Unfortunately, although valuable in many respects, these sources contain very little data on patterns of production and consumption and so it is impossible to know to what extent the analysis here would apply to other Vaupes groups.

3. In practice the Barasana are one of the few exceptions to the general rule that descent and language boundaries coincide among Tukanoan Indians, nevertheless Barasana insist that descent and language groupings should coincide. The practice of linguistic exogamy in the Vaupes area is discussed in Sorenson (1967) and Jackson (1974).

4. S. Hugh-Jones (1974) contains a detailed analysis of initiation rituals and a discussion of the relations between these and both the other types of communal ritual I mention and other types of life-cycle ritual. Apart from initiation, the important life-cycle rituals are held at birth, menstruation and death. These have elements in common with initiation, but they do not involve invitation of outside communities, dancing or beer-drinking.

5. The longhouse as a whole may be regarded as a condensed version of some Indian villages in Central Brazil in which a central men's house, the focus of ceremonial activity, contrasts with a peripheral circle of extended family huts, the domain of domestic activity.

6. The detailed description of the manioc process is important for several reasons. No good description exists for the Vaupes area and the processing varies considerably from one culture to another (see Schwerin n.d.). Added to this is the point, made both directly and by implication throughout this paper, that analysis of primary productive processes is not likely to be useful unless these processes are considered in detail.

7. Many of the chants in which the male community participates on ritual occasions relate the upstream journeys of the exogamous group anaconda-ancestors.

8. Elsewhere (Hugh-Jones 1977) I have attempted a complete analysis of the manioc process using data drawn from myth and ritual as well as the type of data included here. In this analysis I account for the use of starch alone in the manioc bread eaten during seclusion, but to discuss this point here would require introduction of a type of material I have purposely excluded.

9. While the proposition manioc:pepper:: sisters:wives may make sense in the case of initiates it clearly does not in the case of menstruating women or mothers of new-born children — people who also observe the seclusion diet. This suggests that a more general formulation is required, but limited space prevents me from providing the necessary data. Initiation is the most appropriate example here precisely because it is the climax of ritual life and the patterns of consumption are most clearly marked.

References

Bidou, P. (1972). Representations de l'espace dan la Mythologie Tatuyo (Indiens Tucano). *Journal de la Societe des Americanistes*. Vol. **61**, 45–105. Paris.

Goldman, I. (1963). The Cubeo: Indians of the Northwest Amazon. Illinois Studies in Anthropology, No. **2**, Urbana.

Hugh-Jones, S. (1974). Male Initiation and Cosmology Amongst the Barasana Indians of the Vaupes area of Colombia. Unpublished Ph.D. Thesis, Cambridge.

Hugh-Jones, C. (1977). Social Classification among the South American Indians of the Vaupes Region of Colombia. Unpublished Ph.D. Thesis, Cambridge.

Jackson, J. (1974). Language Identity of the Colombian Vaupes Indians, *in* "Explorations in the Ethnography of Speaking" (eds. R. Bauman and J. Scherzer). Cambridge.

Jackson, J. (1976). Vaupes: Marriage: A network System in an Undifferentiated Lowland Area of South America, *in* "Regional Analysis, Vol. II Social Systems" (ed. C.A. Smith). New York.

Jackson, J.E. (1977). Bara Zero Generation Terminology and Marriage. *Ethnology*, Vol. **XVI**, No. **1**, 83–104. Pittsburgh.

Reichel-Dolmatoff, G. (1971). Amazonian Cosmos: The Sexual and Religious Symbolism of the Tukano Indians. Chicago.

Schwerin, K.H. (1971). The Bitter and the Sweet, Some Implications of Techniques for Preparing Manioc. Unpublished paper presented at 1971 Annual Meeting of American Anthropological Association.

Reichel-Dolmatoff, G. (1975). The Shaman and the Jaguar. Philadelphia.

Sorenson, A.P., Jr. (1967). Multilingualism in the N.W. Amazon. *American Anthropologist*, Vol. **69**, No. **6**, 670–82. Menasha.

ASPECTS OF THE DISTINCTION BETWEEN THE SEXES IN THE NYAMWEZI AND SOME OTHER AFRICAN SYSTEMS OF KINSHIP AND MARRIAGE[1]

R.G. ABRAHAMS

I

My purpose in this paper is to try to document and understand a major area of difference between the Nyamwezi and similar systems of kinship and marriage, on the one hand, and others such as the Lozi and the Gonja systems, on the other. All of these systems are of a type commonly, if somewhat uniformatively, called non-unilineal, yet they exhibit two strongly opposed patterns of sexual status definition, namely one of relative equality between the sexes of the Lozi and the Gonja cases, and one of relative inequality among the Nyamwezi. The chief manifestations of the contrast upon which I will focus include rules and practices concerning the holding and transmission of property and, in the Nyamwezi case, a system of bridewealth marriage with concomitant strict rules of unequal filiation. It will be seen that the contrasting patterns involved are similar in many ways to those which Gluckman (1950) analysed in his classical comparison between the Lozi and the Zulu, and it will be recalled that Gluckman's discussion suggests that it is the patrilinearity of the Zulu system which best accounts for many of the differences in question. As I have said, however, the Nyamwezi have no unilineal descent group system, and it is clear that the sexual asymmetry of unilineal descent is only one of a range of possible factors — including, I may add, some which may coexist with it — which might help to explain the sorts of inequalities with which I am dealing here. The nature of some of these factors will emerge in the course of my discussion which will, I hope, also con-stitute a contribution to a more positive delineation of cognatic kinship and its variations than that arising from the use of labels such as non- or quasi-unilineal.

The significance of variation in the treatment of the sexes as a base for such comparative study has been clearly seen by Fortes (1969) when he distinguishes between what he calls the 'equilateral' filiation of the Lozi and the Iban and the more complementary 'bilaterality' of Australian kinship. More generally, the work of Leach (1961) and others, such as Yalman (1967) and Tambiah (1965), on Singhalese kinship has, of course, also thrown a great deal of light on the question of how we may best understand a kinship system which is not characterised by unilineal descent but which nonetheless embodies features often taken to be diagnostic of it, In addition, it may be noted here that Radcliffe-Brown, despite his assertion (1950, p. 82) of the rarity of African cognatic systems, nonetheless provides some interesting insights into the possibilities of a positive character-isation of their structures. I am referring here especially to some of his more 'structuralist' discussions in which he draws out the well-known range of oppositions between joking and avoidance, familiarity and respect, proximal and alternate generations, and so on.[2] Looked at in this fashion, the Nyamwezi kinship system can be seen to form a combination of a number of such oppositions. The most important of these, in addition to those just mentioned, are: a strong contrast between kinship and marriage, which is en-capsulated in a rule that known kinsfolk should not marry and the equally strong contrast between male and female kin which forms the main subject matter of this paper.

II

I have presented a general account of Nyamwezi ethnography else-where, including an outline description of the system of kinship and marriage (Abrahams 1967a and b) and I will therefore limit myself in this section to setting out the main points which appear to be necessary as a background to and substance for my subsequent dis-cussion.

The Nyamwezi are a Bantu-speaking people of west-central Tanzania who together with their closely related and similarly organised northern neighbours, the Sukuma, constitute about one sixth of Tanzania's population. Most of the people are farmers, com-bining agriculture with a variable amount of animal husbandry and supplementing both with migrant labour, though this last has decreased in recent years as profitable forms of cash-cropping have developed. The area was traditionally divided into a large number of chiefdoms and each chief was at the head of a local political and judicial hierarchy of which the lowest level was occupied by village headmen. These arrangements persisted till the early 1960s when the chiefdoms were abolished and a new administrative structure was established in their place. The long term effects of this new structure on the kinship system of the area are likely to be serious, but their exact nature is for the most part not yet clearly visible. It may be noted, however, that the abolition of the chiefdom system did not diminish the support to extensive population mobility and concomitant tendency for kin to disperse, which the chiefdoms had previously given, both through their widely distributed replication of law, order and public services and through their rules of land tenure. These rules, while offering security of individual tenure to the commoners who formed the large majority of any chiefdom's population, nonetheless denied them any clear-cut rights to pass on their holdings to their heirs, and this discouraged the establishment of commoner land-holding kinship corporations. This situation was maintained in the new system which, of course, also continues to provide a replicated territorial framework of the same general sort as that previously provided by the chiefdoms. Under both arrangements, at least prior to 1974, when further changes were introduced through the establishment of new large nucleated settlements, each individual homestead in a village was built within a set of fields allocated to the homestead head by the headman or subsequent relevant authority. Homestead heads are typically married males and most homesteads contained such a head, his wife or wives, their children, and an occasional and varied sprinkling of other kin such as a divorced or widowed mother or sister, a younger brother, and perhaps some sister's children. The residence of children is partly, though not wholly, as we shall see, determined by the locus of jural authority over them, and this in turn depends upon the form of union between their parents and especially upon whether bridewealth or other related payments have or have not been made to their mother's kin.

A number of writers on the Nyamwezi and Sukuma areas, including myself, have pointed out that there is a wide and changing range of forms of marriage custom to be found here. As in the Dahomean case discussed by Bohannan (1949), however, the different forms of marriage concerned fall fairly readily into two major subdivisions of bridewealth and non-bridewealth unions when they are looked at in terms of their jural consequences. The relative incidence of these sorts of marriage in different parts of the country and at different points in time in its history and in the life history of its individual inhabitants is a complex matter with which I cannot deal with fully here. Briefly, however, it appears that bridewealth marriage has been on the increase over the last forty years, that it is generally more common in areas rich in cattle, and that a woman's first marriage is especially likely to be a bridewealth one. It may be noted that, despite some differences between them, divorce in both sorts of marriage is common and that, taken as a whole, men over thirty years of age appear to have experienced an average of about two divorces each.

Non-bridewealth marriages may start with an elopement, though if the wife has previously been married, the marriage may commence more openly than this. Sometimes, however, even quite old people will elope together more or less for the fun of it. After an elopement it is possible, and in the case of a previously unmarried girl it is extremely likely, that her father or other guardian will try to obtain bridewealth. His chances of doing so and of his being able to insist successfully that she return home in default of payment are again especially high in the case of a previously unmarried girl.

The wife in a non-bridewealth marriage should, like her bride-wealth counterpart, receive the wherewithal for the establishment of her own household. Mainly, this will consist of fields, seed, and her own hut with its own cooking hearth. Her residence in her husband's homestead and her engagement in its economic activities coupled with her cooking for him and sleeping with him are all emically important signs that, in spite of the lack of bridewealth and formal marriage ceremony, she is her husband's wife, and it may be noted here that the same basic terms, e.g. *nke* (wife) and *kutola* (to marry, the passive form *kutolwa* being used for a woman), are used with reference to both types of marriage.

Children born of a non-bridewealth marriage belong in Nyamwezi customary law to the wife's kin who are entitled to remove them to their own homestead once they reach the age of about eight or so.[3] The maternal kinsfolk do not always exercise this right, particularly in the case of the daughters of such a marriage whom they may prefer to let stay so that they can help their mother. But exercise it or not, it is a right which they are felt most definitely to possess. Consistently with this, the father of such children has no right to receive the bridewealth from his daughters' marriages, and − for in a sense this is also a right − no right to provide bridewealth for those of his sons. These rights belong to the mother's kin. The sons of such a marriage likewise have no rights to inherit any property left by their father unless other, more eligible kin are absent.

The husband in a non-bridewealth marriage has the right to his wife's household and agricultural labour and to her sexual services and fidelity. He is entitled to take an adulterer to court and the adulterer will be fined but no compensation will be given to the husband who also has no rights to the offspring of his wife's adultery. The wife, for her part, has a right to her husband's participation and support in household and agricultural tasks along the lines of the customary well-defined division of labour between the sexes.

As I have implied, the situation with regard to bridewealth marriage differs mainly with respect to rights in children, although such marriages are additionally often accompanied by a varying amount of ceremonial and the husband is also entitled to receive compensation from an adulterer. The husband in such a marriage has full genetricial rights over his wife throughout the period of their marriage, and people say of an adulterer in this context that 'the casual labourer does not own the field he tills'. The husband has a right to receive bridewealth paid in marriage for his daughters and the responsibility and right of paying bridewealth for his sons. These sons will be the main heirs to his heritable property, such as cash and livestock, when he dies and such property will be divided along 'house-lines' if the sons were born to different mothers. On his death also, a man's kin have a right to the refund of bridewealth if his widow is not inherited by a younger brother or other suitable kinsman, although widow inheritance is rare these days and the right to a return of bridewealth is by no means always exercised. Bridewealth is also returnable – and much more often returned – upon divorce. In both cases, bridewealth is refunded less certain deductions for children born of the marriage. These are greater in the case of daughters than in that of sons since, the people say, daughters are more useful and more valuable as sources of labour, bridewealth, and children. At the time of my fieldwork in the 1950s the amounts deducted were 2 cows and 1 bull for a girl and 1 cow and 1 bull for a boy, 1 cow being reckoned equal to 2 bulls. Bridewealth itself is not customarily fixed in amount, but payments of between 8 and 15 cattle were common in northern Unyamwezi in the 1950s and the amounts paid appear to have risen somewhat since then.

It is possible for a man who married without bridewealth to convert his marriage into a bridewealth one if his wife's kin agree to this. They will usually do so but cases of refusal in special circumstances are found. It is also possible for a man to make redemption payments for children born to him by a non-bridewealth wife or an unmarried girl. In this case the woman's kin have no right to refuse to let him do so providing that there is no disagreement about his paternity of the children. The payments are the same as those deducted from bridewealth when it is returned at death or on divorce.

Mention should also be made here of a payment called *mchenya* which was introduced into parts of Unyamwezi during the 1960s from a neighbouring area of southern Sukumaland. This payment, of one cow, is a sort of fine imposed by a girl's father or other guardian upon a man who elopes with her, especially if she has not previously been married. It is possible for bridewealth payments to be agreed and made after such an elopement and payment of *mchenya*, but the legal situation is to some extent in flux and there is considerable argument about whether the receipt of *mchenya* signifies a father's or other guardian's acquiescence in a non-bridewealth marriage for the girl, and whether the beast paid should be counted in as part of any bridewealth if this is arranged. It is not absolutely clear why the payments started in the area in the 1960s and not before, but it is not, I believe, insignificant that profitable cash-cropping, and a subsequent increment in the cash value of women's labour, also started at this time.

III

The material which I have so far presented contains most of the main points which I wish to draw upon, and expand upon where necessary, in my subsequent discussion. Most generally it serves to illustrate the fact that women are recognised in the Nyamwezi kinship and marriage system as being significantly different from men in a range of interrelated ways which help to give the system its particular character and form.

One fundamentally important point here is of course that rights in the productive and reproductive capacity of women are in large part controlled by and transferred for payment between men. Admittedly, the possibility of asserting jural control over sons through the making of redemption payments, albeit smaller than those made for daughters, also exists, and indeed such *patria potestas* over sons as well as daughters is one of the benefits of paying bridewealth for a wife. The crucial fact remains, however, that bridewealth is a form of payment between men for rights in women, and no comparable payment exists between women for rights in other women or in men. And it is, of course consistent with this that one finds polygyny but not polyandry, in the area, and that a woman's sexual relations with another woman's husband are a recognised offence only to the extent that she herself may be someone else's wife.

Looked at in these terms, the position of women in this system can be seen to approximate much more closely than that of men to the status of perpetual jural minors, and other factors such as restricted direct access to diviners in the field of ritual tend to support this view. The situation is, however, slightly complicated by the fact that a woman's social personality and status is nonetheless a developing one and that her first marriage is, as my discussion has from time to time implied, an important watershed in this developmental process. A woman who has been married theoretically returns under the authority of her father or other guardian upon divorce. The people, however, generally recognise and accept that she is in fact likely to operate much more independently than a previously unmarried girl and that this likelihood increases with the length and number of her marriages. Related to this is a feeling that over time it is increasingly unreasonable for a man to try to insist upon the payment of bride-wealth for his daughter's or other ward's later marriages, and this is partly reflected in the higher incidence of non-bridewealth unions in such cases. It may be noted also in this context that a previously married woman is, especially between marriages, referred to by the special term *mshimbe* which marks her status as a relatively mature, experienced, and independent woman. Such independence, which we have seen to be somewhat paradoxically derived from a woman's marital history, is, however, only relative — with the possible excep-tion of such women who 'escape' to towns — and it should be noted that it is only in the most extremely rare and genuinely exceptional circumstances that a woman can come to possess the property paid for herself or for her daughter in bridewealth or as redemption pay-ments for her children. Almost always there are one or more males somewhere who have the prior right to receive such property if it comes to be paid. Similarly, women either inherit nothing of their father's wealth or they receive at best a much smaller portion than that received by sons, and it may be added that more distant male kin customarily take precedence over daughters in this context. Women are in certain circumstances entitled to hold land in their own right, e.g. as widows or divorcees, but it is significant here that land is not a heritable good. Women may also occasionally become possessors of substantial wealth in cash or cattle through skilled work, such as divination or some craft work, or through other forms of enterprise, but such 'propertied' women are extremely rare, at least in the rural areas, since opportunities are few; and there is considerable male and some female hostility towards them.

It will be clear that the material I have presented has important implications for the filiation of children. The main point to be noted here is that for any particular child at a particular point in time, his or her ties to patrikin will differ significantly from those to matrikin.[4] Ideally, it can be argued, the system is one in which jural control over children is vested in their mother's husband who should be their genitor. This will be the case in the majority of bridewealth marriages, but there are of course complications which arise through non-bride-wealth marriage and, to some extent, through fornication and adultery. If no bridewealth has been paid in marriage for a woman or if she is simply unmarried, any children which she bears belong to her kin unless they are redeemed by their genitor. But their status vis-a-vis their matrilateral kin only approximates to that enjoyed by children born of a bridewealth marriage (or redeemed) vis-a-vis their patrikin. The main differences are twofold. Firstly, the attachment of un-redeemed children to their matrikin is always in a sense only tem-porary because their father, or his representative, always has a recognised right to make redemption payments. Secondly, and relatedly, the rights of unredeemed children to inherit property are considerably weaker than those of their redeemed counterparts. For they can only inherit major portions of property on their mother's side if fully patrifiliated heirs are lacking there, and access for them to paternal property depends upon redemption. Filiation in this system is then always 'complementary' — to follow Fortes' original usage (1953:33)[5] — rather than equilateral; or, to put it more simply, jural relations traced through women as mothers, and indeed as sisters and daughters, differ substantially from those traced through men.

IV

I turn now to the comparison of this material with that collected for some other African peoples, a task which poses certain difficult though not, I hope, insuperable problems. Firstly, it is necessary to acknow-ledge that one is much more likely to be dealing here with variation along some sort of continuum of difference rather than with absolutely clear-cut oppositions between systems. This is in part already built in to the notion of a contrast between different patterns of filiation of the sort which Fortes has, as I have mentioned, tried to draw. For, leaving aside superficial difficulties of terminology (Cf. footnote 5), it is clear that such concepts as 'equilateral', 'bilateral', or 'com-plementary' filiation, like that of cognatic kinship itself, all imply that there is something which can sensibly be identified as a parent-child relationship irrespective of differences in the sex of either party to it and, as such, that sex-tied differences between various kinship statuses are always to some extent counterbalanced by some degree of sex-free unity. I should perhaps add here that I see no reason to doubt the existence of such unity in most if not all African kinship systems, and it may be worthwhile to point out in this context that a very wide range of African languages possess sex-free verbs, which indeed lack any adequate equivalent in English, to denote the process of producing offspring and becoming parents.[6] On the other hand it would be quite unlikely, to say the least, that any kinship system could be found which failed to differentiate status one way or another along sex lines.

This said, it is abundantly clear nonetheless that major differences of the sort to which Fortes has drawn our attention do exist even in societies without unilineal descent. The next problem is to specify more clearly the sorts of differences for which we are looking. Three basic areas of difference can be usefully identified and have underlain my choice above of Nyamwezi data. Firstly, there is variation in the rights which men and women may hold for themselves. Secondly there is variation in the rights which they are eligible to pass on from themselves to others. Lastly there are differences in rights and obligations which accrue to a person by virtue of his or her links to others through men as opposed to women and vice-versa.

Bearing these sorts of variation in mind, I want now to consider the situation which appears to obtain in three other African societies, namely among the Nyakyusa, the Lozi, and the Gonja.[7] I bring in the Nyakyusa because their kinship system is in many fundamental ways closely similar to that of the Nyamwezi. Unilineal descent, at least as the basis of a commoner descent group system, is apparently absent among them, but one does nonetheless find there, as among the Nyamwezi, institutions of bridewealth (and a form of non-bridewealth marriage also) and widow inheritance, a clear distinction between patri- and matri-filiation with a strong jural weighting to the father's side providing bridewealth has been paid, some tendency towards division into houses with regard to property holding and inheritance, and control over main property by men. The Lozi and the Gonja, on the other hand, appear to provide us with a pair of systems which are fairly similar to each other and which contrast interestingly with those of the Nyamwezi and the Nyakyusa in the present context. Gluckman (1950) has, of course, contrasted the relevant features of the Lozi system with those of the Zulu, as I have mentioned, and Fortes (1969) has stressed the relative equilaterality of Lozi kinship. Esther Goody, upon whose Gonja work I draw, has herself remarked upon some similarities between her own and Gluckman's data (1973, p. 306–8), though she has not focussed on the points of variation between systems without unilineal descent which I am concentrating upon here.

Gluckman (1950) tells us that among the Lozi 'the child belongs to both sides' and the courts will not constrain a young boy or girl to live in his or her father's as opposed to mother's place or vice-versa.

This is in some contrast to the Nyamwezi situation where many cases concerning the custody of and the locus of authority over children arise as among the patrilineal Zulu. Moreover, Lozi children do in fact seem to grow up or establish themselves later with a wide range of matrilateral kin including mother's mother's and even mother's mother's mother's people as well as a wide variety of patrilateral kinsfolk. Coupled with this, among the Lozi only token marriage payments are made, widow inheritance does not exist, and the difference between *pater* and *genitor* is not allowed to arise as a jural issue. This last fact, incidentally, which is usually discussed, as in Laura Bohannan's (1949) work in terms of the different rights and powers of different men also has considerable relevance for the status of the women in question themselves. For in the sort of system in which the rights of genitors are more strongly protected, a woman is – unless subjected to rape – personally capable of bestowing paternity upon a range of men of her choice which she cannot do in a situation in which her husband (either living or dead in some societies) is automatically the pater of her children.

Lastly, it appears that among the Lozi women can hold and transmit to heirs considerable property of their own and of the same type as that held by men, in addition to serving as important links between male holders and their heirs. Thus Gluckman tells us that a man, in addition to his having what he calls a general heir, also allots gardens, fishing sites and cattle *pre mortem* to both sons and daughters as they grow up, and these sons and daughters are then able to transmit these holdings in due course to their own heirs. In addition, he tells us that a woman's children are not only heirs to property she may herself have acquired but they may also succeed her brother, father, or mother's brother by virtue of their ties to them through her. It is also of some interest in this context that a Lozi court will uphold a divorced wife's right to half of the conjugal estate she shared with her husband. Nyamwezi courts have customarily only done this in the case of the collapse of a non-bridewealth marriage, and their doing so is apparently a relatively new thing even in such cases.

The Gonja material presents, as I have said, a similar constellation of features. No more than nominal bridewealth payments are made, a child belongs to its genitor rather than its mother's husband, women appear to be entitled to hold and transmit property which passes down a line of siblings more or less irrespective of sex, and widow inheritance is impossible. Moreover, the fostering system seems to involve an ideal linkage between children and their parent's cross-sex sibling, admittedly with some sex-linkage so that

theoretically a son should go to his mother's brother and a daughter
to her father's sister, and in reality an even greater variety of links
are made use of so that in this context of filiation, as in other contexts noted, Gonja women appear to be much the same sort of
persons as men at least in comparison to their counterparts among
the Nyamwezi. In the field of ritual also, Gonja women seem to be
more similar to men and less dependent on them than are Nyamwezi
women, though there is admittedly a marked distinction among the
Gonja between attitudes to male and female witchcraft. (E.N. Goody
1970 and 1973, pp. 104–5).

V

My discussion so far has served to bring out a range of substantial
differences between the relative statuses of women *vis-a-vis* those of
men in a number of African systems of kinship and marriage which
lack unilineal descent. The fact that such 'non-unilineal' systems contrast with each other in so fundamental a respect is, I believe, a point
of no mean interest in itself which highlights the need which I expressed earlier for a much more positive approach to their description
and analysis; and it is perhaps worth stressing here that I have
focussed in this paper simply upon one main basis of distinction
between them. It is, for example, also possible to contrast the rules
within such systems with regard to marriage between kin, and it may
be noted that the four societies I have discussed fall into a different
pattern of similarity and contrast when considered in this light. Thus
whereas Nyamwezi and Nyakyusa contrast with Gonja and Lozi with
regard to men's and women's statuses, we find Gonja permitting
marriage between cross-cousins while Nyakyusa, Lozi and Nyamwezi
disapprove of such marriages (Gluckman 1950:173; Wilson 1950:114;
E.N. Goody 1973: 76–81). A further point of some significance is
that the differences which I have paid attention to are as I have
observed, clearly similar to many of those which Gluckman emphasised
in his account of contrasts between the patrilineal Zulu and the Lozi;
and the Nyamwezi data, like that on the Nyakyusa, clearly raises
serious issues concerning the overall explanatory power of patrilineal
descent and lineage organisation with respect to matters such as bridewealth and related features of inheritance and concomitant patterns
of inequality between the sexes.

But if descent provides no explanation – at least in the four cases
under consideration – of the differences I have outlined, what if anything further can be said about them? Why should women among the
Lozi and the Gonja be relatively similar to men as status-holding

persons in the kinship system whereas their Nyamwezi and Nyakyusa counterparts possess the very different and in certain ways inferior status of the sort I have described? While one would clearly by unduly sanguine to expect that there are any single, simple answers to such questions, it may nonetheless be useful to try to speculate a little more about them here.

One initial problem in this context is that the actual formulation of questions to be answered is by no means as straightforward as it might at first appear. For example, if it were the case that one of the situations which I have contrasted is somehow more 'natural' than the other, then there could be a danger that at least some of one's questions might be reducible to a more general one of 'why male and female?' which no particular ethnographic analysis is, of course, likely to elucidate! If one tries, moreover, to sidestep this problem, as I shall have to do in the present circumstances, it becomes clear that there are at least two different though not necessarily wholly separable issues in the data. One of these relates to factors which may be present among the Gonja and the Lozi, and absent in the other two societies, and which might run together with the relative equality of women's status there. The second asks what factors among the Nyamwezi and the Nyakyusa, which are absent among the Lozi and the Gonja, might help us to understand why rights in the productive and, especially, the reproductive powers of women are valued highly enough to be 'marketable' in a system of exchange controlled by and between men.

This said, let me first try to clear the ground of factors which appear to have no bearing on these issues. We have already seen that differences in the patterns of marriage prohibitions are not in any way correlated with those under consideration here, and the same can, I think, be claimed for the division of labour between the sexes and some other features of the mode of subsistence. The division of labour is broadly similar among the Nyamwezi, Nyakyusa, and Lozi who differ collectively from the Gonja with their more typical West-African pattern of predominantly male agricultural labour (Gluckman 1941, Chapter 7; Wilson 1951:261; E.N. Goody 1973:52, 103). More generally, all the societies in question are agricultural and the main form of production is hoe-cultivation with no substantial development of fixed crops except in the case of the Nyakyusa who keep relatively large plantations of bananas. The situation with regard to cattle-keeping, which Engels (1972) and others have considered significant in such contexts, is rather more problematic. It is true that the Nyamwezi and the Nyakyusa are keen cattle-keepers whereas

the Lozi and the Gonja have less interest in them. But it is by no
means clear that there are significantly serious differences in the
number of cattle among the Nyamwezi, Nyakyusa, and Lozi, though
it is, in fact, likely that there are rather fewer among the Gonja, and
it seems probable that the emphasis on cattle follows from the interest
in bridewealth rather than vice-versa (Gluckman 1941:20–1; Wilson
1951:257; E.N. Goody 1973:24). In addition, there is of course the
fact that alternative forms of property could no doubt be made
available for bridewealth among the Gonja if they so wished, and it
may be noted here that payment in money and at an earlier stage
in hoe blades is reported for those Nyamwezi areas in which cattle
have at different times been scarce. Moreover, even though the
institution of non-bridewealth marriage in the Nyamwezi and the
Nyakyusa cases appears to be associated with problems of the mal-
distribution of cattle and other property over time and space and
between individuals, it is nonetheless a totally different institution
from marriage among the Lozi and the Gonja where the possibilities
of conversion to bridewealth marriage or of redeeming children
simply do not arise.

So much then for a range of what appear to be non-explanatory
variables. I turn now to consider two further features of the
situation, one mainly political though with economic implications
and the other rather more directly economic, which may perhaps
prove to be a little more illuminating. Taking the political field
first, I will start from Esther Goody's discussion of its possible
significance for kinship in the Gonja case and that of other states
such as the Lozi kingdom which she cites. She notes that there
appears to be a category of important states in Africa which are
'characterised not only by the virtual absence of unilineal descent
groups (although they often have dynasties recruited agnatically),
but also by a series of other features of the kind noted for the
Lozi and the Gonja' (E.N. Goody 1973:307). Here she is referring
to such features of their kinship and marriage system as low bridewealth and the absence of widow inheritance which I have
documented earlier in this paper, and she goes on to ask what connection there might be between politics and kinship in such states.
'Any answer must be tentative', she writes 'But enough has been
said of kinship in central Gonja to show that it is marked by a
continual circulation of men, women and children between compounds whose heads are members of different estates and which are
located in different villages' (1973:308).

Esther Goody herself seems to be interested in this context in the way in which this feature of the kinship system operates as a cohesive force within the complex division of the Gonja state and she also pays particular attention (Cf. also J.R. Goody 1970) to the idea that the 'bilateral component' of the kinship system may be understood as a sort of lowest common denominator in such an ethnically and otherwise culturally mixed situation. This is an interesting argument, though I am uncertain to what extent its view of cognatic kinship as a residue can take into account the sorts of differences within that field which interest me in this paper, and as such to what extent it is basically a theory to explain the absence of unilineal descent groups rather than the presence of particular forms of domestic and wider kinship structure.

However this may be, I want here to suggest, albeit very tentatively, a possible further line of argument relating to the patterns of open connubium and subsequent kinship linkages among the Gonja. This would stress fairly heavily the idea that rank and relative status of various kinds are matters of considerable and wide-ranging importance to the Gonja. It would also involve an assumption that 'open connubium' may permit the raising of a woman's status through her marriage to a rich and/or politically important man and/or a man of high estate, and that additionally the sisters of such a man or of his wife may often provide kinship links for their own children of a value at least equal to, if not greater than, that of links traced for such children through their fathers. In such a situation, the fact that women tended overall to have a kinship status relatively similar to that of men would seem to make considerable sense. I emphasise the tentative nature of this argument because Esther Goody herself has tended rather to play down such considerations in her own analysis, but I have thought it worthwhile to present it on the basis of some part of her own discussion (Cf. 1973, p. 208–9) and also on that of J.R. Goody's (1967) account of the political importance of women of the ruling estate both in their own right and as crucial links between their sons and an apparently substantial number of 'Sister's – son' commoner chiefships.

If such an argument can in fact help us to understand the Gonja situation, it can perhaps also be further developed to throw some light on the comparative problems at issue here. For it can, I think, be plausibly suggested that the Lozi and the Gonja states differ seriously from their Nyamwezi and Nyakyusa counterparts in a range of possibly significant ways such as in their overall size, the size of their ruling groups, and more generally the elaboration of their internal hierarchies. The multi-chiefdom nature of the

Nyakyusa and the Nyamwezi, the lack of any complex division into estates and the absence of highly elaborate patterns of status differentiation such as that involved in the hierarchy of Lozi 'mats' is significant. As a result, the multiple chiefdoms of the Nyamwezi and the Nyakyusa for the most part appear, in comparison to these states, as relatively small-scale and undifferentiated units. Open connubium is a feature of all four societies, but it can be argued that the sorts of effect which I have tried to attribute to it will be much more marked in large and elaborate states than in smaller and less complex structures of the Nyamwezi and Nyakyusa variety.

The second feature of the situation, which I now wish to discuss, concerns patterns of residence and land-tenure in the four societies in question. Starting with the Lozi and the Gonja, we may note the slightly paradoxical fact that although both of them are organised, as I have noted, in powerful, complexly stratified state systems, some of their fundamental groupings at lower territorial levels are essentially assemblages of cognatic kin. This appears to be true of most Lozi mound villages and it appears also to be true of Gonja compounds some of which are quite large units. Esther Goody (1973 pp. 5, 52–5, 257) has described some of the main features of Gonja land-use which may bear upon this. Land is, in an absolute sense, not at all scarce but people seem nonetheless to feel constrained to cluster and co-operate together in bounded local settlements. The productive system itself seems to involve a need for fairly regular co-operative labour particularly when land is being cleared, and it is possible that other ecological, cultural, and social-structural factors work together to encourage such co-residence. Whatever the cause, however, the overall result is a situation in which access to agricultural land and reliable labour is effectively limited and is mainly handled through the kinship network. Membership of compounds turns on kinship (with the compound head an apparently crucial focus of relationship) and, with kinship fostering, provides the main sources of extra-familial labour. In the Lozi case, the mound-village system provides a comparable, though differently based, situation of cognatic kinship 'islands' to which access is typically limited to those who can claim kinship ties of one sort or another to existing members. In both cases, I would suggest that the culturally and ecologically based 'scarcity', in the special sense outlined, of land on which a viable livelihood can be obtained fits sensibly with a kinship system in which ties through men and women are in many respects similar so that there is maximum flexibility of access for the members of statistically fluctuating domestic groups to co-residence with an co-operation from kin.

Turning now to Nyamwezi and Nyakyusa society, we find that the situation there is interestingly different in a number of ways. Probably the most important single point in the present context is the fact that both peoples work much more closely to straight-forwardly territorial principles at the local level, with their combination of village headmanship, neighbourhood co-operation and, traditionally in the Nyakyusa case, coevality in non-kinship villages. As such, access to land and labour is not seriously dependent on the kinship system there, and apparently in both cases, and certainly among the Nyamwezi, individuals and domestic groups have moved relatively freely from one local area to another, gradually opening up new territory in the process, in response to a variety of social and ecological pressures, on the one hand, and largely ecological attractions on the other.[8] What exactly in their land-use system makes it possible (if that is the right question) for households in these areas to rely so much upon themselves, the chiefdom system, and help from mainly non-kin neighbours is by no means altogether clear. Certainly the ecologically-based boundedness of Lozi mounds is not a problem there, and it is possible that differences of soil quality, water supply, and associated population densities might partly account for differences with the Gonja.

So far, I have tried to suggest two aspects of Gonja and Lozi political and economic organisation which might be interestingly consistent with the relatively high status of women in the kinship systems there. I will, I hope, be clear that the influence of either one of these two features does not preclude that of the other and that, if anything, it would be stronger in conjunction with the other than alone. I turn now finally in this section to the further question, noted earlier, of what if anything in the Nyamwezi and Nyakyusa cases might help us further understand the fact that rights in women are a highly 'marketable' commodity. I have already mentioned the possibility that such a fact, or its opposite, might be conceived of as an almost natural feature of human society, and of course Levi-Strauss and others have come fairly close to such a view in this case. I have also noted, however, that it is doubtful that particular ethnography can throw much light on such a general question, and what I wish to do here is simply to look for some of the con-comitants of such 'marketability' in the Nyamwezi and Nyakyusa cases. Once again, I would suggest that such an exercise, if useful can be seen as complementary to my earlier discussion rather than as necessarily alternative to it.

There are several aspects of the situation which may deserve further attention in this context. It is clearly likely to be relevant, for example, that the women and children, over whom the payment of bridewealth gives a man control, may be an important source of labour and/or income to him, and there is the further fact that bridewealth payments also involve a process of redistribution of wealth to a significant extent, though of course not wholly, between generations. Again, it is at least initially tempting to note that both Nyamwezi and Nyakyusa have for a long time engaged in the extensive labour migration of relatively young males which has helped *inter alia* to provide bridewealth and other funds for redistribution affines and kin (responsibility to the latter having been largely determined by former bridewealth payments), whereas such migration does not constitute a serious element of Gonja life (Gulliver 1957; E.N. Goody 1973:23). On the other hand, however, it must be admitted that a high rate of migratory labour seems to be a major feature of the Lozi situation and, as such, does not appear to be tied in any automatic way to a system of bridewealth marriage and bridewealth-dominated filiation (Gluckman 1941:113). Nor, one may add, is the apparent investment in a woman and her children, as a source of future labour, income, and – in the case of daughters – bridewealth, a particularly safe one among the Nyamwezi given such further factors as the high rate of divorce, the apparently related extent to which young men tend to move away from their fathers (Abrahams 1976)[9], and the chance that a daughter may not be married with bridewealth or even be born at all. But it is perhaps possible to argue that it is, nonetheless, the best investment which men appear to have in the circumstances, and it may be noted additionally here that although bridewealth marriages are not especially stable, those in which children have been born do seem to last longer than others, and thus 'childwealth' reverts, as it were, to being bridewealth inasmuch as a woman tends to be tied to some extent to the place where her children are jurally affiliated.

I have suggested that the payment of bridewealth may be an uncertain but nonetheless attractive investment. One important background point to such a suggestion is, I suspect, a feature of the Nyamwezi and Nyakyusa systems which I have emphasised above, namely the fact that local communities there tend to be essentially communities of neighbours. For one corollary of this point is the further fact that such local communities are, equally essentially, relatively loose congeries of individual male-headed households. The system is, then, one in which individual males tend to establish their own domestic units on the basis of their marriages and, at least with regard to residence and everyday domestic economic organisation, it is these marriage-centred units — co-operating on occasion with largely unrelated similar units — which predominate rather than any wider kinship-based associations. Bridewealth marriage then begins to appear as one of the main cohesive forces, though not in any sense a perfect one, whereby a man may try to bind the members of his own domestic unit to himself in this somewhat individuating system. The existence of non-bridewealth marriage in these areas may appear at first sight to run against this argument. Without going into further details of its incidence, however, I would argue that there is good evidence that in many cases such marriage is in fact best understood as a surrogate for bridewealth marriage and that it makes most sense in such cases when viewed as a form available for the relatively in-digent, enabling them to establish households of their own which they will typically hope eventually to convert by subsequent bride-wealth or redemption payments into more clearly viri-focal units.[10] As such, the existence of non-bridewealth unions can in fact plausibly be argued to support the case that marriage, and especially bridewealth marriage, really does lie at the core of the local domestic system as I have suggested. It may be noted, moreover, in further support of this that, in these Nyamwezi and Nyakyusa systems, the main avenue for a man to extend his domestic field of action seems to be polygyny (although the actual rate is not especially high), whereas Gonja men, at least, appear to operate rather more through attempts to attract kin to them, and one may also note here the high proportion of men (17% in one area) whom Esther Goody (1973, pp. 82–3) found to be unmarried in her surveys.

One further point is also perhaps worth making in this context. This is that the very tendency to male individuation which I have mentioned — i.e. the tendency for men to build their domestic world upon the basis of their marriage rather than their sibling ties — per-haps contributes to local perceptions of the attractiveness of bride-wealth as investment. The point here is perhaps comparable to that which can be made about lotteries or other forms of gambling in which many people are attracted to participate despite the fact that only a few are likely to win. The overall statistics of the situation are likely to appear less relevant than is the hope of winning in such con-texts where the main concern of the investor is his own benefit and salvation rather than that of the total body of investors.

This last point brings this paper to a close. I have tried to explore some of the possible concomitants of the differences which I have identified between the systems in question and I have focussed mainly on a range of features within the broad fields of political stratification, land-tenure, and the relative importance of kinship, neighbourhood and marriage in the local 'domestic' sphere. In this last context, it may be noted that my arguments suggest that the very isolation of kinship-linked male-headed households from each other may be at least as consistent with patterns of bridewealth marriage, viri-focality and unequal filiation as would be the unification of such households in a local patrilineal descent group framework. More generally, I would hope that my material also raises the possibility that (as has long been recognised with regard to kinship terminologies) an approach to kinship systems as a whole which would concentrate upon the way in which they handle the allocation of roles and statuses along such fundamental lines as those of sex – and, I might add, age, though I have not dealt with this here – might ultimately be more fruitful than one which takes as its starting point the presence or absence of particular patterns of descent.

Footnotes

1. The fieldwork during which material was collected for this paper was carried out in 1957–60 and 1974–75. I am grateful for comments on earlier drafts which I have received from Dr J. La Fontaine, Professor M. Fortes, and Dr E.N. Goody and for helpful discussions with Professor J.R. Goody.
2. Cf. especially the papers on joking relationships in Radcliffe-Brown (1952).
3. The wife's kin in question will vary according to her own jural attachment to her patrilateral or matrilateral kin.
4. The Nyamwezi kinship terminology is highly consistent with these jural patterns (Abrahams 1967b).
5. In this usage filiation in general appears to be spoken of as 'complementary' whereas later usage commonly attaches the adjective only to the filial tie through which descent is not traced.
6. This is, for example, true of all the languages which I have used in the field, i.e. Swahili *zaa*, the related Nyamwezi *byala*, and the unrelated Luo form *nywolo*. It is not difficult to document the point more widely.
7. See Gluckman (1950), E.N. Goody (1973) and Wilson (1950) for the main source data. It may be noted that Professor R. Frankenberg (1976, pp. 17–21) has recently reviewed the Lozi material and has highlighted some features of male/female inequality there. The contrasts and relative differences which I note in this paper still appear to be valid ones, however.
8. See Abrahams (1976) for some documentation of this.
9. The point is that adult sons very rarely stay with their fathers if their mother has been divorced.
10. The nature of non-bridewealth marriage appears to vary to some extent

according to whether it occurs at an early or a late stage in an individual's marital history. My comments here refer especially to relatively early marriages of this kind.

References

Abrahams, R.G. (1967a). The Political Organization of Unyamwezi. Cambridge University Press, Cambridge.

Abrahams, R.G. (1967b). The Peoples of Greater Unyamwezi. (Ethnographic Survey of Africa, Part XVII). International African Institute, London.

Abrahams, R.G. (1976). Time and village structure in Northern Unyamwezi. *Cambridge Anthropology*, Michaelmas Term 1976, **3**, 26–42.

Bohannan, L. (1949). Dahomean Marriage: a Revaluation. *Africa*. Vol. 19. No. 4.

Engels, E.F. (1972). The Origin of the Family, Private Property and the State. Pathfinder Press, New York. (First published 1884.)

Fortes, M. (1953). The structure of unilineal descent groups. *American Anthropologist*, **55**, 17–41.

Fortes, M. (1969). Kinship and the Social Order. Aldine Publ. Co., Chicago.

Frankenburg, R. (1976). Economic anthropology or political economy – the Barotse social formation. To be published *in* "The New Economic Anthropology (ed. J. Clammer). Macmillan, London (forthcoming).

Gluckman, M. (1941). The Economy of the Central Barotse Plain. (Rhodes-Livingstone Paper No. 7). Rhodes-Livingstone Institute, Livingstone, Northern Rhodesia.

Gluckman, M. (1950). Kinship and marriage among the Lozi of Northern Rhodesia and the Zulu of Natal, *in* "African Systems of Kinship and Marriage" (eds. A. Radcliffe-Brown and D. Forde). Oxford University Press, London.

Gluckman, M. (1951). The Lozi of Barotseland, *in* "Seven Tribes of British Central Africa" (eds. M. Gluckman and E. Colson). Oxford University Press for the International African Institute, London.

Goody, E.N. (1970). Legitimate and illegitimate aggression in a West African state, *in* "Witchcraft Confessions and Accusations" (ed. M. Douglas). *Assoc. soc. Anthrop. Monograph*, No. **9**. Tavistock Publ., London.

Goody, E.N. (1973). Contexts of Kinship. Cambridge University Press, Cambridge.

Goody, J.R. (1967). The Over-kingdom of Gonja, *in* "West African Kingdoms in the Nineteenth Century" (eds. D. Forde and P. Kaberry). Oxford University Press, London.

Goody, J.R. (1970). Marriage policy and incorporation in Northern Ghana, *in* "From Tribe to Nation" (eds. J. Middleton and R. Cohen). Chandler, Scranton, Pennsylvania.

Gulliver, P.H. (1957). Nyakyusa labour migration. *Human Problems in British Central Africa*, **XXI**, 32–63.

Leach, E.R. (1961). Pul Eliya. Cambridge University Press, Cambridge.

Radcliffe-Brown, A.R. (1950). Introduction, *in* "African Systems of Kinship and Marriage" (eds. A.R. Radcliffe-Brown and D. Forde). Oxford University Press, London.

Radcliffe-Brown, A.R. (1952). Structure and Function in Primitive Society. Oxford University Press, London.

Tambiah, S.J. (1965). Kinship fact and fiction in relation to the Kandyan Singhalese. *Journal of the Royal Anthropological Institute*, **95**, 131–173.

Wilson, M. (1950). Nyakyusa kinship, *in* "African Systems of Kinship and Marriage" (eds. A.R. Radcliffe-Brown and D. Forde). Oxford University Press, London.

Wilson, M. (1951). The Nyakyusa of South-western Tanganyika, *in* "Seven Tribes of British Central Africa" (ed. M. Gluckman and E. Colson). Oxford University Press, London.

Yalman, N. (1967). Under the Bo Tree. University of California Press, Berkeley.

SEX, AGE AND SOCIAL CONTROL IN MOBS OF THE DARWIN HINTERLAND

BASIL SANSOM

'Presently we got that problem agin: too many young girl running round'. In the fringe camp sited near Wallaby Cross,[1] a busy cross-road in Darwin, this statement would be recognised as a comment on the state of affairs within a population of Aborigines who distinguish themselves from all others by calling one another Countryman. The Countrymen, as they put it, *run* in mobs and their mobs are associated with the camps of a particular North Australian hinterland.

The urban fringe camp at Wallaby Cross is one of these camps and belongs as much to the hinterland as to the city. Given its urban location it is, for the Countrymen, of particular importance for it serves as a regional centre and Aboriginal *serai*. About 80 people spend most of their time living as fringe dwellers at the Cross. The 80 serve as Darwin hosts to some 400 others – their Countrymen whose mobs are based on hinterland camps. In this population, 'how many young girl you got running round' is an index of good times and bad times and the good and the bad are seasonally phased. The velocity of sex in the population increases with the scarcity of cash so that off-seasons of work in the local pastoral industry are seasons, too, for 'that running round business'. In bad times some previously married women of the population are released from marriage to become girls again. This has the effect of potentially making of any marriage what is known as 'that on and off business' – a relationship that is prone to dissolution but, if things work out that way, open to resumption.

I have first in this paper to show that both 'on and off business' and 'running round' are aspects of the same thing: a redistribution of the Countrymen between mobs and camps that, in thin times, effects efficient redistribution of scarce cash. The people have adjusted to seasonal fluctuations of cash supply by reconstituting mobs in response to scarcity so that the Australian welfare dollar can be equitably though thinly spread. Equity in the welfare dollar is secured but at the cost of the stability of marriages.

The circulation of men and women between mobs and camps and the on-and-off character of marriage, raise issues of social control. Locally, the problem is viewed in terms of women and their sexuality and has two dimensions. In the first place the males of any mob currently associated with a camp must be able to offer protection to mob women. The test of protection is whether the women of a mob are open to abduction or to being sexually abused by envious or predatory outsiders. Then, and secondly, the sexuality of women within a mob must be contained: intra-mob sex cannot be allowed to disrupt the current order of the mob, an order which specifies the terms of the relationships between the mob's male and female members. Within a mob, the relative availability of each person to all others of the opposite sex must be formally defined while individuals must be held to the given definitions.

In the matter of control, there is a sexual division of labour. Men are protectors, women chaperones. Men protect all mob women and all current mob marriages from outside interference. Women organise to guarantee one another's sexuality and, by a system of chaperonage, police the rule that the only legitimate sexual relationships in camp will be between persons currently joined in mob-approved marriages. Potentially disruptive sexuality is thus directed outwards. Any 'young girl running round' will not be permitted to run round with men of her own mob and camp. On the other hand, her person will be protected when she has dealings with outsiders. All mob members move within a range, a locus made safe because relevant others know that that place is policed by a mob's Fighting Men. A woman should, then, at any time be able to rally her mob's Fighting Men to her defence.

Wage Dollar and Welfare Dollar

The population of Countrymen I discuss all have cattle station backgrounds and, further, come of ethnic stocks whose members have an eighty year history of dependency on the white supply of rations and/or wages. Countrymen is a term that stands for a new ethnicity. In the Darwin hinterland Aborigines drawn onto white-controlled properties to work as hands in rural enterprises have merged together to form a loose-knit inter-tribal association. The Countrymen now belong firmly to a region and they dominate a set of cattle stations and farms between which they regularly move. In sinking linguistic differences, they have adopted and developed an Aboriginal English which, in an area of linguistic diversity and tiny traditional speech aggregates, now serves as *lingua franca*. Nor for these Aborigines do traditional foraging and hunting pursuits serve significantly to supplement the rations that, through the year, the Stockmen buy or draw from an employer's store. Dependency on cash income is total.

When in the 1870's Anthony Trollope visited the outback of New South Wales, he was prompted to call the men of the itinerant white rural proletariat, members of a nomad tribe. And in this, Trollope emphasized the sporadic demand for labour in sheep-rearing country which promoted proletarian movement. His white nomads moved about the outback to find work where work was to be had (Trollope 1876: 69). Today, Aboriginal Stockmen in the Northern Territory are the functional equivalents of the men who worked a century ago in New South Wales as shearers, ringers, fence builders and so on. In the Darwin hinterland, two major activities are significant – cattle raising and buffalo shooting. In addition there are other bush jobs such as tree cutting, estuarine fishing, farming, work in abattoirs and sporadic small scale mining and prospecting activities in each of which Aborigines find occasional employment. The terms and conditions of work in these secondary pursuits are matched to the terms and conditions proffered to employees by graziers, the leading employers of Aborigines in the Territory.

Employment of Aborigines in the region is then systematically sporadic. First there is a seasonal rhythm – the alternation between the active Dry Season and the Wet Season when, with the onset of rain, communications become difficult and an industry bogs down. Second there is a year-to-year fluctuation in the demand for labour in a region where the leading industry has a history of boom and bust.[2] The period of my fieldwork was a time of depression: one of the two regional abattoirs closed down while the other worked at a reduced rate. In this period cattle-station employers were also less willing to build fences and make improvements on their properties. Among Aborigines dependent on a rural labour market with a fluctuating demand, the Countrymen of the Darwin hinterland have experienced the periods and seasons of unemployment directly and keenly. The outcome of the structure of employment is that men who work do not command steady wages, but, instead, have an interrupted supply of cash. This condition of the interrupted cash supply is chronic. During the off periods men have to find the means to fund themselves into the next period of work and wages.

While the wage dollar does not stand for a steady flow of cash, the welfare dollar does. The welfare dollare stands for a range of payments, first the old age pensions given to both men and women;

second pensions given to widows and third child endowment payments. There are also a few people who have gained awards due to industrial injury. For the population at large, the welfare dollar
represents the steady and reliable cash flow wholly predictable in an
area of otherwise sporadic income. The welfare dollar has a wide and
general significance: welfare payments are not monopolised by those
who receive them but are treated as a communal asset.

One has thus to discuss the dynamics of the redistribution of the
welfare dollar, the rules for its reallocation and the social effects of
these rules. The rules relate cash to status in a direct way and serve as
the basis for organising money into social worth. Identity is endowed,
sustained and transformed on social criteria that link men and women
to the cash supply. I shall first discuss the relationship between income
and the maintenance of marital status and then go on to show how
further differentiations of status within a mob are managed.

Wrong Kitchen Business

Constitutive rules that govern the sustained recognition of individual
marriages are means that serve the economic management of scarcity
within the population of Countrymen. In times of scarcity the number
of independent commensal units is reduced while the size of such
units is increased. The effect is to lower the general rate of consumption and, as economic scarcity becomes acute, a proportion of extant
marriages must be sacrificed. To explain how this overall adjustment
is accomplished, I discuss how a marriage is established, maintained
and, in certain circumstances, brought to an end by the studied with-
drawal of collective support for its continuance.

To announce that a marriage has taken place (or been resumed) a
woman defines herself as wife by rising early and setting a hearth. Then
with ostentatious diligence, she cooks a meal for the man who is
established as her husband when he accepts the food she has prepared.
The act is celebrated in the camp by subscription to an activity I call
the business of *remarking*. Everyone verbally registers the fact that
'Clovis bin get up early and cook for that ol' fella Tommy. Them
twofella marrit.' The marriage is publicly established as this message
is generally remarked. Each person confirms to each other member of
the camp that, indeed, a couple have entered into marital commen-
sality. In this way the camp's membership becomes witness to the
marriage. The message about a marriage is then taken outside the
camp to be further promulgated. Annoucement that Clovis and
Tommy are married is among the first things said to any Countryman
that camp members encounter. Promulgation continues until all

Countrymen have been informed. And the marriage is a marriage
because it has mob backing. Thus the assertion in any relevant context: 'Themfella really marrit: we witness for that.' A mob is clearly
a collectivity with the capacity to attest to the marriages of its
members. The definition of marital status is, hence, a mob
prerogative.

If a marriage is challenged, the parties to the marriage turn to the
mob of their current allegiance and call for witnesses to support their
claim. Men and women can easily divorce by ending marital commen-
sality, an ending usually accompanied by one or other of the parties
moving out of camp and going elsewhere. If either a husband or a
wife makes an outright declaration of divorce, this too will be
promulgated. However, the ending of marriages can, by the indirect
effects of the action of third parties, also be brought to an end. This
can happen when a couple are so circumstanced that some other has
the power to deny them not their marriage, but the means towards
its continuance. The general principle is that a marriage cannot survive if both parties to it enter into a state I call cooking-pot dependency.
In local terms, this state is given as: 'Marrit fella taking tucker' or,
otherwise, as that 'wrong kitchen business'.

To continue in a marriage, a wife should be able from day to day to
reassert the grounds that were initially entered as her claim to wifely
status. She should cook and give tucker to her husband and any other
members of the commensal group made up of people who take
tucker from her kitchen. Tucker is cooked food and tucker is to be
distinguished from unprepared food and the category word for all
unprepared food is rations. Recognition of a marriage is not at risk
for as long as the parties to it are self-sustaining: turning their own
rations into tucker. The grounds for denial of a marriage by members
of a mob are that a once-married couple are no longer self-sustaining.
Married people who have no rations find that their unions are at
risk.

While this principle can be simply stated, commensal arrangements
admit complications. Several married couples can pool their resources,
establish a single hearth and the women of this grouping will then
together share the work of cooking and preparing food. Such combinations of the commissariat are normally based on a notion of
symmetrical exchange. Each married woman with a right to her own
hearth is, in principle, contributing a fair share towards the rations
that are cooked. The tucker provided is then cooked food made with
pooled rations. Again, the pooling of rations can be based on debt
relationships. People presently in funds can support those short of

cash without degrading those they support, always provided that the arrangement is represented as one in which debt is being accumulated. The relationship between the parties then remains symmetrical. Rations can also be given in exchange for services and within combined kitchen groups such mutual accomodation is, as might be expected, not done by assigning actual rations to wives but by notional calculations. A crisis can be precipitated in a combination based on indebtedness if, in the judgement of the actual purchasers of rations the other parties have extended their credit to the full and, therefore in the local idiom, now need to 'level up'. From this point on, any further withdrawals from the cooking pot will be 'taking tucker'. Taking tucker is an act of asymmetrical exchange that signals (as Marriott has it in another context) 'routine dependence on the food provider' (Marriott 1968: 144).

The shift from symmetrical to asymmetrical exchange (from 'level' to 'not level') alters the balance in a relationship of close co-operation between parties who are known in camp as allies. The business can be accomplished privily. However, those desperate for food often try to hang on, to persuade the person in funds to continue to extend credit. 'We not taking tucker, we gonna pay.' The further recourse of an unwilling lender is to make a public declaration, to announce that tucker is being taken or, more strongly, to sing out with curses and declare that 'bloody wrong kitchen business' is afoot. Announcement of 'wrong kitchen business' causes people in the came to murmur about the marriage of those who are pretending to marital status and yet are without the means to get rations and, thereby, to sustain their pretensions. At this juncture, indebted spouses have two choices: if they have hopes of either reclaiming a debt or finding another source of credit, they can take their marriage to another combined kitchen. Failing this, they must both enter a state of cooking-pot dependency. And, generally this means that the parties to the marriage go separate ways and end up in different camps and mobs.

I should hasten to add that while the grounds for action are clear and the principles are explicit, the style in which the transformation of a cooking-pot partner into a cooking-pot dependant is achieved is fractious. Those about to be degraded make appeals. They voice allegations of old debts unpaid, cite the obligations of kinship, and, finally, beg.

In the camp at Wallaby Cross, one middle-aged widow who had recently found a new husband, battened onto her brother's hearthgroup. She stubbornly refused either to leave the camp or to accept that her relationship with her new husband, Bosun, was not based in propriety. She asserted her marriage – the camp denied it: 'Themfella not marrit, jus living together'. The widow, Mabel, became that Wrong Kitchen Mabel and took tucker from one kitchen after another, resisting violent attempts to keep her away from cooking pots. She was able to survive in this way because she was a woman with a long history of close association with many of the people at the Cross and could state that she had special claims to their continuing support. While Mabel and Bosun were, in the end, not denied sustenance, Mabel had each day to fight for food and, hence, pay her way in bruises. She was subject to everyday, routine humiliation. Even children in the camp felt free to address her as 'Wrong kitchen'. Mabel and Bosun were rescued by Welfare authorities. Appointed Hygiene Lady for the camp, Mabel drew a small wage for collecting garbage. Two days after her entry into employment, I made the mistake of speaking of her as 'Wrong Kitchen': the campers made me abject for hours. The nickname no longer had currency and to denigrate a person so recently redeemed was counted an act of compound insult. I not only impugned Mabel but also the whole mob of those who now regarded Mabel and Bosun as properly married.

For the time that Mabel was Wrong Kitchen Mabel, she and Bosun lived poorly, eating what could be begged or snatched. In a camp of heavy drinkers, the couple entered a dry period of existence. Those who go into recognised cooking-pot dependency rely on the generosity of their suppliers. Mob members may, from time to time, proffer drinks but the person in dependency is excluded from renewal of clothes, swag and kit. By the time they reach the dependent state, people who take tucker have normally already yielded up their possessions in return for food and in settlement or part-settlement of debts. There is, in the mob, an ideal of the fully kitted couple. Such people have good clothes, use domestic tools and utensils of quality and can vaunt complete swags, including portable tape recorders and radios all wrapped up in the swag blanket that Australian frontiersmen call a 'bluey'. The stockman outfit with $60 boots, tooled belt, slough hat, 'Merican check shirt and riding denims is costly. Camp life is hard on clothes and all the appurtenances which need constant renewal. During seasonal lows of employment when cooking pot dependency is at its peak, the younger people of the camp become decrepit. Any remaining good clothes circulate so that those who wish to go to town or do something special can wear them. The whole stock of things within a mob during the period of scarcity is run down. The degrading of the cooking-pot dependants is important to those still able to maintain

kitchens. The person defined as 'taking tucker' would be presumptuous to ask for more than food. A moral threshold is established so
that a definition of what is asking too much of a mate or kinsman can
be used to choke requests in mobs whose members subscribe to a
general mutual-aid ethic. If those who have cash are not themselves
to be mulcted into penury, they must establish limits to their liability
to help others on demand. In the camps this is achieved by working
to redefine a debtor's social worth.

A public debtor is a person who has been shown to be 'not level'
when the balance of dealings in his relationships with others is
'reckoned up' and, furthermore, is shown to be a person who 'gotta
pay whole lot' (i.e. much to many). There is also a characterisation
for the style of a declared debtor's further transactions that rests on
the distinction between the making of legitimate demands and the
entering of appeals. When people make demands from strength or
when, uncompromised by debt, they make requests, they *ask*.
Appeals, on the other hand, are acts in which there is supplication.
The cooking-pot dependant has thus to *cry* either for tucker or for
other favours. In commensal groupings that are enlarged by the
accretion of dependants, there is a distinction between those who
are there to appeal and the rest. The general rate of consumption can
be made to fall because declared dependants are established as the
purposefully deprived. Receiving basic food by favour, they cease to
share in the range of other things that would be shared among all
those in a commensal combination that is 'more level'. In hard times
there is within a commensal grouping a divide between two styles
of consumption, between those who subsist sparely and the
dominant others who establish that luxury items are their own 'very
private' acquisitions. In all this food is treated as a symbolic focus.
The current pattern for the provision, preparation and consumption
of food is explicitly referred to as the template for all relationships
of sharing within a grouping centred on a hearth. People reduced to
crying for tucker are thus excluded from a range of dealings and
reduction of the overall rate of consumption finds its justification
in the results of work that has been done to lower individual worth.

Sex, Age and Social Control

People of Wallaby Cross and their Countrymen distinguish between
two states of persons. One is either *in control* or *out of control* and
these designations are used in ways that can be described as mob-
relative. The person deemed to be in control currently poses no
challenge to the order of a speaker's mob. To be in control is to

accept both mob-backed definitions of situations and the communally established terms that define current states of relationships between mob members. To defy mob definitions is to challenge an order of statuses, to defy protagonists of a collectively defined order and thus go out of control. When too many people are out of control, a general order of disorder or state of total uncontrol is recognised. Such generalised uncontrol is *noise*. Contrariwise *quiet* stands for a general state of order presently maintained. In labelling persons, noisy and out of control, quiet and in control can, in appropriate contexts, serve as synonyms.

Employing these words of order and disorder, the people themselves translate the problem of economic scarcity into a problem of social control via the other recognised proposition that you can, at times, have too many young girls running round. The problem, when the proportion of people in cooking-pot dependency increases, is to check out of control behaviour and prevent noise. The problem, again, is presented by men in authority as the problem of being hard on others who want you to be easy and yet sustain an order of mob and camp that is not made chaotic by individuals who enter noisy protest against invidious discrimination. A whole organisation for the abatement of noise is structured on ground rules that divide the work of control between the sexes. The maintenance of order is, in consequence, activity that confirms and reconfirms social differences between men and women by consistent emphasis on sexually divided responsibilities. With recourse to a sexual division of labour for the organisation of enforcement, separate male and female ideologies are promoted so that, eternally, the sexes as categories are socially opposed. To demonstrate that this proposition holds, I have now to discuss discriminations of authority and the roots of inequality in mob and camp. The first task is to account for the prominence of the leading men of mobs. I refer to these leaders as Masterful Men even though, in local usage, this term is employed as an occasional honorific and not a label of entitlement. The economic base of the power of Masterful Men who emerge as camp comptrollers is in their secure access not to wages but to the welfare dollar.

The fringe camp at Wallaby Cross has special significance for Countrymen not only because of the urban location which makes it a good place 'for holiday' when one is in funds. When money is scarce and the consumption opportunities of the city scene serve only to emphasise a lowered state, the camp at the Cross still attracts Countrymen. The reason is that the camp is a place of the concentration of the welfare dollar. Among the permanent fringe dwellers, recipients of constant welfare payments are over-represented. Further, in times of scarcity, the absolute number of recipients of welfare money in the camp increases as hinterland pensioners take refuge in town. The people call all welfare recipients 'pensioners' and pensioners are attracted to the fringe camp because, on the outskirts of town, they can rely on the Masterful Men for protection. In smaller mobs or camps of the hinterland, an unfavourable ratio between welfare recipients and rationless people can lead to acute difficulties — the over-reliance of too many on an under-protected few.

In the language of the camp use of the verb *to organise* is restricted and reserved to special purpose. Organising is actively conducted within a world of Aboriginal business that is distinct from the domain of black-white relationships. Masterful Men are organisation specialists and they dominate camps in which the welfare dollar is concentrated. Concentrations of the welfare dollar allow the Masterful Men to become fulltime specialists who opt out of wage labour. Settled in particular camps, Masterful Men move about only to promote Aboriginal business. Minute to minute availability of a Masterful Man is crucial and the absence of a camp's Masterful Man is a threatening condition. In the absence of a leading man, outsiders could 'sneak up' and have dealings in camp without reference to authority. Unless a camp's mob is always to move about in a body, a mob rich in pensions requires more than one leader. Three men dominated organisation at Wallaby Cross, a triumvirate whose members continually consulted one another to rotate the responsibility for watching out for trouble in the camp.

Above all, Masterful Men are protectors. Supervening in camp affairs to check out of control behaviour, they must also secure and command a set of Fighting Men who will be employed to guarantee the camp's security from outside threat. The bargain between a Masterful Man and the set of pensioners whose interests he represents is that a pensioner contracts into protection, yielding up part of the pension money so that personal retention of the remainder will be guaranteed. If pressed for cash by any other, the protected pensioner's recourse is to refer the matter to the Masterful Man. The pensioner disclaims any personal holding of cash and usually disclaims all control over the pension earnings as well. 'Better ask that ol' fella (Masterful Man). He got all that money, you know that.' If further pressed, the pensioner calls for help. He demands and gets the decisive act of intervention that saves his cash and is itself the price a pensioner demands for his economic subvention of authority. When applications for help are regularly referred to Masterful Men, they become the arbiters who discriminate between 'asking for' and 'crying for', between appeals and legitimate demands. One measure of a Masterful Man is the relative impenetrability of the screen he establishes between 'his' protected pensioners and a world of demanding others.

To find Fighting Men and hence secure the camp, a Masterful Man needs clients and his clients will be drawn from Stockmen who, between contracts and spells of work in the Dry Season are to be found in the camps of pension concentrations. While the Dry Season is the season of wages and employment, it is still a time of movement between countryside and the Darwin camp. At the time of the annual muster there can, in fact, be indirect competition between employers and Masterful Men. Both draw on the same set of men, the one to recruit a Mustering Mob and the other to ensure that a camp is not unguarded. If a camp's fighting force is presently depleted, a man should gain a release from the camp before taking off for work. Those wage earners who are endeavouring to sustain marriages generally take their wives to the cattle station or buffalo camp of their employment. Stockmen who double as Fighting Men are also the wage-earners who, when out of work, run the risk of drifting into cooking-pot dependency and thus entering an 'off' phase of marriage. Each 'off' phase carries the risk that a one-time wife may not resume the relationship but find another man instead. During any period of wage earning, Stockmen, in fact, make considerable contributions to an economy of conspicuous ceremonial consumption and also finance the festivities for which, again, the Darwin camp is famous. The importance of public ceremony can be gauged by the fact that music masters, like Masterful Men, can become full-time specialists and make a living without wage income. The Wallaby Cross mob was willing to draw on the pool of pension earnings to support a married Singing Man and an instrumentalist (a Bamboo Man or didgeridoo player) who was a bachelor.

I have discussed the position of the Stockman and the Fighting Man to lead to a discussion of sexual opposition. What I have to show is that, whatever contribution he may have made to camp festivities during his wage-earning period, the Stockman without a large fund of savings at the end of his work period cannot sustain a marriage on the basis of long-term indebtedness for rations. Masterful Men are in a sense disempowered. They cannot, in times of scarcity, divert funds to support a set of favoured Stockmen for they face female opposition. In hard times it is women who discriminate between candidates for tucker. In making their choice, married women select those other women who can be held in mob control because the women of the mob can guarantee that their sexuality will be diverted outwards. Briefly, the choice is this. The grouping about a Masterful Man will receive appeals for help from one set of women who relate to the group as wives of stockmen clients and from a second set who relate to the group as kinswomen of those wives whose kitchens will be sustained throughout the year. And it is kinswomen, not Stockmens' wives who generally are chosen. The rationale that dictates this trend in discrimination is one of chaperonage. What is required is the containment of running round.

The dissolution of marriage is made a regular consequence of cooking-pot dependency because husbands and wives standardly modulate the state of their marital relationship by conducting extra-marital affairs. For the Countrymen, marriage does not stand for the containment of sexuality within the relationship. It is expected that all husbands and all wives will want lovers. Extra-marital sexuality of either partner to a marriage disturbs the marriage least (a) if the affair is conducted with discretion and not publicised and (b) if there is no strong economic component in the extra-marital relationship. Either the publication of affairs or the diversion of cash from a domestic economy lead to marital disputes. Wives protest when their husbands spend cash on other women while husbands interpret a wife's receipt of economic favours from a lover as a threat to the marital relationship. A man who overwhelms a woman with gifts and good-time spending is making a bid for a more lasting association with her. The people thus distinguish between harmful and harmless extra-marital affairs. And a particularly female form of protest is for a wife, though still married, to shame her husband by public 'running round'. A woman then uses the publicised fact of her relationship with a lover as a reproach, either to check a husband's disbursements or because he is, in her view, failing as a provider. A highly disturbed marital relationship is usually the prelude to cooking-pot dependency. Once degraded, a couple if they continue to live together, are usually regarded as out of control. An ill-provisioned wife is a danger. Other women of the camp object to her behaviour and a husband who for the duration of his marriage should be able to negotiate a quiet adjustment with his wife is proved incompetent. Out of control behaviour is also translated into fighting. Thus to gain each day's supplies, Wrong Kitchen Mabel had to exchange a daily round of blows with other women.

Women who come out of ill-provisioned marriages find succour with sisters, with brothers' wives and with older women, especially mothers and mothers' sisters. These women accept those they call their '*lations* into cooking-pot dependency on the understanding that any woman who becomes dependent will in no way cause trouble in a camp by sexual indiscretion and misdemeanours. In such arrangements, it is advantageous if a marriage or incest ban is associated with the relationship between any attached female dependant and her sponsor's husband. Further, genealogy and kinship category do not offer the only grounds for funded safe relationships. Women who spent their childhood together and the daughters of such women value the relationship of being reared up together and value also the relationship between an older woman and a younger whom the former has helped to rear. What relationships a dependent woman has with men outside the mob are her own business for as long as the effects of her liaisons do not rebound back to disturb mob order. Chaperonage is active and a collective responsibility of all camp women. Led by wives who sustain hearths, punitive squads act against any dependent woman who infringes the rule that neutralises her sexuality in her relationships with the men of the mob. Each woman thus has a set of female kin, the core of her '*lations*. These are the women with whom she can join in the asymmetrical relationship of cooking-pot dependency either as a senior or junior partner. Theset of a woman's female '*lations* represent continuity over time, for these woman-to-woman ties transcend the fleeting though absorbing corporateness of mobs.

The mob as presently constituted is of absorbing importance to men. However, mobs as units do not endure for their composition changes seasonally and, as I have indicated, mobs contain marital relationships that are themselves inconstant. Masterful Men who dominate camps rely, in the end, on the sets of female '*lations* that a sister or wife recruits to their mob. The set of pensioners on whose continuous earnings one Masterful Man relies is no chance combination but a group of older men and women together with widows and women in receipt of child endowment monies who are all '*lations*.

The ideological divide between men and women is expressed and recognised locally as one of the truisms of social life. Women 'worry for' their '*lations*, men 'worry for' mobs. Men are concerned with instant realisations of status, with striving to be someone, trying to sustain a marriage or attain social recognition within the current order of some mob. Male triumphs are inherently short-lived and the history of any man's career is a story of ups and downs. Women consistently devalue the short-lived excellencies of a man's past performance to make the inconsistent pattern of male careers the grounds for vocal reproach. In mocking men and denigrating them either for the commission of overt wrongs or for failing as providers, women cite and list the occasions on which 'lations have helped them while men have failed. With their reliance for status on a seasonal and fluctuating labour market, men are fated to be inconsistent providers. Their identities as Stockmen are seasonally spoiled and, hence, the social grounds for male and female opposition are rooted in an imposed structure of racial inequality. In the end, the opposition between male inconstancy and the fealty of a woman's 'lations is a function of the opposition between wage dollar and pension dollar.

The Defeat of a Gerontocratic Ideal

The fluctuating wage dollar is further relevant to an opposition between ol' fellas in authority and the Stockmen whose identity seasonally is spoiled. Because young men can be good Stockmen and, for their period of working, gain wage equality with any other working man, it is not within the power of any Aboriginal authority to deny the maturity of young men by ensuring that youngsters have unequal access to wages. Yet, as things used to be, North Australia was a region of the promise marriage. Infant girls were generally promised to future spouses who often were already adult men and the promisee was required to play an economic part in 'rearing that young girl up'. Instituted promise marriage was used by older men to delay the social maturity of those who, ultimately, would become their successors. Again, the deprivation of younger men and the prolongation of bacherlorhood was the condition of the polygyny of their elders.

In his discussion of social transmission *From Generation to Generation*, Professor Eisenstadt considered the relationships between younger and older men among the Murngin of North Australia. He characterised Murngin organisation as 'a complete and extreme case of gerontocracy' (Eisenstadt 1956: 249), while he also posited delayed maturity as one of the preconditions that, when fulfilled, tend to cause age groups to arise within the structure of family or descent group (Eisenstadt 1956: 248). What I have now to describe is the social action of groups of young Fighting Men who arise within the structure of mobs, not because their maturity has been delayed, but to ensure instead that no ol' fella will presume to monopolise the person or sexuality of any young girl.

In August 1975, the man I call Tommy Atkins who is well known in Darwin as a mob leader or ol' fella Masterful Man of the mob at

Wallaby Cross, tried to secure Clovis, a young girl, to wife. Clovis, he claimed, was his promise. After negotiations with Clovis's mother and with the step-father of the girl (whose own father, the original promiser, was long dead), Tommy Atkins sortied from Darwin in the company of older members of his mob. The party commandeered the anthropologist and his truck and thus, in company, we set out for the camp at Blue Grass Station where Clovis and her parents were living and working with the station mob. Tommy Atkins went laden with gifts. We left these behind with the station mob and brought Clovis back to the Darwin camp. The marriage linked May and November for Tommy Atkins was fifty-three while Clovis was seventeen years old. The marriage was a marriage for nineteen days. It ended when Atkins let Clovis go because his marriage had brought an order of threat to the Darwin mob and its female members refused any longer to live in fear. To bring this about, youngfellas of the Darwin mob entered into a conspiracy of youth with a company of Fighting Men from Topside Mission. The terms of the conspiracy were these: the Darwin youngfellas would make themselves scarce, find time-consuming things to do either in or out of town and generally be unavailable. With the disappearance of Fighting Men, the women and older men of the Darwin mob found that they had no safe refuge and that theirs had become an open camp. One of the Darwin mob's Fighting Men was, as it happens, Clovis's brother. Young men from Topside Mission rather than any others were brought to the scene because one of their number wanted Clovis and the girl's brother approved the suit of his young mate. Trouble began four days after Clovis had been brought to Darwin.

Women of the Darwin mob who went unescorted out of camp to shop, to visit the pub or in search of friends, were intimidated by youngfellas of the Mission mob. As the days wore on the verbal abuse of initial intimidation gave way to jostling and, later still, the jostling (which was gang jostling) served as cover for rabbit punch and hard elbow nudge. A state of fringe camp siege was established in which only women were the objects of attack. The women described their situation thus: 'We got that very danger'. With no Fighting Men to act as escorts or to be rallied as a force, the danger could not be reduced. Further the Mission fellas were selective. They chose as special targets those women within the camp who were closest to Tommy Atkins, the ol' fella Masterful Man who has presumed to take Clovis, that young girl, to wife. In the state of 'very danger' night-long watches were kept in camp; the remaining camp residents left camp only in parties. Atkins declared a ban on all visits to the pub where, he said, the youngfellas were waiting to bash any older male mob member who, after drinking, would be less than able to stave off attack. Clovis who, in the meantime, had been strictly confined to the camp, stopped cooking for Tommy Atkins and declared that she wanted a divorce.

There were lulls in Mission mob action. The intimidators would withdraw for a day or two only to return and show increased determination and toughness. Finally, women in the camp went to Atkins in a body to tell the ol'fellas that the next thing that would happen would be the victimisation of one of their number by gang rape. On that day Tommy Atkins let Clovis go.

In February 1977 I learnt that Clovis was still married to the suitor her brother had approved. After being released by Tommy Atkins, she had repaired at once to Topside Mission and her present marriage thus dates from the day of the termination of her sojourn in the Darwin camp. I say sojourn for now, in retrospect, the brief union of Clovis and Tommy Atkins is remembered by both parties as an event of small significance: there was, in short, no marriage. Similarly, the details of the trouble, now that it is finished up, are generally not talked about. Mention of the finished trouble is consistently suppressed.

During the period of my research there were five attempts by older men to gain young girls. These were all defeated and by the means I have described: the intimidation of women of each presumptuous ol'fella's mob by a company of Fighting Men. Attempted marriages are described by these hopeful ol'fella suitors who initiate them as 'tries'. Young men and others who disapprove of the attempt say 'that ol'fella jus bin sneaking up to grab young girl' while the defeat of gerontocratic purpose is represented as 'youngfell bin pull'm ol'fella off young girl'. The general success of youngfella action is reflected in the fact that of current marriages in the relevant population, none were regarded as 'ol'fella 'n young girl marriage'. And in eliminating ol'fella to young girl marriage as a type, the young men of a population have thus wholly defeated the gerontocratic ideal represented by the tradition of promising. One of the other older and leading men of Wallaby Cross was able wryly to count up fourteen promise marriages that he had been unable to realise. Unrealised promises are said to have been 'missed' and, quite clearly, the era of the missed promise has arrived. Nor now when girls are born do fathers bother to promise their daughters to future sons-in-law.

Conclusion

In conclusion let me try to account for the importance of sex and the relative unimportance of age as principles of social differentiation among Countrymen of Darwin and the city's hinterland. My accounting is an elaboration of two general observations, the first is negatively and the second positively phrased.

Firstly, then, the Countrymen work within a frame of organisation in which biological aging is not treated as a given process that can serve socially to provide criteria for the differentiation of a population into recognisable categories of coevals in whose hands social power and access to resources can be differentially concentrated. Instead, the social consequences of aging differ radically from individual to individual which is to say that they are contingent and that (with regard to grounds for entering claims to formal status) the consequences of aging are structurally indeterminate.[3]

Secondly, a low degree of stability characterises relationships of all the categories contained in the total social field within which Countrymen relate to one another. A low degree of stability in social relationships has profound consequences for actors' perceptions of the significance of time in all their activities and more particularly, a low degree of stability in social relationships vitiates the possibility of making relationships with others conform to prescriptions that are enunciated on the assumption that certain categories of social relationships have a determinate time-bound future.[4] This explains why in a short essay that cannot be exhaustive, I have chosen to leave issues of paternity and the bonds between mother and child out of account. Social continuity in the conduct of parent-child relationships is for the younger children of Countrymen and their wives a function of parental constancies and inconstancies. In an individual's later years, relationships with surviving parents are sometimes close, sometimes distanced. The quality of any parent-child relationship is, in sum, the outcome of what the relevant actors achieve in relation to one another. The same can be said of the marital tie. What now remains is to establish a link between the structural indeterminacy of the consequences of aging and a low degree of stability in social relationships. To achieve this I refer briefly to the way in which labels are attached to persons and to the everyday relevance of a myth-backed taboo.

As the people themselves announce, their problem is the containment of the disruptive sexuality that is represented by 'too many young girl running round'. And any woman who in appearance is under, say, fifty will be called a young girl if she enters into dependency. Should she while unmarried choose to enter into casual sexual relationships with white men in order to get money, she will be called a 'working girl'. On the other hand, for as long as a marriage is sustained, a wife is a *marrit woman*. A younger wife could also be called *young marrit*. *Girl*, then, denotes marital unattachment and, with on-and-off marriage, a woman can every now and then return to her girlhood. Again the term ol'fella is related more to a person's current standing than to age. An ol'fella is some male to whom a speaker concedes that, on any one of a variety of grounds, he owes respect. A man of fifty may be ol'fella to his son but if not a Masterful Man will not generally be called ol'fella in the camps. He will be Billy Marrit Man, or Billy Stockman or Billy Fighting Man. Such terminological usage is, in fact, highly consistent: what a person is called is referred to that person's current social standing and current social worth. As worth and standing derive from current dispositions within camp and mob, use of labels that are attached to persons accurately defines shifting social realities. A low degree of stability in relationships *requires* that shifts of the order of the one-time wife's return to girlhood be given explicit recognition. With the absence of a model pattern for marital careers, a married man of thirty presently sustaining his marriage has greater claim to worth than a man of forty-five who has just lost his marriage.

In all this, the Countrymen in organising their perceptions of shifting social realities have, from time to time, to reconcile anomalies. The man of forty-five who has lost his marriage and is currently less worthy than some younger men may, in addition, be white-haired. And anomaly is perceived when younger men outshine those who bear the physical signs of age. The stock response to this particular incongruity is to refer to a sacred place and a taboo. Washing or bathing in certain sacred water holes is the prerogative of those who have gained access to them with due observance of the religious properties. For those that illegitimately wash in sacred places, the consequence is a premature whitening of the hair. The significance of explanations of this sort brought down on everyday anomalies and the use of terms of reference and address deserve more extended discussion than space permits. However, my brief examples are indicative. Countrymen define their social reality in terms of on-and-off relationships and, by secondary elaboration, explain away perceived discrepancies between signs of age and achieved worth. The consequence is that they do not entertain time-bound definitions of relationships and endow them with futurity.

Age when aging is made socially definitive is associated with notions of futures that are determinate. In the Darwin hinterland futures are indeterminate and the indeterminacy of futures is reflected and expressed in the degree of instability that pervades all categories of relationships. This aspect of what I have had to say can be phrased in terms that Dr. Woodburn (unpublished paper read at the conference) has supplied. In the Australian region of the promise marriage, promises of young girls to older men once represented futures – and I use the word in the investment sense. A traditional system in which there was deferred and delayed return has, over time, been altered to become a system of more immediate reciprocities in which six months stands for the longest stretch of time for either the realisation of investment or the recovery of debt. The men who no longer realise what locally are known as promises have lost their futures and their transactional time is become a season for they have found no new futures with which to replace traditional promises. Theirs is a frame for social organisation in which relations between the sexes continually provide grounds for social differentiation. As principles for organisation, age is as age does while sex is dominant.

Acknowledgement

For their pointed comments on an earlier draft of this paper I owe debts to Dr. J. La Fontaine and Dr. James Woodburn.

Footnotes

1. A pseudonym as are the names attributed to Aborigines in this paper.
2. Detailed accounts of recent developments in the cattle industry in the Northern Territory have been provided by Kelly (1971) and by Stevens (1974).
3. Cf. Pehrson (1966) who uses the notion of structural indeterminacy with reference to the consequences of cousin-marriage among the Marri Baluch.
4. Elsewhere I have discussed situations in which there is a low degree of stabilisation in social relationships by referring degrees of stability to a proposed measure that I called the tempo of sociation (Sansom 1972).

References

Eisenstadt, S.N. (1965). From Generation to Generation. Routledge and Kegan Paul, London.
Kelly, J.H. (1971). Beef in Northern Australia. ANU Press, Canberra.
Marriott, McKim. (1968). Caste ranking and food transactions: a matrix analysis. *In* "Structure and Change in Indian Society" (eds. Milton Singer and Bernard S. Cohn), Aldine, Chicago.

Pehrson, R. (1966). The Social Organisation of the Marri Baluch. Viking Fund
    Publications in Anthropology No. 43, Chicago.
Sansom, Basil. (1972). When witches are not named. *In* "The Allocation of
    Responsibility" (ed. Max Gluckman), Manchester University Press,
    Manchester.
Stevens, F. (1974). Aborigines in the Northern Territory Cattle Industry.
    ANU Press, Canberra.
Trollope, A. (1876). Australia and New Zealand. Melbourne.

conform – in cases of 'successful socialisation' or become deviants, in cases of 'failed socialisation'.

As has been pointed out (McKay 1973: 29), the very dichotomy adult/child has been borrowed from the common sense world of Western twentieth century culture and viewed as a theoretical formulation. 'Under the formulation of the world as a process of socialisation, children as a phenomenon disappear, and sociologists reveal themselves as parents writing slightly abstract versions of their own or other children' (*ibid.*: 28). The view of children as passive raw material for the grist-mill of socialisation does not derive from descriptions of children extant in the ethnographic literature (e.g. Bartels, 1975; Erikson, 1950; Fortes, 1938; Mayer, ed., 1970; Mead, 1928; Raum, 1940; Read, 1959; Whiting, 1963). However, many anthropological accounts omit certain questions because of their concern with socialisation, educational methods, and the relationship between culture and personality. As Aries (1962) and others note, this conception of the child is relatively recent even in the West. It has developed as children's participation in processes of production has become more and more irrelevant. We have, after all, passed from a period in which children performed important economic roles in small-scale production units based primarily on kinship, to a period of labour intensive industrialization in which children were exploited outside the kinship context as cheap labour,[2] to a period in which unemployment and a capital intensive industrial economy have made the contribution of children negligible in most economic sectors (but not all – e.g. fruit picking in the U.S.A.). The concept of childhood as a period of non-productivity has also developed as part of a reaction of moral indignation to the participation of children in nineteenth century industry. It has gone hand and hand with the development of formal educational institutions and the transfer of some of the responsibilities for child-rearing to the school. The prolongation of schooling itself has also removed children further from participation in most arenas of adult social life.

Thus while there has been an increasing concern with childhood as something distinct from adulthood, the emphasis on socialization has trivialized childhood as a social status. Children rarely enter descriptions of social systems, any more that they enter the system of production (although they do, of course, enter the economic system in an important sense, as consumers). Increasingly, however, the traditional socialization approach has come under criticism, particularly from those social scientists who take an interactionist approach, influenced in part by the theoretical orientation of phenomenology (see Dreitzel, McKay, O'Neill and Raffey in Dreitzil, ed. 1973; M.P.M. Prebaids, ed. 1974; J. and E. Newson, 1974 for examples. See also White 1975, for a study of children's economic roles in Jaura.).

An interactionist approach is of interest for cross-cultural research since it enables us to suspend the presumption that adult culture, or even social structure and culture themselves, are independent variables. If one focusses on the interaction of people of different ages, all as dependent variables, without assuming that one group or the other 'makes the rules', one is *forced* to reexamine the society itself and study the significance of the participation of people of different ages. It then becomes possible to study the 'value of children' in sociological terms.[3]

In industrialized Western societies, fragmentation of institutions according to age has meant that interaction of persons of different ages occurs less and less frequently and is of diminishing social significance. The separation of institutional structures according to age — i.e. age segregated schools, geriatric homes, age homogeneous communities — has its own social and psychological import and is well worth critical evaluation (e.g. Illich, 1971). In those societies where this institutional fragmentation is absent or less marked it is important to look at the interaction of people of different ages and not simply the progression of the individual from one age class to the next. The relevant questions then are, for example: what would happen to the adult world (other than its extinction) if there were no children? In what ways are adults dependent upon children? What is the significance of children in maintaining the relative status of men and women? Why do people want or need children? Other questions concern imminent processes of socio-economic and cultural change.

For example, in those societies undergoing rapid industrialization and socio-economic change, what may be the effects of changes in the roles of children consequent to the introduction of universal Western education and prolonged institutionalization of children in schools? In what ways does industrialization itself threaten to alter the roles of children, and how will this affect the family and the social-psychological development of the child? While the last two questions are now being asked by historians of the Western family, little has been done to apply this perspective to contemporary developing economies, where quite different cultural conditions may affect the direction of change.

If we ask these kinds of questions and look at children as children, not as the next generation's adults, we open up the possibility of finding out a great deal about the society in question. Both children and adults can be studied as social actors, as independent and mutually interacting variables. We cannot assume that dependency goes only from younger to older and we cannot let such an assumption distort our approach. The social irrelevance of children in certain societies: the advanced industrial economies and among hunters and gatherers, as James Woodburn pointed out at this conference in reference to the Hadza, and their social significance in other societies, such as that of the Hausa, deserves our attention.

Hausa Society

There is no way of giving a brief, yet complete description of a society as complex as that of the Hausa, and the reader is referred to the existing literature for further detail.[4] However, certain characteristics of the society of relevance to this discussion may be summarized.

Long before European contact at the end of the nineteenth century, Hausa society had become politically and economically complex. Even before the Jihad in the early nineteenth century, which established the political hegemony of the Fulani over the Hausa ruling class, long distance trade and economic specialization occurred alongside an agricultural economy which produced the basic means of subsistence as well as a number of exports, particularly cotton and leather goods. For centuries, the agricultural areas of Hausaland have been deeply involved in an economy based on trade and in the production of crops and craft items for sale in distant and local markets. The complex nature of this economy has led to considerable economic specialization and to the common practice of men being simultaneously farmers, craftsmen, and traders with more or less emphasis on one or the other occupation. This has been true in the rural areas – i.e. those of lower population density, where farming was, and is, the primary occupation, and also in the urban centres which were established by the eighth century.[5] Kano is now the largest of these centres and the most important commercial centre in northern Nigeria. Despite the effects of industrialization and Westernization, and the influx of southern Nigerians and foreigners, the old walled city of Kano is spatially, socially and culturally delimited within the metropolitan area. It still possesses many of its older characteristics; its population is almost entirely Muslim Hausa, and although culturally homogeneous, it exhibits patterns of economic specialization and socio-economic stratification which have their roots in the pre-colonial era (see Tahir 1976). The old city of Kano (estimated population in 1963–64 was 165,455 [cited in Paden 1973: 18]) is divided into 127 administrative wards (the number having increased with successive local government reforms in this century), two of which provided the sample for this study. These wards are of somewhat different characters, depending upon their particular histories, the dominant occupations of their inhabitants, and their traditional political roles and statuses. Of the two wards in which the present study was conducted, in one most men were salaried civil servants, mainly in local government. Formerly these people were in varying degrees part of the traditional Fulani ruling class, and their connections to the tradtiional aristocracy are still of some social, cultural and political importance. They still hold offices in Kano Emirate, on the district, municipal and village levels (see Paden 1973: chapters 6 and 9). Although the Fulani assumed political control in Kano only in the early nineteenth century, the ward itself, like other parts of Kano city, was settled earlier. The original Hausa inhabitants have been absorbed into the settled Fulani population (see Bashir 1972). The other ward studied was probably settled even earlier, long before the Fulani entry into Kano political history. The men are mainly artisans, butchers, and merchants, many in the cattle trade but nowadays also in businesses such as the importation of building materials, transport, and contracting. Although the inhabitants in these two wards may be described and describe themselves, as Fulani or Hausa, and although there are some cultural differences between them,[6] these are not so great as to affect the broad generalizations which follow. What is referred to henceforth as 'Hausa culture' refers to the culture of the Hausa native speakers in Kano city, regardless of ethnic distinctions between Fulani and Hausa. These may indeed for a very long time have been more of political than cultural significance. Given the increasing hegemony of national bureaucracies and Federal institutions over local ones, and the long term effects of mass education, one must indeed question whether the distinction will for long retain any significance at all.

Due to the economic complexity of traditional Hausa society, not to mention changes in this century, and the complex political history of the area, there are today multiple ways of evaluating status, of which ethnicity is only one and no longer the most important. Occupational status, in the traditional and modern sectors, wealth, education – both Islamic and Western, past and present political, economic and kinship connections, relative age, and gender all are important. The relative status of individuals is an issue of great significance in Hausa society, as is the etiquette of deference and respect which expresses this. While there are multiple status systems (see M.G. Smith, 1959, on male and female hierarchies), in actual situations rules will operate to define the priority of various aspects of status. Thus although their situational importance cannot be stated *a priori*, that is, outside a real context where they always interact with other components of status, two aspects of Hausa personal identity are always relevant: distinctions based on age and on gender. As in all other status hierarchies, the person in the superior position (in these cases the elder, or the male) commands respect, deference and obedience from the person in the inferior position. But this way of stating the matter is too simplistic, because age and gender, like other aspects of identity, never operate in isolation. For example, men can be stated categorically to be of higher status than women, but a male servant owes deference and respect to the wife or daughter of a man of high political rank. A mother, or almost any older woman, up to a certain point in time, has authority over young boys, and women in certain kinship positions will never lose the right to respect and deference from male relatives, although they do lose authority over them. While women, on the whole, must show respect to men, this is only enforceable (in the sense that sanctions are available) between husbands and wives. In fact, the respect relationship may be reversed when a woman (not a wife, for men never marry older women) is older than a man provided other factors, such as political status, are equal. Thus, even in dealing with the relatively clearcut dimensions of age and gender, if one examines behaviour in real situations, simple hierarchical rules, while not irrelevant, will be affected by other aspects of status evaluation.

In the following sections I first set out some of the main characteristics of male and female roles within the Hausa family and then turn to age, and the significance of children in Hausa society. One of the main arguments of this paper is that 'sex roles' in Hausa society could not be defined as they are without children performing certain roles which are distinct from and complementary to adult roles. Children are crucial in maintaining the institution of purdah in certain economic classes, and in maintaining the present definition of female roles. Changes in the roles of children, consequent to such innovations as universal primary education, will have far reaching effects, not only on the children themselves, but on the whole structure of the Hausa family.

In pointing out the independence of the female status system from the male, M.G. Smith brought out the fact that there are many domains in which adult men and women are virtually autonomous.[7] Among adults, there is a very strong notion of modesty (*kunya*) which governs female deportment and male/female interaction. *Kunya* also refers to an avoidance relationship based upon respect associated with sexual relations, between a man and his affines, or even between a man and his wife or wives. It is particuarly evident in the marriage ceremony, in the deportment of young spouses, and between parents and their first born children.[8] While adulthood implies sexuality and sexual activity, it also imposes strict limits upon the interaction of men and women in non-sexual contexts. This is, of course, expressed in and reinforced by the institution of purdah, which puts limits on both men's and women's spatial mobility. Women in purdah (the vast majority of married Hausa women in Kano city) do not generally leave their compounds except for the specific purpose of visiting relatives or close female friends, attending ceremonies for the occasions of births, marriages and funerals, or going for medical treatment or to visit the sick. Men also do not have free access in and out of each others' houses. Even kinship does not open the door, for a man would not normally enter the house of a younger married sister. He might, but probably only with the husband's permission, enter the home of an older married sister, but even then once both siblings are fully grown their statuses as male and female take precedence over the kinship relationship, and the man does not normally enter his sister's house (Cross-cousins, however, who are joking partners, may enter each others' houses regardless of age). Nor does a man feel free to enter the female section of his younger brother's house.

In general there is very little daily interaction between adult men and women in Hausa society, even between spouses, at least in the city where most men work away from their homes. Men eat separately from women, often outside the house, where they share food with neighbours and friends. Men often go out in the evening, but rarely with their wives, and when married women go out, this too is without men. These patterns are beginning to change among the Western educated, but the traditional mode of deportment is still evident.

In naming ceremonies, marriages, and funerals, the activities of men and women are quite separate, although both are crucial to the completion of the ceremony. Among many people, particularly the Western educated, parties in which both men and women are present are becoming more common, but even on these occasions men often do not bring their wives. The marriage ceremony takes a week to perform and the portions relating to the bride and to the groom are held separately. Men, as a group – the friends of the groom, interact with women as a group – the friends of the bride, in certain rituals which clearly express this sexual opposition. For example, in the section of the marriage ceremony known as 'selling *fura*' the friends of the groom have to bargain with the friends of the bride to buy a symbolic calabash of *fura* – millet porridge. The money finally agreed on depends upon the status of the bride, including her age and education, and may come to several hundred Niara (one Niara is, as of February 1978, equivalent to 84 pence), which is then shared between the friends of the bride. These elaborate and protracted ceremonies are one of the major bridges between the male and female domains outside of actual marriage and it is particularly on these occasions that prospective spouses are sought and pursued.

Very few household tasks are performed jointly by men and women in Kano city, but there is a clear division of responsibilities according to gender. On the whole, men have very little contact with infants, although they do spend time with children, especially those under six years. Grandfathers and other men who may be home more often, spend considerable time playing with children in the entrances of their compounds. Men are responsible for providing a house, or room, food and clothing for their wives and children, and for paying school fees.[9] In fact, it is the capacity to meet these economic obligations and not simply reproductive capacity, which makes a man eligible for marriage.[10]

Some Kano residents have farms outside the city, but these are worked by hired labour. Women take no part in actual production in meeting the essential needs of the household (except in female-headed households or when the husband's income is insufficient), although they often have of their own separate incomes. But these productive activities are clearly distinct from their conjugal roles: in cases, for example, where women cook food for sale, even the fire-wood is likely to be distinct from that used for the family cooking – the two domains are conceptually and functionally separate although credit, gifts and debt may operate between them. Within the family, women are responsible for cooking, daily in the case of monogamous households and in rotation in polygamous families. The evening meal is cooked at home in most houses[11] but food in the afternoon is very often purchased with money given by the husband for this purpose. Women are responsible for caring for children and cleaning the house, but they receive help, both from outsiders (employees) and from children – the relative balance of help from these sources depending upon income. Laundering is a man's occupation and in most families washing and ironing, particularly of the husband's clothing, is given to a washman. Some families have paid household help consisting of Qu'ranic students (*almajiroi*) who do chores and errands in exchange for room and board; or divorced or widowed women, often from rural areas, who help with cooking, carrying water or minding infants. In many households some of the most arduous tasks associated with food preparation, such as pounding grain, are given out to women who do this for an income. Grinding machines have replaced much manual labour, and one of the daily tasks of many children is to take ingredients for grinding. Some husbands help with shopping while other men give their wives money for all purchases and the wives rely on hired help, or more commonly on children, for shopping. Many purchases can be made locally, from other houses, from small shops, and from children and unmarried women selling items from house to house. However, certain purchases inevitably require a trip to one of the large markets.

Women have the right to earn and control their own incomes as long as they do not violate the obligations of marriage including purdah. They obtain capital from many possible sources: from gifts from their husbands, parents, or siblings, from savings from house-keeping money (sometimes with the husband's knowledge), from spending money given by the husband, by borrowing, or, as a last resort, by selling part of their dowries. There are a limited number of economic activities open to women in purdah which do not require the assistance of children: pounding grain, hair plaiting, embroidering men's caps and trousers, embroidering bedsheets and horse trappings, sewing (on a machine if the woman has the capital), cooking food for sale, or trading from within the house. However, even these activities require assistance from people not in purdah, for purchasing materials, delivering and selling the final products. Women who are not in purdah have other options open to them including fetching water, working as housemaids, midwifery, trading – for themselves or as brokers for women in purdah, or prostitution. Although none of the women in the present study had businesses ranging in thousands of Niara, it should be born in mind that women do inherit property, including real estate, and that there are wealthy Hausa women involved in large scale trade (including the gold trade), and in transactions involving land, houses, and in organizing the annual pilgrimage to Mecca. This summary does not include salaried jobs, such as teaching or nursing, which are open to a very small but growing number of Western educated Hausa women.

Married women with children old enough to help them have a much wider choice of occupations, particularly if the children can help through street trading, or *talla*. Women's occupational histories cannot be studied in isolation from their marital and child-bearing histories. Changes in occupations are correlated time and again with changes in the age, gender, and number of children available to women. The lack of child helpers is the most frequent reason for stopping a particular occupation. With children to market their produce, women sell cooked food outside their houses, and may invest in other commodities such as detergent, kola nuts, sugar, salt, fruit — just about anything that can be transported on a tray and sold in small quantities. Women need not necessarily rely on their own children, however. Some women foster relatives' children; others may employ Qu'ranic students; and some employ neighbouring children on a commission (usually ten percent) basis. The availability of children to help is correlated not only with choice of occupations, but also with income. Of the two wards studied, in one — the predominantly Fulani ward — many of the girls, and almost all of the boys, were in both Arabic and Western school, and not doing *talla*. There, women's occupations were mainly embroidering caps, and their incomes averaged only about ₦5 to ₦15 per month. In the other ward, where very few girls attended Western school, the children were actively engaged in street trading and the women's incomes were considerably higher, often double or triple the average for the other ward. The independent income of women serves as an insurance for divorce, which is frequent; it may supplement the income of the husband, if not for basic subsistence, then for the purchase of 'extras' including clothing for the woman and her children. But the incentive for women to engage in independent economic activity does not depend entirely on the husband's income. Even wealthy husbands ration the money they give their wives, and even among the more affluent, a woman's expenses often far surpass her allowance. Moreover, there are certain areas of female expenditure which men rarely contribute to at all: one consists of gifts given to other women, known either as *biki*, within the context of friendships which entail reciprocal gift-giving, or as *barka*, on the occasions of births. Gifts are also given to friends and to the daughters of friends and relatives at marriage. The other major area of expenditure has to do with the provision of dowry. This is in the form of furnishings (a bed, mattress, cupboard, pillow and sheets provided by the bride's father) and a collection of enamel bowls and dishes known as *kayan daki* (literally, things of the room), provided by the bride's mother. *Kayan daki* are important indicators of status, as well as being a form of savings for women (see Bashir 1972). They remain the property of the bride until she bequeaths them to her daughters, or otherwise disposes of them. The provision of *kayan daki* is directly related to the use of female children in trade. Except in the poorest families, where the child's economic activity contributes directly to subsistence, the profits of most girls' trading goes towards the purchase of this dowry. The cost of a set of *kayan daki* varies considerably depending upon its size, but it is common for women to spend ₦300 to ₦500 for one set, and among the wealthy, as much as ₦1000 to ₦3000. For the less affluent this expense often far exceeds a year's income. Nevertheless, despite the importance of *kayan daki* to most Hausa women,[12] not all girls engage in street trading, for this depends upon the attitude of the parents, their income, and sometimes, on the inclination of the child.

Children in Hausa Society

As discussed above, age is an important component of Hausa status, but this refers more to relative than to chronological age. Hausa society is still one in which traditions, both cultural and religious, are revered more than, or at least as much as, change. Wisdom is a quality which is felt to come from experience, and older people receive respect, deference and obedience from the young. The status attaching to seniority applies across the broad divisions of generations, but it is particularly relevant within the categories of child, adult and old person. Even among twins, birth order is significant and kinship terminology consistently differentiates between older and younger, male and female, siblings. Mothers know the chronological ages of their very young children, particularly in the first two months after birth when they must, for forty days (or fifty for first deliveries) take hot baths in a particular manner and observe a number of special prescriptions to regain their strength. With each successive birth a mother may lose track of the exact ages of her children, although if they were born close together she can usually calculate their age by computing the age of each child, in relation to the time elapsed since it was weaned, at the pregnancy of the next.

Many people do not know their chronological age, but they almost always know who, among close associates, is older. It is important for people to know who their age mates (*sa'a*) are, for only between age mates (and certain categories of kin)[13] can deferential behaviour be replaced by familiarity and equality. Among adults in many situations other components of status are more important than relative age in defining social relations. Among children, however, relative age and later, around puberty, gender,[14] are the most important aspects of social identity and are usually more important than other factors,[15] which gradually assume greater significance. Children learn the importance of relative age from adults and from other children. In relations between children, they are not particularly concerned with deference and respect, which they learn to show towards adults very early, but older children do demand (but not always command) obedience, delegate tasks, and attempt to discipline younger children. Play groups reflect the significance of age divisions very early, and by five years these further divide on the basis of gender.

Although lack of space precludes a detailed discussion of ante-natal customs and the details of infant care, a number of points about the attitude to infants and child development may be made (see also Trevitt 1973). Some Kano Hausa women deliver their babies in hospitals and clinics, particularly the first birth, but many deliver at home with the help of female relatives or a mid-wife. The notion of *kunya* discourages a woman from discussing her pregnancy or labour with others and it is common for a woman who lives in a small compound to deliver alone, sending for the midwife after the delivery. Almost immediately after the birth the mother begins receiving female visitors who hold the baby, admire it, and particularly on the third day, the day of *barka*, or greeting, bring gifts for the mother and child. During the first week the child is given a name. The selection of the name, *huduba*, is done by the father who by the third day (sometimes the fourth for girls), whispers the name to the malam. The formal naming ceremony, in which the malam publically announces the name, occurs on the seventh day.[16]

During pregnancy, in her post-natal baths, and during the period of breast feeding, the mother uses a number of medicines to ensure her health and the child's, a successful delivery, and healthy milk. The traditional medicines, now often supplemented by those prescribed in modern hospitals, are in two forms: *laya* (pl. *layu*), charms made from inscriptions of Arabic texts, mainly the Qu'ran, bound in leather or from objects such as shell or animal tails, and herbal medicines. Besides ensuring physical health, some are to protect the child against the jealousy of others, to protect against witchcraft, to ensure popularity, to ensure that a daughter attracts many suitors, to ensure that the child develops an honourable character, and many other things. Childbirth and infancy are recognized as dangerous periods in which all types of medicinal and spiritual protection are needed.

On the third day after birth, most fathers call the *wanzam*, or barber (traditionally the specialist who does all sorts of cutting operations, including circumcision) to perform the excision of the uvula (*beli*). On females, part of the labia minora (also called *beli*) is removed as well.[17] This operation, although performed soon after birth, is part of the preparation for marriage in that it is said to facilitate sexual intercourse and make it more pleasureable for women.

The child is born without a definite character, although the birth of a Muslim child is a promise to Allah that the person will become a worthy Muslim. Parents are criticized for spoiling their children by being too indulgent (after infancy) or by setting bad examples. A number of proverbs express the attitude towards character building in childhood: 'character is like writing on a stone' and 'a stick should be bent when it is raw'. When a child grows, physical and characterological resemblances between it and its parents may be noted, but there is a strong sense in which upbringing is regarded as crucial in shaping a child's behaviour. This is so even though on another level of awareness people attribute many major events to fate, to the will of Allah, and to the mystical intervention of spirits or of humans.[18]

The period of infancy is said to last five months and is terminologically differentiated. The terms for male infant, *jinjiri* and female infant, *jinjiniyya*, are replaced at about the time the child can sit, with the terms for boy, *yaro* and girl, *yarinya*. During infancy the child is almost never separated from its mother. Until forty days after birth neither the child nor the mother leaves the house, except to go for medical care, or, in the case of girls, for ear piercing. At the end of the forty day period, the mother, if she can afford it, announces the completion of her ritual bathing by distributing rice and wheat cakes to other women in her compound and to close relatives and friends. Similar gifts are again distributed by the mother when the child first sits, and when it begins to walk.

Children are said to begin to develop intelligence, awareness or cleverness (*wayo*) during infancy. A child who discriminates between breast and bottle and rejects the latter is said to have *wayo*. This quality does not necessarily develop from experience or from the process of learning, but it refers to the child's capacity to mature and learn on its own. Each new accomplishment is approvingly noted by adults and older children. When a child begins to talk it is taught new words, and its mistake may be laughed at, but adults never use

'baby talk' to speak to children. Older children and adults set
examples and young children follow them by being eager and
accepted participants in group life. In fact, the term for imitate and
the term for learning derive from the same root, *koyo*.[19] Once the
hurdle of weaning is over, children appreciate and enjoy the freedom
and mobility of childhood, and younger children are as eager as their
parents are for them to join the world of those older than themselves.
Once children are about seven they are expected to be able to do
things on their own, assume responsibility, and carry out tasks
independently.

In addition to *wayo* Hausa children are said to develop wisdom
(*hikima*) and creativity (*dabara*) quite early. A four year old who
shaves a large stick to fit it into a small hole is said to be demonstrating *hikima*, while older girls who invent new embroidery
designs, or boys who build airplanes and cars out of millet stalks or
old tin cans, are demonstrating *dabara*.

By about seven years, children are said to develop *hankali*, understanding or sense.[20] Before age six or seven, children rarely are said
to have *hankali*, and boys are said to attain this, as well as other
characteristics of maturity, later than girls, partly because girls are
'constantly exposed to their mothers'. By seven, both boys and girls
should have *hankali*. Unlike *wayo*, this develops from experience,
although not from direct teaching. It relates to − among other
things − the beginning of an understanding of correct behaviour
associated with gender. Boys are usually circumcised in the
harmattan, or cold season of their sixth year, although traditionally
the age was later, nine for the Hausa and seven for the Fulani, and
today it is occasionally done earlier, even in infancy. By the
traditional age of male circumcision, both boys and girls are
supposed to understand some of the rules of avoidance between males
and females. The boy is a 'grown up child' and he knows he cannot
sleep near his mother. Girls can still sleep near their mothers, but not
where their father sleeps. For both, *hankali* implies the ability to
discriminate between actions that are morally good and those that
are bad. This understanding is said to develop with and be part of
the understanding of the significance of male/female differences. The
strictness with which this avoidance behaviour between the sexes is
enforced among children varies from family to family, and from
village to city. Many parents watch the movements of their daughters
closely, and the daughters are often kept more busy and given less
freedom than the sons.

After circumcision, and generally about the time that *hankali* develops, children are expected to show much more independence and responsibility. Once a child has reached this stage, punishment for misbehaviour may be more severe than earlier, for the child is expected to understand the purpose and meaning of discipline. Corporal punishment, in moderation, is felt to be educational, but too much is felt to be counter-productive, in that the child gets used to it and simply ignores it. After circumcision, a boy is expected to be able to stay away from his parents, for example to follow a malam to another town for education. Kinship fostering for both boys and girls also often begins at this age, except in cases of crisis fostering – that following divorce or the death of a parent.

Another important Hausa character trait *kunya*, or modesty, is also developed in childhood. Before age four, children do not know about *kunya*, but by this age they are expected to begin learning gender specific behaviour associated with the expression of *kunya*. Girls, for example, are supposed to wear clothing and sit in such a ways as to cover their thighs. The most commonly heard reprimand, said even to infants who are not expected to understand (although the adults around do note such rhetorical statements) is *maras kunya*, which can be roughly translated as 'without shame' or 'without modesty'. But this is a mild reprimand; it does not communicate the idea that the child has done anything for which he or she would be punished, but rather that he or she should know better and should exercise self-control. Thus a four year old girl was told 'maras kunya' when she tugged on her mother's breast. The mother laughed as she said this, and the child protested and laughed at the same time (she had long since been weaned but was the youngest of eight children). The expression is used to correct what is felt to be regressive behaviour, and it is also used in teaching certain specific manners such as eating with the right hand, or in toilet training (a noticeably untraumatic process – see also Dry, 1949).

The major trauma in the life of most Hausa children is weaning, particularly if this is immediately followed by another birth. Until weaning, the child is given the breast on demand and when the mother feels the need to breast feed. By five months, other foods are added to the diet, and breast feeding becomes less frequent as the child grows, but it does not cease until formal weaning (*yaye*) has taken place. Boys generally are weaned at seventeen to eighteen months and girls at twenty to twenty-one months. The earlier age for boys is said to be because of *karatu*, reading. The sooner they are made independent from the mother, the sooner they are ready to start attending Qu'ranic school. Also, too much milk is said to be bad for their memories and an impediment to learning. It is important that a child should be weaned soon after it can walk, for if another birth follows right after, the child can then join the group of older children, in and around his or her own compound. Most children are physically removed from the mother's presence for one week, from one Friday to the next. The woman who cares for the child in this period may be the maternal grandmother, or another woman of her generation. During the *yaye* the child is given various medicines to ensure its strength and to help it forget the breast. In fact, if there is no new birth, some children continue to reach for the breast (this is one of the privileges of the *auta*, the last born). Most mothers are fairly indulgent about this behaviour although they do not encourage it. For the child who is displaced by another birth,[21] the transition may be more difficult. These children may be morose and sullen for a short time, but they soon become absorbed into the older sibling group and begin to enjoy the freedom and mobility characteristic of Hausa childhood.

Hausa children enjoy a freedom that no other group in the society commands – the right to wander in and out of people's houses. Children are not expected to observe formal greeting behaviour, and they casually walk into the houses of neighbours, relatives, friends and even strangers, to look for playmates, to make purchases, to offer things for sale, or to carry messages. There are many important implications of this including the educational experience the children gain by observing many facets of the society that they will be excluded from as adults. All children, even when they come from small families,[22] can join a large group of children their own age and older, consisting of siblings, cousins, neighbours and schoolmates. Within this children's world, older children do a great deal of direct and indirect teaching of younger ones. Given the restrictions on the spatial mobility of adults, this is a vitally important part of Hausa traditional education.

Parents also specifically delegate the care of young children to older ones. Until about the age of seven or eight, children are not usually allowed to carry babies on their backs or pick them up. However, as soon as they can walk, children act out the carrying of babies. Until about age four both boys and girls can be seen carrying plastic dolls, cushions, bits of firewood, or just about any object they can find, on their backs in the manner in which women and older children carry babies. Boys generally cease this form of play by about four years, but girls continue until they are entrusted with the real responsibility which they assume with pleasure and pride. By nine and ten, boys and girls will be entrusted with the care of young children, including infants. Older children bathe younger ones, play with them, and take them when they do errands. Young children who can walk accompany their older siblings to Arabic school. There the children sit with their age mates and the malam gives each age group lessons according to their capability.

By the time a girl marries, then, she has already had considerable experience with many aspects of child care. However, caring for young children is only one of the many tasks which children perform for adults in Hausa society. In the next section, the distribution of rights over children, and the nature of the services children perform for adults are discussed.

The Hausa kinship is cognatic, but with a strong patrilineal emphasis. Women are said to bear children 'for their husbands' and in cases of divorce, any children already weaned remain with the husband or someone he delegates. In fact, men sometimes allow one female child to remain with the divorced wife, but they are not obliged to do this. Fostering is common and occurs mainly between relatives; a child's older married sibling, a parent's (usually father's) sibling, a grandparent, a father's wife other than the mother (particularly after the divorce or death of the mother) and occasionally more distant relatives or non-relatives, such as malams, are delegated the responsibility of raising the child. The term *riko* refers to raising someone else's child, while a *mariki* (male) and *marikiya* (female) may be distinguished from a *mahaifi* (genitor) and *mahaifiya* (genitress). The biographies of many children, particularly those whose parents are divorced or deceased, include several changes of residence and caretakers. Note that fostering of this type is not to be confused with adoption, which if it occurs at all, is rare except in cases when both parents are deceased (see Schildkrout 1973). Parents do not give up all rights in their children, nor do children give up all claims upon their parents, although responsibility for caring for children and rights to children's services may be delegated.

Rights over children's services belong with its parents and or guardian but all other relatives, and many other adults living in the same compound, or even neighbourhood, may use the services of a child, for limited tasks, without asking permission of the parents. Even strangers ask children to do errands, however, although when there is no relationship to the child, the adult will reward the child with a gift (*lada*) of a small amount of money. Thus, even given restrictions based on adult status, there may be dozens of adults who have rights to the services of a child. In the same way, adults other than a child's parents may discipline children. Adults have these rights by virtue of being adults, not by virtue of being parents. Children, on the other hand, are taught very early to obey the orders of adults, and they almost never directly refuse to do what is asked of them. They may, however, devise numerous means of non-compliance, such as claiming that another adult has already co-opted their time, or simply leaving the scene and ignoring the command.

Although rights over children are, in the formal sense noted above, vested with fathers, it is mothers, and women in general, who have the greater use of their services, simply because women and children spend most time together. Were this not the case, women, except in the wealthier families, where paid labour can replace the services of children, could not remain in purdah and carry out their domestic responsibilities, not to mention their independent economic activities. It should be noted that the restriction of child participation to the female domain relates to the fact that Kano city is an urban setting with most men working away from their homes, and many children attending both Arabic and Western schools.[23] In farming families children are likely to be given more tasks to perform in association with men such as weeding, minding animals, and carrying farm produce. However even in Kano city, the large markets are filled with children, girls doing *talla*, and boys, about eleven and twelve, who are not attending primary school, who accompany their fathers to market to learn their trade.

In Kano city both male and female children grow up, at least until about age twelve, primarily under the authority of women. Numerous household tasks are performed by children, and the degree to which these are gender specific depends to some extent upon the number, ages and gender of the children available to help. Certain tasks, such as sifting flour, or virtually anything to do with food preparation, are done by girls, but if there are no girls available boys may be called in to help (although they may be ridiculed by other children). Girls more often mind younger children, but boys may also do this, in which case there is no ridicule, for men also play with children. Boys more often take out refuse, but both boys and girls shop, take food for grinding, fetch water, carry goods and messages, and sell food. Girls more frequently accompany women out at night, bathe younger children, wash dishes and sweep. Both boys and girls wash their own clothes. Thus, although differences in gender are not absolutely crucial in determining the allocation of tasks to children, certain spheres of activity are defined as male and female, and children gradually fit into this. Once gender becomes an determinant of the assignment of roles, the transition to adulthood has occurred.

I have noted that gender is not crucial in determining the tasks that children perform for adults. However, in interaction among children, it becomes increasingly important from about age seven, In play, children often imitate adult roles, which are inevitably gender specific. Thus little girls spend a lot of time 'cooking' with mud and sand; boys build tiny cars and airplanes, engage in sports and games which test strength, physical endurance and tolerance of pain. Boys gamble (often for food or playing cards) and nowadays play cards, while girls play clapping and singing games. The play of boys is, in general, much more competitive and aggressive than that of girls.

As pointed out above, adult female dependence on children is apparent not only in the domestic sphere but also in women's independent economic activities. Many men object to their daughters doing street trading, or *talla*, and in some families *talla* is specifically forbidden. In one of the two wards studied, where most of the men were in salaried government jobs, most of the girls were in both Arabic and Western school and there was a strong feeling on the part of the men against their daughters doing *talla*. In the other ward, where the men were traders, butchers or artisans, most girls were doing *talla* and attending only Arabic school. In some cases women send their daughters to trade over their husband's objections. One, for example, sent her four year old, and explained. She said that until the child was of school age, she had 'nothing to do' at home, and moreover, the small income would help. Older girls, although they risk being 'spoiled' before marriage, also attract prospective husbands in this way. This is a major reason why some parents encourage it. They realize, too, that children learn many valuable skills by trading, in making mathematical calculations, in learning about trade, and in dealing with people.

There is some evidence, from the life histories of adult women, that the prevalence of children doing *talla* has increased in the past twenty years in Kano, perhaps as the scale of women's independent economic activities or even the institution of purdah itself, has increased. At the same time, the massive enrolment of children in primary school is increasingly removing children from trade. Whether or not a specific child does *talla* depends on many factors, but in particular on the economic position of the family, their attitude towards Western education for girls, and the mother's occupation. Girls in fatherless families inevitably help their mother by trading, either for the purpose of providing money for subsistence or in preparation for their own marriages. In Kano, boys who have left their families in rural areas as they have followed a malam to the city may do *talla* on a straight commission basis in order to support themselves. They also do other work such as cleaning gutters, carrying loads and begging.

All children become highly involved in the cash economy very early. Besides their participation in it for adults — shopping and selling — they also participate in what might be termed a 'children's economy'. Children have their own money, from school allowances given them daily for the purchase of snacks, from gifts, from work they may have done for strangers, and from their own investments. Most children regard the economic activity they do for profit, such as *talla*, as work done for themselves, even though they may hand over the money to adults for safe-keeping. Besides doing chores for adults, boys make toys for sale, and they rent out valued property (such as slide viewers or bicycles). By the age of ten many girls begin to practice cooking. They do not help very much in the preparation of the family food, for this is strictly the wife's responsibility, but they do sift flour, wash dishes, and help with other tasks. By age twelve many girls help their mother's in all stages of preparing food for sale. By ten, many girls cook food for sale on their own. With initial help from their mothers, or other adult female relatives, who may give them a cooking pot, charcoal, or a small stove, they purchase small amounts of ingredients and prepare various snack foods. These are then sold in very small quantities to other children. As the sellers will sell for less than the price of any item of food sold by an adult woman, and as the quantities are extremely small, the customers are mainly children. These child sellers extend credit to other children, which is usually honoured. In one case an eleven year old girl began doing *talla* but did not enjoy it and rarely made any profit. In fact she began losing money and went into debt to her grandmother in order to pay back her mother's original investment in the goods she was supposed to sell. After some time, she began to sell miniature *waina* to children and in four months she made enough money to buy herself a new dress and begin saving for a pair of shoes (the mother was divorced and she and the daughter were self-supporting).

All children are expected to gradually assume more and more responsibility in performing socially significant tasks which are complementary to tasks performed for adults. Many tasks are delegated to children, and some can be performed only by children, or by other persons who for one reason or another, are not bound by the 'normal' adult roles of husband and wife. This includes domestic servants, elderly women, and divorced women who are not in purdah. However, it should be noted that children's roles are to some extent dependent upon the economic status of their parents, particularly their fathers. In Kano city, the income producing work of most men is done away from the home, and most children grow up as economic dependents, contributing little or nothing, directly, to subsistence. With the increase in time spent in formal educational institutions, children are in fact becoming more dependent, for longer. However, even when children are dependent, when their 'cost' exceeds their productive capacity, the errands and household chores they perform are still of economic significance, for were there no children to perform these tasks, hired labour would be required. In this sense, except in families where hired labour does in fact replace children for tasks such as shopping, taking errands, and minding young children, children's roles, even when non-income-generating are economically significant. Moreover, there are, in Kano city, children who are partly responsible for their own subsistence – the *almajirai*, or Qu'ranic students who often live with malams away from their families (who often are in rural areas), and children of very poor families, sometimes in female-headed households. Other children, while not responsible for supporting themselves, still generate income which is part of their preparation for adulthood. Many boys provide the expenses for their weddings, after they become self-supporting and capable of supporting their own families. Girls who do *talla* contribute to their dowries. Thus growing up is not a transition from being an unproductive member of society to becoming a productive one. In Kano city, children participate in socially and economically significant activities as children, gradually assuming greater responsibilities and more independence from their parents. At the same time, they gradually observe certain modes of behaviour that socially mark them as fully adult, for example, performing greetings properly, praying regularly and, in the case of boys, attending mosque, and most important, avoiding frivolous contact, in public, with the opposite sex.

The symbolic transition from childhood to adulthood really comes about when the freedom to move inside and outside houses, between the male and female domains, is restricted. This transition is associated with the full assumption of adult sex roles, and it occurs somewhat differently for boys and for girls. Until puberty, both boys and girls live primarily in the sphere of women, although they may move in both domains (very obviously spatially delimited in Kano). For girls, the transition to adult status occurs at marriage which ideally coincides with sexual maturation, specifically reproductive capacity. Marriage for girls takes place generally between twelve and sixteen, but sometimes as young as ten, and sometimes particularly among girls receiving Western education, later.[24] At marriage, all girls move into their husband's house. This may or may not be with the husband's parents, who, in first marriages especially, are often relatives – for a large proportion of first marriages are between cross-cousins. If a girl is married as early as ten, she may not cook for her husband or have sexual relations with him for some time, but she enters purdah and loses the freedom associated with childhood.

For boys, the transition to adulthood does not immediately involve marriage, for a boy rarely marries until he is economically productive, often in his late twenties or older (although this varies with the economic status of the father particularly for first marriages). However, although he does not immediately marry, after puberty a boy must move out of the sphere of women into the world of men. Boys whose fathers are traders or artisans may apprentice themselves to their fathers or to other adult men by age eleven or twelve. But even those going to school and planning on higher education spend less and less time at home after puberty. The process of separation begins by age ten. A boy of this age refuses to eat with his sisters and carries his food outside to share it with his male friends. He spends more and more time outside, reporting in from time to time to see if the women have errands or chores for him. And the women depend on him less and less for performing household chores; younger children or female children of the same age will more and more take over the chores the boy performed previously.

Adulthood means separation, even avoidance, between male and female in all non-sexual activities, while childhood is a period in which these boundaries are not important. Children in fact are the only persons entirely free to cross the boundaries between the male and female domains. Until they develop sense, *hankali*, they are not expected to understand the full significance of these boundaries, but once they do understand they are expected to demonstrate this understanding through behaviour exhibiting the quality of *kunya*, modesty. If children were not free to cross the boundaries between the male and female domains, women, quite obviously, could not take the major responsibility for raising all of their children, male and female. For boys it is important to note as well that being a child implies being jurally and economically dependent, and being under the authority of adults, male and female. But as men in Hausa society, although they may in some respects remain under the authority of men of higher status than themselves, they cannot remain under the authority of women. Inevitably, then, the transition to manhood means moving out of the domain of female authority, into the world of men, and ultimately into the relationship of marriage, where male dominance is as yet unchallenged.

At this point one may enquire as to the extent to which Western education is changing the role of the Hausa child, and the roles of adults who interact with children. Hausa children have been attending formal schools, in Qu'ranic studies and Arabic, for several centuries and continue to do so. In the North of Nigeria, Western education has been slow to take hold on a large scale mainly because of a colonial policy which, for a number of complex political reasons (Hubbard 1975; Hiskett 1975) discouraged the establishment of schools in the region. Since much early Western education was indeed Christian education it engendered resistence among the educated Muslims. The British, in order to preserve the special political relationships they had built up in the North, catered to the most con-servative of these interests, which included not only the religious leaders, but also the traditional aristocracy which was less than enthusiastic about mass non-Islamic education. Moreover, the traditional educational system in the North provided judges (*alkalis*) and scribes in sufficient numbers to run the administration and the courts. Therefore, given the resistence to Christian mission schools, the colonial government was able to carry on without investing heavily in education. The result of this policy was an increasing im-balance in the extensiveness of Western education in the former three regions of Nigeria (now superceded by the nineteen states). With the intention of correcting this imbalance, the present Federal Military Government has embarked upon a program of universal free primary education (known as U.P.E.) aimed at full enrollment at the primary level by 1982.

The number of children in school has indeed increased in the North, although it is still relatively low in rural areas and lower for girls than for boys. Between 1968 and 1975 the number of primary school children more than tripled in Kano State, and this was before the massive enrolment campaign associated with the U.P.E. program. In the same period, while the number of girls in school has tripled, the enrolment of boys has almost quadrupled, and there were still, in 1975/76, more than three times as many boys as girls in primary school (*Educational Statistics for Kano State 1975–76*). In Kano metropolitan area, in 1975–76, approximately one out of three boys was in primary school (106,792 out of 647,229 school age children – both sexes) while only approximately one out of six girls attended school (45,205).

For the purpose of this paper, I will restrict this discussion to a number of observations on the changes that Western education makes in children's roles, and the effects of this on the family, omitting any comment on the significance of Western education for the individual child's future, or on the problems, foreseen by many, of a rapid expansion of primary education in the context of an economy which may not be able to offer continuing education on a large scale or absorb the products of the educational system in meaningful employment.

Since the vast majority of Hausa children continue their Arabic education while attending primary school, they are now busy, almost full time, with formal education. This explains the resistence on the part of some parents to Western education, for it deprives them of the presence of their children. This objection depends upon other factors, for men with salaried jobs are less likely to miss their children's daily presence than are men who are farmers, traders or artisans – men who traditionally would have handed down their skills and their assets to their sons. Since more boys than girls are attending school another consequence is that the burden of household tasks performed by young girls has increased, and the interchangeability in the allocation of tasks to boys and girls below a certain age, noted above, is becoming less noticeable. Among children, and adults, to the extent that Western education is more a prerogative of males than of females, it adds a further dimension of inequality to the relationship between men and women.

In Kano city, I have noted that in those neighbourhoods where the majority of children are in school, one notes that it becomes more difficult for married women to pursue independent economic activities. Their incomes are lower, and their position within the institution of purdah is more difficult. While women do manage to get their household tasks performed, by employing the services of children in non-school hours, and by employing those children who do not attend school, the children are kept very busy (with little time for studying) and the women are able to use them only for the most essential tasks. Without children around, women in purdah are more cut off from information and communication with the outside world. In families where paid labour can be employed to assist in household tasks, adults are not as dependent on children and women do not suffer as much from the loss of their services. Nevertheless, unless they have a great deal of capital, their independent economic activities are likely to be curtailed. Western education, then, besides changing the opportunities for and roles of children, also in a very direct and practical way challenges the position of women within the institution of purdah, particularly in the lower classes. While very few people object to what are perceived as the long term benefits of Western education, such resistance as there is (and it is not as great as has been made out), is very often based upon those very realistic appraisals of its immediate socio-economic consequences.

In summary, this paper has stressed that in studying children it is important to take a perspective in which one views children and adults as complementary participants in the social system. In Hausa urban society, although most children do not play a significant role in providing basic subsistence, they are crucial in social structural terms: the social, economic and political definition of adult roles, particularly those based on gender, cannot be understood without taking account of the roles of children. In Hausa society, in all but the wealthiest and most non-traditional families, certain tasks are inevitably relegated to children, for adults cannot perform them, limited as they are by the social definition of gender. The Hausa child does not simply imitate adult behaviour in rehearsal for adult life. Childhood is qualitatively different from adulthood, for the child does not have to observe many of the rules that regulate the behaviour of adults. The suspension of these rules is a crucial part of the learning process, for it gives the child particularly the boy, whatever insight and understanding he may later have of the lives of women.

Footnotes

1. The following organizations have provided financial support for this research: the American Museum of Natural History, the National Science Foundation, the Social Science Research Council, and the Wenner-Gren Foundation for Anthropological Research. The University of Lagos and Bayero University, Kano, have provided institutional support in Nigeria. Dr. Ibrahim Tahir, Dr. Musa Abdullahi, Malam Sule Hamma, Alhaji Mohammadu Lawal Iro, and Mr. Joe McIntyre, and my assistants Bilkesu Bashir and Alpazazi Namairage all read and commented upon various versions of this paper, and I am grateful for their many suggestions.
2. Also, children's small fingers were those best suited for operating early

textile machinery, while their small bodies were 'ideal' for cleaning chimneys.
3. With few exceptions, the emphasis in most of the 'value of children' studies is demographic, concerned with the issue of population growth and limitation.
4. There is a large bibliography relating to the Hausa, including numerous works in Arabic and Hausa, cited in the bibliographies of Tahir (1976) and Paden (1973), works related to economics cited in Hill (1972), and items regularly noted in the bibliography of the journal *Savanna* published by Ahmadu Bello University. Works related specifically to this paper include: Adamu (1976); Barkow (1972); Bashir (1972); Dry, E. (1949); Dry, D.P.L. (1950, 1953); Greenberg (1946); Hill (1969, 1972); Jaggar (1973); Madauci, Isa, Daura (1968); Mortimore and Wilson (1965); Paden (1970, 1973); Palmer (1928); Smith, M.F. (1965); Smith, M.G. (1952, 1959, 1962, 1966); Tahir (1976); Trevitt (1973); Trevallion (1966).
5. See Paden (1973: 46) and Palmer (1928, iii, pp. 100–1) cited in Hodgkin (1975: 92).
6. For example, details of the marriage ceremony differ. There is also a greater emphasis on the notion of *kunya* among the Fulani, and possibly a greater emphasis on patrilineality and first-child avoidance.
7. I would also suggest that as a result of this Hausa women do not develop the psychological dependence on men typical of Western women. However, the areas in which they are able to exercise this independence are severely limited.
8. Dry (1950: 103) suggests that the notion of *kunya* as applied to the first-born child is an extension of its importance for a young married couple, where the greatest modesty must be shown in all matters related to sexuality. This, he suggests, is done so that the young couple will not seem too eager to advance quickly vis-a-vis the older generation.
9. In Qu'ranic schools this consists of *kudin laraba* (money of Wednesday), a nominal fee of about 10 kobo (8.4 pence) per week, and gifts to the malam depending upon the father's status and income.
10. According to Dr. Ibrahim Tahir (personal communication) the age of marriage for both men and women has lowered considerably in recent years. In the last century, as today, however, the affluent married earlier than others.
11. Except in those houses where food is received from patrons or more affluent relatives, or in those in which the husband is absent and the wife is helped by relatives or friends.
12. Western educated women also have *kayan daki* but its content is changing to include more dishes and fewer enamel and brass bowls. Formerly, calabashes were used.
13. Joking partners- cross-cousins and grandparents and grandchildren, but in the latter case the authority that comes with age is not entirely absent.
14. Dry (1953: 40) observes that 'in childhood authority is conferred by age not sex, and girls give orders to boys younger than themselves . . . The unmarried girl is not obliged to observe respect to younger adult males, especially if they are not married.' However, I would note that since girls

marry around age twelve, and since boys are thought to mature later than girls, these younger males would not be regarded as adult.

15. The major exception noted so far was the ostracism and bullying applied to one boy whose mother was not married and who was said to be a prostitute. Increasingly, status differences among children based on Western school attendance are noted. The ways in which school-attenders and non-school-attenders spend their time is so different, that the division among children is inevitable. Also, they do not fail to note the future status differences education may lead to.

16. If a child dies before the naming ceremony, it is buried, a prayer said, but no funeral held.

17. This is not always done (but usually is in Kano city), and may be limited to people from certain areas of Hausaland. In the literature reference is made to clitoridectomy, but I have some doubts as to whether this was practiced, even in the past. The description of 'cutting' may have been mistakenly translated as clitoridectomy.

18. Spirit possession, as institutionalized in the *bori* cult, remains from pre-Islamic Hausa religious beliefs (see Greenberg, 1946; Tremearne, 1914). Humans are thought by many people to be able to cause harm either through witchcraft or through the maleficent use of Islamic charms.

19. The word for imitate is *kwaikwaiyo*, a reduplicated form of *koyo*, to learn.

20. It is interesting to note that these Hausa concepts correspond closely with the developmental stages outlined by Piaget (1967). *Hankali*, at age seven, corresponds with the stage at which Piaget says children develop a sense of morality, and *kunya*, at about age four, corresponds with the stage at which Piaget says children understand the notion of respect.

21. The traditional period of post-partum abstinence is eighteen months to two years, but in reality it is often less.

22. There is a great range in family and household size, from the three person 'nuclear family' to large polygamous families and extended families living in a single compound of up to one hundred persons or perhaps more among the very rich.

23. In Hausa, both Arabic school and 'Western school' are known as *makaranta*, distinguished as *makarantar Arabia* and *makarantar boko*. This dualism in the educational system of the north is a result of the imposition of the Western education on a highly developed and formal traditional educational system. Attempts are being made by the educational authorities to unify the system. The Islammiyya schools, in fact, are government approved schools which combine the curriculums of the two types of education.

24. In recent years there has been a campaign launched on the part of the Kano State Government to discourage early marriage.

References

Adamu, M. (1976). The spread of Hausa culture in West Africa, *Savanna*, **5**, 1, 3–15.

Aries, P. (1962). Centuries of Childhood. Random House, New York.

Bartels, F.L. (1975). Akan indigenous education, *in* "Conflict and Harmony in Education in Tropical Africa (eds. G.N. Brown and M. Hiskett). George Allen & Unwin, London.

Barkow, J.H. (1972). Hausa Women and Islam, *Canadian Journal of African Studies*, **6/2**, 317–328.

Bashir, M.K. (1972). The economic activities of secluded married women in Kurawa and Lallokin Lemu, Kano city. B.Sc. thesis, Ahmadu Bello University, Zaria.

Dry, E. (1949). The social development of the Hausa child, *Proceedings of the Third International West African Conference*, 164–70.

Dry, D.P.L. (1950). The family organization of the Hausa of Northern Nigeria. B.Sc. thesis, Oxford.

Dry, D.P.L. (1953). The Place of Islam in Hausa Society. D. Phil., Oxford.

Dreitzel, P. (1973). Introduction *in* "Childhood and Socialization" (ed. P. Dreitzel). Macmillan, New York.

Educational Statistics for Kano State 1975–76. Government Printer, Kano.

Erikson, E. (1950). Childhood and Society. Reprinted, Penguin, London, 1963.

Fortes, M. (1938). Social and psychological aspects of education in Taleland, Supplement to *Africa* **II (4)**, Oxford, London.

Greenberg, J. (1946). The influence of Islam on a Sudanese religion. Monographs of the American Ethnological Society, New York.

Hodgkin, T. (1975). Nigerian Perspectives (2nd edn.), Oxford, London.

Hill, P. (1969). Hidden trade in Hausaland, *Man*, Sept.

Hill, P. (1972). Rural Hausa: a village and a setting. Cambridge University Press, Cambridge.

Hiskett, M. (1975). Islamic education in the traditional and state systems in Northern Nigeria, *in* "Conflict and harmony in education in tropical Africa (eds. G.N. Brown and M. Hiskett). George Allen & Unwin, London.

Hubbard, J.P. (1975). Government and Islamic education in Northern Nigeria (1900–1940), *in* "Conflict and harmony in education in tropical Africa" (eds. G.N. Brown and M. Hiskett). George Allen & Unwin, London.

Illich, I.D. (1971). Deschooling society. Harper & Row, New York.

Jaggar, P. (1973). Kano city blacksmiths: precolonial distribution, structure and organisation, *Savanna*, **2, 1**, June, 11–27.

Madauci, I., Isa, Y., Daura, B. (1968). Hausa customs. Northern Nigeria Publishing Co.

Mayer, P. (ed.). (1970). Socialization: the approach from social anthropology. A.S.A. Monograph No. 8. Tavistock, London.

McKay, R. (1973). Conceptions of children and models of socialization, *in* "Childhood and Socialization" (ed. P. Dreitzel). Macmillan, New York.

Mead, M. (1928). Coming of age in Samoa. Morrow, New York.

Mortimore, M.J. and Wilson, J. (1965). Land and people in the Kano closed settled zone. Department of Geography, Ahmadu Bello University, Zaria.

Newson, J. and E. (1974). Cultural aspects of childrearing in the English-speaking world, *in* The Integration of a child into a social world (ed. M.P.M.

Richards) Cambridge University Press, Cambridge.

O'Neill, J. (1973). Embodiment and child development: a phenomenological approach, *in* "Childhood and socialization" (ed. P. Dreitzel). Macmillan, New York.

Paden, J. (1970). Urban pluralism, integration and adaptation of communal identity in Kano, Nigeria, *in* "From tribe to nation in Africa: studies in incorporation processes" (eds. R. Cohen and J. Middleton). Chandler, Scranton, Pennsylvania.

Paden, J. (1973). Religion and political culture in Kano. University of California Press, Berkeley.

Palmer, H.R. (1928). Sudanese Memoirs, Vols. I–III, Lagos. Reprinted in one volume, London, 1967.

Piaget, J. (1967). Six psychological studies. Random House, New York.

Rafky, D.M. (1973). Phenomenology and socialization: some comments on the assumptions underlying socialization theory, *in* "Childhood and socialization" (ed. P. Dreitzel). Macmillan, New York.

Raum, O.F. (1940). A Chaga childhood. Oxford, London.

Read, M. (1959). Child of their fathers: growing up among the Ngoni of Nyasaland. Methuen, London.

Richards, M.P.M. (ed.). (1974). The integration of a child into a social world. Cambridge University Press, Cambridge.

Schildkrout, E. (1973). The fostering of children in urban Ghana: problems of ethnographic analysis in a multi-cultural context, *Urban Anthropology*, **2**, 1, 48–73.

Smith, M. (1954). Baba of Karo: a woman of the Muslim Hausa. Faber and Faber, London.

Smith, M.G. (1952). A study of Hausa domestic economy in northern Zaria, *Africa*, **XXII**.

Smith, M.G. (1955). The economy of the Hausa communities of Zaria. Colonial Research Studies, **16**, HMSO, London.

Smith, M.G. (1959). The Hausa system of social status, *Africa*, **XXIX**.

Smith, M.G. (1962). Exchange and marketing among the Hausa, *in* "Markets in Africa" (eds. P. Bohannan and G. Dalton). Northwestern University Press, Evanston.

Tahir, I. (1976). Scholars, sufis, saints and capitalists in Kano 1904–1974. Ph.D. thesis, Cambridge University.

Tremearne, A.J.N. (1914). The ban of the Bori. Reprinted, Cass 1968, London.

Trevallion, B.A.W. (1966). Metropolitan Kano: Report on the twenty-year development plan, 1963–1983). Greater Kano Planning Authority, Glasgow.

Trevitt, L. (1973). Attitudes and customs in childbirth among Hausa women in Zaria city, *Savanna*, **2**, 2, 223–227.

White, B. (1975). The Economic Importance of Children in a Javanese Village, *in* "Population and social organizations (ed. M. Nag), 127–147. International Congress of Anthropological and Ethnological Sciences, 9th Congress 1973, The Hague.

Whiting, B.B. (ed.). (1963). Six cultures: studies of child rearing, Wiley, New York.

GERONTOCRACY, POLYGYNY AND SCARCE RESOURCES[1]

URI ALMAGOR

I

The connection between gerontocracy and polygyny has been pointed out by almost every anthropologist dealing with gerontocracy, and goes back to Frazer and Rivers.[2] It seems to me that this connection can be divided into two extreme models. One is shaped on the metaphor of a ladder, and was recently elaborated by Spencer to describe the social organisation of the Samburu.[3] Indeed, the Samburu are typical of this type of society in which age-sets are ranked in order of seniority and their position on the ladder is parallel to the various demarcated age-grades, i.e., stages of the life cycle. The division of the life cycle into such 'sociological ages' determines the privileges, rights, and obligations of each age-set and therefore its status and relative strength. This model attributes qualitative differences to age and the gradual advancement of the system, like that of the life-cycle, means that whenever a set reaches a certain stage, all its coeval members assume privileges to which the new stage entitles them and for which they had until then not been eligible.

It is true that in such a society marriage (and quite often polygyny) is the privilege of elderhood, but this has to be seen in conjunction with another aspect, namely, the 'sacred tradition of the group', which is what Weber described as the source of elders' power in a geron-tocracy.[4] Spencer calls it a 'mystical component', but whatever the term employed, it refers to a supernatural power which elders possess only by virtue of their age-set occupying a particular rung on the ladder. The sacred prerogative means, for example, the power 'to bless' to 'to withhold their blessing', to 'control their [young men's] destiny' and so forth. Although such powers may remain latent, they must nonetheless be viewed as a complex whole in a situation of polygyny among Samburu elders, where it fulfills 'the task of holding young men in check for a while so that elders can retain their monopoly in marriage'.[5] In other words, in such a model power devolves upon each of the 'sociological ages' and, *inter alia*, determines, leads to, or is associated with their access to women, but not vice versa.

The other model is one of a society in which privileges, rights, and obligations are not associated with the ranking order of demarcated age-groups, nor does common age or common stage in life serve as a principle of group organisation, let alone determine the relative strength of any group or its access to women. In practice, the process usually goes the other way round: small corporate kin groups are connected through the formation of marriage alliances and the Tiwi are a representative case in point.[6] Here it is women, either through bestowal or through widow remarriages, who serve as the main invest-ment in building up one's status as well as for the accumulation of political power. Gardner calls this type of power accumulation through wives 'gerontogamy',[7] to indicate that political success is based on the attainment of a large number of wives and is affected by demo-graphic factors such as entering into the first marriage late in life for males and early for females. There is a gap of at least a generation between the spouses; consequently, a man is a senior elder by the time he fathers daughters whom he may bestow upon young men in order to make them dependent on him, and he thus reaches the peak of his political power at elderhood. In such a society there is no 'mystical component' in elders' power.

The first model can be termed 'ascriptive gerontocracy' in the sense that a man's status and claim to power emanates from his membership in an age-set and age-grade. The second model may be termed 'achieved gerontocracy' since it is an individual achievement through the useful alliances and judicious investment of bestowed daughters which brings reward, neither of which depend on the ascension of groups through progressive ranks.[8]

Note, however, that the two models described above only indicate different paths to power, but they are not mutually exclusive. Each type incorporates certain elements of the other. In the first type, for example, there are in each age-set elders who are more prestigious and politically prominent than others thanks to their having established a more successful polygynous household. Similarly, in some societies of the second type, elders are not absolutely devoid of a sacred or religious component in their power, which they may use to 'control the younger [men] through the elaborate system of male initiation found in Australia', as Rose pointed out.[9]

These two models were described in some detail so as to enable me to discuss the connection between gerontocracy and polygyny among the Dassanetch of Southwest Ethiopia who display features of both models. To be more accurate, Dassanetch society formally represents the first model in the sense that age is the main principle of social organisation and the age system is hierarchically ranked in generation sets, but within the system the main mechanism of power accumulation is the one described in the second model, i.e., through marriage alliances and patronage of young men — power accumulated by individuals. The result is a divided gerontocracy: on the one hand, we have the ascriptive aspect of gerontocracy — elders, called 'bulls', who are the senior elders of the senior generation-set in power; their power contains the sacred and mystical components described above, and they are the formal political and religious leaders to be succeeded by the generation-set occupying the rung below them on the ladder only upon the demise of all incumbent 'bulls'. The other element of gerontocracy is achieved — it refers to the power an individual achieves through his own endeavours by creating a self-selected network of social relationships over a long period of time which cuts across the lines of generation-sets. The achieved gerontocracy of the Dassanetch contains elders of three of four generation sets who are not 'bulls' and who become influential members of the community. Unlike 'bulls' whose status derives from the very structure of the age system and whose position is therefore unassailable, the position of influence achieved by other, non-'bull' elders is vulnerable to outside influences. However, this is not entirely relevant at the moment.[10] It should be noted, however, that the distinction between 'achieved' and 'ascribed' gerontocracy is not clear-cut. For example, not every elder who belongs to the senior generation-set in power is necessarily also a 'bull'. The number of 'bulls' is limited, and an elder is elected 'bull' on his personal merit — usually as a result of lengthy political efforts and alliances and after having accumulated credit throughout his lifetime. But for the sake of simplicity the terms are here used in their broadest sense, i.e., to denote the mechanism whereby elders occupy positions either by virtue of the age-set to which they belong or as a consequence of individual power accumulation. In this essay I shall only discuss the mechanism of power accumulation in an achieved gerontocracy, and must postpone the discussion of the ascriptive gerontocracy (the 'bulls'), its power and control over certain aspects of Dassanetch life, and its inter-relations with other powerful elders who are not 'bulls', to another occasion.

I shall begin with a brief sketch of some features of Dassanetch social organisation and age-system which are relevant to the present analysis.

II

The Dassanetch number about 15,000 souls and inhabit the area north of Lake Turkana (Rudolf) on both sides of the Omo River in Ethiopia. The annual inundations of the Omo River allows cultivation and this water, augmented by rains, enables the Dassanetch to practice pastoralism. The Dassanetch economy is based on a balance between transhumant pastoralism and flood retreat agriculture. The inundations of the river are irregular, varying from one year to another in extent and duration, so that land is not a stable cultivable resource and is not owned by collectivities of people. A complicated system of allocation of strips of land along the river banks was developed, in which no one can acquire permanent exclusive rights.[11] This allocation system permits a maximum number of people to cultivate land at any point in time, but it also bestows certain rights (albeit of a transient nature) upon individuals who are entitled to sub-allocate their strips to others.

Although Dassanetch society is formally based on the patrilineal principle, patrilinearity itself is not used to delineate corporate groups. The Dassanetch do not have lineages.[12] Kin groups are not localised and do not function cooperatively in political, economic, or ceremonial activities. There are no large corporate kin groups and close cooperation among kinsmen is limited to the household level where a father, his wife or wives, and his unmarried sons and daughters form a single unit of production and consumption. When a man marries, he usually leaves his natal household, withdraws the stock in which he has rights, and establishes an independent neolocal residence. Once the younger sons are all married, there is little cooperation between brothers and between them and their father, since they are not usually co-resident. Only the first-born son is obliged to remain with his father even after marriage and until the latter's death.

The mixed economy of the Dassanetch requires a great deal of mobility between pastures throughout the year and also imposes a burden of labour which must be divided and shifted between pastoral and agricultural tasks. Although a young man becomes the head of a household upon marrying, a newlywed man is not entirely independent since he and his wife alone are unable to bear the burden of pastoral and agricultural activities. For many years, therefore, a person remains dependent on the labour of others.

When a boy is born he is given a cow and a few head of female small stock by his father, as the nucleus of his future herd (women have no rights in stock). The adult male has the right to all the progeny of the beasts he received at birth, although until he marries his beasts remain part of the household herd. The life-cycle of a household can be viewed from the angle of availability and control of, and access to the three main desirable resources: land, labour, and stock. Generally speaking, the main preoccupation of an adult's life cycle is the manipulation of social ties in order to obtain cultivable land, labour, and cooperation with other households. These, in addition to the growing responsibilities of the head of a household to his dependants, result in the gradual disposal of stock and acquisition of a useful social network. In these networks, affinal ties and bond partnerships play a crucial role. A full exposition of the short- and long-run consequences of such ties is beyond the scope of this paper; here I shall only outline some aspects relevant to the following analysis.

Marriage is not an alliance between groups but an individual venture to establish affinal ties that will provide a man with co-operation in the future. Affinity must be carefully cultivated and nurtured if it is to be effective, and relationships between affines are established and maintained through a long and gradual process of bridewealth allocation over twenty to thirty years. In other words, bridewealth is not transferred *en bloc* to a group of bride-givers; it is passed on piecemeal in a lengthy series of individual transactions between the bride-receiver and those of the bride-givers (i.e., cognates of the bride and bond partners of her father; this will be elaborated below) who are entitled to receive it. Bridewealth generates no competition within the household as a man can only allocate beasts as bridewealth out of his own herd, i.e., from stock to which he can lay claim by right of ownership. Not only is a man prohibited from using stock belonging either to his sons or to his father's household for this purpose, he cannot prevent his son from utilising the stock belonging to him (the son) as bridewealth. Furthermore, one marriage into a family excludes the possibility of other marriages into the same family. Two brothers for example cannot marry related women. Although this rule considerably limits the range of brides available to a man, it disperses affinal ties instead of concentrating them within a group of bride-givers. This often means that there is little political cooperation or community of interest between a father's set of affinal ties and that of his sons. In addition, since the establishment of affinal ties opens a new field of social relationships for a bride's kin, fathers and sons may often find themselves in opposing factions in clashes over the marriage of nubile girls belonging to the household, because their interests may conflict when it comes to a decisions on how to invest the resource of a nubile girl in future affinal ties. Each party strives to invest the same asset in a different manner in order to accomplish a different aim: fathers tend to prefer marrying their daughters to elders, while their sons would rather their sisters married other young men.

Young men and girls are fairly free to choose their spouses, and although senior adults can try to direct or influence their daughters' choice their success is limited at best as youngsters often marry by elopement and present the girl's family with a *fait accompli*. On the other hand, an elder who wishes to marry a young girl as his second or third wife must secure the marriage by negotiation with her father. Consequently, an elder's chance of securing such an alliance improves if the girl's father is still alive. Ordinarily, the combined interests of the two elders in bolstering their networks of social ties suffice to conclude the negotiations successfully. However, if the girl's father is dead, her brothers will prefer a young brother-in-law who is directly engaged in economic activity and with whom it will be possible to develop reciprocal relationships. Such relationships bring, in the short run, the advantage of direct cooperation between the affinally related households, and − in the long run − future cooperation as the brothers-in-law become elders together, linked by ties of long standing.[13]

The gradual allocation of bridewealth by a young man is consistent with the building up of a network of useful relationships, and is especially important in the early stages of a household's life cycle. On the other hand, the affinal ties established by the second or third marriages of an elder serve to reinforce his existing social network. Due to the rule that forbids the establishment of affinal relations within an already existing affinity, second and third marriages extend a man's field of social relationships. The well-established and selectively developed network of an elder gains new strength by additional marriages simply because it enables him to broaden the scope in which he can function as mediator. This subject of social mediation brings us to another aspect which concerns the building up of a man's social and economic position, namely, bond partnerships.

The process of creating bonds starts at birth and continues up to elderhood. Bonds are established voluntarily by two individuals and once the ritual of bonding has been performed a bond cannot be dissolved. There are six kinds of bond partnerships, which differ in duration, in the ages of the partners, and in their content. I am unable to go any further into this subject and will have to restrict myself to three bonds, the most important ones which I call the 'strong' bonds.[14] These are connected with events in an individual's life cycle: 'name giving' is the bond established between an adult and a newly-born boy; 'smearing' is the bond which takes place at the physical maturation of a youth, between him and an adult man; and 'holding' which takes place upon a man's circumcision between him and an adult who 'holds' him. Each of these bonds has a senior and a junior partner, and they entail reciprocal (but not symmetrical) rights and obligations. What distinguishes these three bonds from the rest is that these three endow the right to claim bridewealth. When a bond is established, each partner acquires rights to bridewealth from the other's son-in-law. It should be noted that a person can be a junior partner in only one strong bond of each type, but may act as senior partner in any number of bonds; custom and etiquette dictate that the initiative for partnership should come from the junior partner or his father. Finally, a sizable quantity of stock (both cattle and small stock) is disposed of in establishing bonds, either transferred as gifts or slaughtered for hospitality.

The Dassanetch slaughter stock lavishly — for food, for ritual purposes, and for hospitality. Once a first marriage has taken place, a lengthy process of slaughtering commences, reaching its peak in the *dimi* ceremony, an annual communal event in which every man who has fathered a girl 8–10 years earlier participates. This is a ritual obligation in which every father must bring his first daughter to be blessed. Though the celebrant of *dimi* gains a great deal of prestige, the ceremony requires him to slaughter almost his entire herd, often leaving him with not much more than a bull and a few cows. It is therefore virtually impossible for him to recoup his economic losses as the ceremony also plunges him deep into debt owing to the obligation to entertain multitudes of guests (and slaughter more and more beasts) and return the *dimi* debts. Most men 'go to *dimi*' in their forties or fifties, after which they usually retire into prestigious (but materially destitute) elderhood; but since their first-born son remains with them until their death, their subsistence is secured. The *dimi* ceremony is not a condition for elderhood; elderhood is socially defined, and anyone can become an elder when he can afford to retire from an active economic life and settle down in a permanent settlement. Most men take this step in their forties.

Unlike a young man, whose lengthy process of bridewealth allocation was described above, when an elder marries he is required to transfer at least twelve head of cattle before marriage so as to ensure the legitimisation of any children born of the union. Dassanetch explain this by saying that since when a man dies bridewealth payments are 'written off', and sons cannot pay their fathers' debts, it is justified to expect an elder to secure such legitimisation beforehand.[15]

To sum up and compare the marriages of young men and elders, the picture apparently presents a paradox: a young man, upon marrying for the first time, possesses a large herd, is under few obligations to dispose of his stock, and is not required to transfer bridewealth immediately and *en bloc* to his bride-givers. But an elder, who has usually already 'gone to *dimi*' and consequently is left with a greatly depleted herd, and in addition faces mounting pressures to provide hospitality, is required to transfer a large number of beasts *en bloc* and immediately. Furthermore, an elder can secure marriage only by negotiating with the bride's father, whereas the most common form of marriage is elopement, practiced only by young men; besides, many nubile girls have no living fathers − yet another apparent advantage for young men. In other words, polygyny is not a privilege of elderhood. Elders usually have two or three wives and compete among themselves and with young men for access to women. However, the tendency is to establish a polygynous household upon entering elderhood, and if we take the age of 40 for men as a rough average of the age at which they enter elderhood we may obsever in the following table (taken from my census of 174 households) a clear relationship between elderhood and polygyny.[16]

Monogamy and Polygyny, by Age Group

Age	Monogamous	Polygynous	Total
Under 40	68	14	82
Over 40	35	57	92
Total	103	71	174

X^2 = 36.16   p = 0.001

The age-system of the Dassanetch is divided into six named generation sets ranked by order of seniority, that come to power in sequential order (A_1, A_2, A_3, B_1, B_2, B_3). The six generation-sets are divided into three pairs, each of which forms a single continuity linking a man and his descendants. Generally speaking, a generation-set is a special type of age-set. It has a longer period of recruitment and sometimes long intervals between inaugurations. Its main characteristic is that it determines the affiliation of individuals to a certain set because they are offspring of a member of another set.[17]

Among the Dassanetch, a man's generation-set is determined at birth and he always joins the alternate generation-set to the one his father belongs to. Thus, for example, the sons of a member of A_1 will all be members of B_1, and B_1's sons — members of A_1. Similarly, the sons of A_2 will be members of B_2 whose sons, in turn, will belong to A_2, and so on (see Diagram).

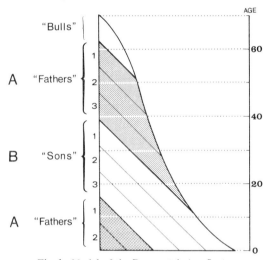

Fig. 1. Model of the Dassanetch Age-System.

It must be stressed that recruitment to generation-sets is simultaneous (as illustrated in the diagram) and independent of other generation-sets. There are, of course, differences in the ages of members of the various sets which inevitably affect their opening and closing. Since the opening of a generation-set depends only on when the members of the alternate set start fathering children, the more senior the generation-set the earlier its alternate set is opened. Hence the perpetuation of the age differences between the oldest persons in successive generation-sets. Members of one generation-set need not wait for the inauguration of their set until the set senior to them ceases to recruit members. For example, during the period of my fieldwork, the eldest members of A_1 were about 65 years old, and approximately 10 years older than the eldest of A_2. Similarly, the eldest members of A_2 were about 8–10 years older than the oldest members of A_3. Both A_1 and A_2 had young members in their twenties, so that evidently both recruited members simultaneously.

Termination of recruitment to a generation-set is determined by the number of circumcision ceremonies performed by that set. Each generation-set holds its own series of ceremonies independently of other sets. Men are circumcised late in life, usually in their late twenties or early thirties. Consequently, the first circumcision ceremony of a given set may take place as long as thirty years after the set was opened. The interval between ceremonies ranges from 4 to 6 years, each generation-set holds four circumcision ceremonies, and recruitment stops after the fourth.[18]   Thus, a set that started its recruitment earlier will also cease to recruit earlier than sets that started later. The younger members of each set are therefore older than the youngest members of the generation-set immediately junior to them. All in all, in spite of the general feature of age differences between the eldest and youngest members of successive generation-sets, there are two points that characterise the age-system. First, the age differences between members of any generation-set may be 40 years or more, so that each generation-set is not, strictly speaking, a set of coevals. Secondly, there is a considerable overlap of age across generation-sets, in that men of similar age are affiliated to different generation-sets or, to put it slightly differently, several sets that are ranked in order of seniority may in fact contain men of similar age.

The senior surviving generation-set is the one in authority, and its members are called 'bulls'. But since the process of recruitment to any generation-set is drawn out over many years, changes of power are not frequent. The present generation-set of 'bulls', for example, has occupied that position of seniority for at least the past 40 years. In other words, the process of advancement in the age system is very slow and at any given time may give the impression (and in fact really is one) of stagnation, as senior elders of successive generation-sets may not survive to become 'bulls'. Furthermore, taking into consideration the fact that apart from the 'bulls' the age system offers very few institutionalised positions of authority, a clear and vigorous tendency has developed among members of all generation-sets to seek power mainly through the establishment of individual networks of social ties that cut across the demarcated lines of generation-sets.

III

A polygynous household is not a sufficient condition for power, since affinal relationships are not alliances between groups but a selective web of individual social networks gradually spun over a long time. However, the establishment of a polygynous household is a necessary condition for power, which brings us to the following question: What are the mechanisms in affinal ties that lead to the accumulation of power? and why should the establishment of a second and third set of affinal ties lead to the attainment of further power?

Cooperation, trust, affection, and reciprocity are expressed in various forms of exchange, and individuals only maintain enduring relationships with selected affines. Thus, it is not mere affinity as such that leads to power, but rather specific and carefully cultivated relationships whose distinction is in their potential for use or manipulation in time of need. Furthermore, the actual position of influence and credit that a man may gain by mediating affinal ties between his kin and bond partners on the one hand and those of his in-laws on the other, depends largely on the nature of the cooperation, reciprocal relations, and credibility resulting from such ties. Indeed, there are enormous varieties of power and influence even among heads of monogamous households. Obviously, then, the establishment of a first set of affinal ties by young men can potentially be elaborated, but only with time, whilst this is not so in the case of an elder's second or third marriage: in the latter case, new affinal ties are added to an already established, articulated, and selected network, and need only a short passage of time before becoming effective. The successful head of a polygynous household thus occupies a position from which the activation and manipulation of relationships can provide access to various resources for others.

A young man starting an independent household cannot rely only on his own affinal relationships that still require careful cultivation; he needs additional support in order to sustain his mobile household. Such a young man may be assisted by an elder, a person with multiple networks of affinal ties, with whom the young man establishes a bond partnership, a bond that is individually and voluntarily established. A young man can, of course, enter into a bond partnership with a monogamous elder who has useful affinal ties; indeed, some young men do exactly that. However, the prospects opened by a bond partnership with a polygynous elder, both in terms of the number of relationships maintained and in terms of the credit a attributed to him, make polygynous elders more attractive bond partners for a young man.

Strong bond partnerships, those that include rights to bridewealth, cannot be entered into by the mere whim of two persons seeking to

strengthen their relationship; they can only be cemented on socially
defined occasions such as the birth of a child (the bond of name-
giving), the physical maturation of a youth (the bond of 'smearing'),
and circumcision ('holding'). A man is thus limited in the strong
bonds he can establish by the relative rarity of such events, and must
therefore calculate and invest them carefully and wisely. Events such
as the birth of children and circumcision appear to occur mainly
during the crucial decade in a man's lifetime, i.e., the decade
following his first marriage. It is in this decade that a newlywed man
is constrained in his endeavours to increase his affinal ties because
he is unable to infuse his limited range of relationships with sufficient
stability and cooperation to gain the credit to secure a hold in a new
set of affinal ties. Thus, young married men must rely on other means,
and these are bond partnerships. Note, though, that regardless of
whether an elder gives his name to a baby or 'holds' a man in
circumcision, the young man is the junior partner and the elder is the
senior one. A bond, once cemented, provides the junior partner with
rights to bridewealth from the marriages of the elder's daughters, and
he (or his father) can claim cooperation and assistance from many
people as part of the rights acquired. The immediate economic
benefit that a young man derives from such a partnership is obvious.
But the elder, senior partner, is not in need of immediate and close
economic aid, nor is he likely to live long enough to enjoy bridewealth
rights upon the marriage of his young partner's daughters. What he
does gain is a debt relationship with his young partner (or his father),
who owes him mediation or access to new fields of social relationships
through rights to bridewealth. Every bond that an elder cements
creates new ties which may be activated in the future, and thus
entails the accumulation of brokerage power and credit. The elder
usually takes advantage by requesting that his junior partner (or the
latter's father) cooperate with certain individuals in the elder's network. Such a request is often spelled out during the negotiations
prior to the establishment of the bond, and the young partner is
usually well aware of the cooperation involved and its possible consequences.

It is theoretically possible to accumulate bonds without enlarging
one's range of affinal ties, but this is unlikely to occur in practice as
there is usually a sequence where enlarging one's ties of affinity
generates further bonds.

The fact that power accumulation involves the discriminating use
of two types of scarce resources — nubile girls and the relatively rare
occasions in which bond partnerships can be cemented — is the crux

of the matter. Nubile girls are potentially available to all. The seemingly paradoxical fact that any Dassanetch can enter into competition for women without any initial restriction (apart, of course, from incest prohibitions) is misleading, since it is only participation in the quest for power that is open to all.[19] Even if all men succeed in marrying, not all can achieve a position of influence or high credit. Thus, it is less a question of obtaining the scarce resource as such, and more one of the subsequent use to which that resource is put. The point is that the open participation is essential in order that young men should play the game and abide by rules that give elders an automatic advantage. Elders compete with young men for a finite number of nubile girls. One result of this competition is that it is economic need that imposes on young married men the burden of vigorous economic activity and puts them into debt. Elders, on the other hand, can take full advantage of the ties they have accumulated in the past in order to influence and marry nubile girls, resulting in even greater influence and power by bridging existing affinal ties and bond partnerships with new ones.

The dependence of married young men on elders brings us to bond partnerships.[20] Theoretically, the reasons for cementing bond partnerships can be legion. Sentiments, for example, between any two persons, are not uncommon. But temporary or partial interests tend to be difuse, numerous, and may disappear with time or alter their character. However, events that occur only once in a lifetime (e.g., circumcision) are by definition structurally scarce because they relate to a limited number of singular events in the social structure, and these are the only occasions open to establish strong bonds.

All in all, the number of nubile girls available each year for marriage and the number of boys born or men undergoing circumcision is finite – and more-or-less stable over the years. Thus, we are dealing with finite sources of power, and a central point in the present analysis is not only the access to these resources but also the sequence of their use, as Blau pointed out: 'differentiation of power arises in the course of competition for scarce goods . . . At first, all members of the collectivity compete against all others, but as status differences emerge in consequence of differential success in the initial competition, the object of the competition changes, and exchange relations become differentiated from competitive ones.'[21] Indeed, these two consecutive stages correspond to the different use of scarce resources, i.e., nubile girls and bond partnerships.

Entry into the system is not easy owing to the fierce competition, but once a person enters, the cost to him for the first entry into the system is fixed, and in fact low. Though the first aim of a young man is to engage in economic activities of his household, he is unavoidably caught up in a political game in which he is forced into dependence upon elders. Elders use the power they already have in order to tie down young married men and perpetuate their dependence. In allying themselves with elders, young men may solve some of their immediate and pressing economic problems, but now the price comes high: once a bond is cemented it can never be dissolved and re-used. Thus, young men are prevented from re-allying themselves with others. In other words, the power an elder invests in bond partnerships aims at the accumulation of additional power, but such patronage cannot manifest itself unless sought out and invited by young men who marry. The prohibition on dissolving bonds and the resulting perpetuation of the junior partner's dependence on his senior partner has two more aspects: first, what Blau states comes 'to assure the continued dependence of others on the services one has to supply by barring access to alternative suppliers of these services.'[22] Such alternative suppliers of social mediation and services are other elders. Furthermore, the inability of junior partners to re-use the bond for re-alignment means that whenever the investment fails for any reason (uncooperative senior bond partners, for example), the resource is lost as far as the original holder is concerned.

At this point the question that comes to the fore is why should young men object to their sister marrying an elder whose network they can use so as to gain access to cooperation, labour, and land which they need?

The answer lies in the fact that a young man has virtually no chance of entering an enduring relationship with an elder who is not a bond partner or an affine. This means that young men can only obtain support and cooperation by openly acknowledging their subordinate position in a ritual or affinal tie. Obviously, and as pointed out above, young men prefer a young brother-in-law so as to enter into relations on an equal footing and with a long-term investment in mind, rather than enjoy the advantage they may gain from an elder consenting to mediate a resource they may need. Furthermore, young men prefer to obtain such mediation and access to resources through bonds with elders rather than through elders who are affines, primarily because of the stress laid on the senior and junior positions in such affinal relationships (i.e., an elder marrying a young girl as a second or third wife). True, having an elder as a brother-in-law may lead to entrance into new fields of relationships, but the price borne by the young man may sometimes border on extortion. In affinal relations, reciprocity and cooperation are only vaguely defined; they tend to be diffuse and general, and the specific content of such relationships evolves out of a feeling of trust, the careful activation of other persons, practice of social tact, close cooperation, and an over-all reluctance to employ one's real power. Affinal relations between an elder bridegroom and his young affines are inherently somewhat tense because they are based almost exclusively on the parties' awareness of the fact that these relations are essentially a short-term undertaking. The young man has nothing to invest in a long-term relationships whereas the elder tends to seek an immediate return.

On the other hand, a bond partnership between an elder and a young man is more concretely defined — it grants each partner specific rights and prescribes the legitimate purposes to which each partner may manipulate the other. In addition, bond partnerships are usually based on the assumption that the tie will endure for a reasonable length of time.

The second point arising out of the dependence of junior upon senior partners is obtaining security against possible deterioration in an elder's credit. A major part of any influential or notable elder's social credit is his reputedly large number of useful social connections, a reputation that can either be augmented or diminished. The image of a person's social network combines both the possession of numerous and varied ties and the mutual trust deriving from cordial cooperative relations. This very combination means that any particular action is judged from both effective and moral standpoints. Thus, any bond that could be dissolved would be vulnerable on two counts: it would damage the reputation of an elder as a person of influence which, in turn, could diminish his actual influence since it depends partly on public credibility. In the competition for resources, one's credit is always relative to the credit possessed by others, so that the permanency of cemented bonds grants elders a certain amount of security against any deterioration in their credit.

IV

The common tendency among societies, whose organisation is based on the principle of age to view their social structure as a broadly-based dichotomy between elders and juniors, probably derives from the fact that this principle relies on the notion of the life cycle. The Dassanetch, too, have a variety of terms to express this dichotomy, e.g., 'fathers' and 'sons', 'neck' and 'back', the 'bush' and the 'house', etc.: elders who are seniors, settled, in a position of responsibility, and generally at the top of the ladder, as against youngsters who are unsettled, 'wild', and at the bottom of the ladder.[23] But such a general dichotomy cannot, in itself, distinguish between the different nuances of power differentiation; it treats elderhood and youth as homogenous categories, as Mair does in referring to the Karimojong: 'The defence of herds and grazing grounds — and raiding those of neighbors — [was given] to *all* the young men of the tribe', while 'the settlement of disputes and ritual approach to divinity for blessing on people and cattle' was the responsibility of '*all* the elders'.[24] We begin treading on thin ice only when we assume that such categories, or any other category based on age, must have a specific function. Such an analysis is likely to be partial and artificial because an age-system does not stand apart from other social institutions, and age relationships between age groups are not just another category of social relationships that can be placed alongside political, economic, and social relationships. To say that relationships are based on age categories says little about their content. Indeed, if we choose not to view the age system as a separate entity and try to analyse its division into sets and grades in connection with the issue that Spencer raised, namely, the 'problem of social control relating to the distribution of scarce resources',[25] we may reach different conclusions, may point to the individual differences, the absence of clear-cut and demarcated dividing lines between age categories, and the discrete aspects of elderhood, rather than treating it as an undifferentiated whole. This, I suggest, is particularly applicable to societies with a generation-set system and a long and/or simultaneous process of recruitment such as those found in East Africa (the Gada, Karimojong, and Jie, for example).

I indicated at the beginning of this paper that there are two kinds of elders in the Dassanetch gerontocracy — the senior generation set in power, which derives its authority from the fact that it occupies the top of the ladder, and the group that was the subject of this paper, selected elders who reached positions of power through individual achievement. I have referred to these two types of ascriptive and achieved gerontocracies, and perhaps the term 'power' does not apply equally to both. I have suggested throughout this paper that 'social credit' seems to be a more appropriate term since it includes the various aspects of such achievement, i.e., its own inherent worth and credibility as well as the attributes of age. Power and credit also correspond to the contrast pointed but by Gulliver, following Parsons, between 'power' or 'authority' on the one hand and 'influence on the other.[26]

The Dassanetch mode of seeking influence or credit across generation-sets in the form of alliances between individuals, and the pattern of dependence of young men on elders perpetuates itself. In other words, it is always elders who replace other elders, and they do this because they have achieved influence or credit and not because of an orderly sequence of power transfer as in the case of one generation-set replacing another as 'bulls'. The Dassanetch do not employ special terms to designate elders who have achieved power. The terms with which they refer to such elders, such as *ma fargogo* ('a powerful man') or *ma gudu* ('a big man') do not necessarily imply elderhood as they can apply equally to young men. The only term which combines authority with age is 'bull', and this in itself reinforces the premise – though an illusory one – on which the age-system is based, namely, that everyone will achieve the position of authority if only he waits for his generation-set to ascend to the rank of 'bulls'. The formal aspect of the ladder in the Dassanetch age-system to which I referred earlier is reflected in this very assumption that the system operates on the succession of generation-sets rather than on the age, qualities, and assets of its individuals.

This begs the question of how the young men accept the perpetuation of achieved gerontocracy which is not 'naturally' transmitted to them and is not anchored in supernatural sanctions such as the ability to curse or bless.

Young men generally have ambivalent attitudes towards elders. Clear antagonism and resentment is mixed with admiration for the elder of high credit and influence. This ambivalence may throw some light on the acceptance by young men of the prominence of elders. Resentment and hostile attitudes stem from the notion of equal competition for women as against the actual advantage enjoyed by elders. An elder who has achieved great influence and dominance is admired as an example to emulate. Accordingly, an elder who has no credit or influence is regarded as a failure and is the subject of pity.[27] In the final analysis, however, the structure of achieved gerontocracy is accepted by young men because influence and predominance are not hereditary. The inability to attach ascribed features to achieved credit gives the young participants the impression of an on-going, open competition without prior restrictions and voluntary choice in which no one enjoys an initial advantage. Finally, the purpose of this paper was not to add another model of age organisation but merely to suggest a new critical appraisal of some feature of existing models, along lines described by using the Dassanetch as an example.

Footnotes

1. The fieldwork on which this essay is based was carried out in south-west Ethiopia during 1968/70. I wish to thank the Hebrew University of Jerusalem and Friends of the Hebrew University in England for their generous financial support. I am also grateful to the Victoria University of Manchester for the award of a Simon Research Fellowship during 1974/75 which enabled me to work on the subject of age-systems in Manchester. I would also like to thank J.S. La Fontaine for her useful comments and R. Levine and K. Keating whose mimeographed essay 'Rethinking Gerontocracy' and valuable comments helped me to sharpen the focus on some of the points raised here.
2. Cf. Frazer (1919: 200–201); Rivers (1914, Vol. II: 47–48, 58–59, 69).
3. Spencer (1975) (1965).
4. Weber (1943: 346).
5. Spencer (1975: 165).
6. Hart and Pilling (1960).
7. The dissatisfaction with the generality of the term 'gerontocracy', which literally means 'rule of old people' is shared by many anthropologists, and Gardner's attempt to introduce this term is one example. Cf. Gardner (1968: 209), Woodburn (1968: 209), Rose (1968: 204, n. 6), and Levine and Keating 'Rethinking Gerontocracy'. The latter is, to the best of my knowledge, the first comprehensive attempt to critically reevaluate the misconceptions surrounding the concept of gerontocracy.
8. In a sense the introduction of the terms 'ascriptive' and 'achieved' in relation to gerontocracy comes to fill a gap in the use of the concept of gerontocracy which is applied to both. See Levine and Keating, 'Rethinking Gerontocracy', (mimeograph), p. 3.
9. Rose (1968: 207).
10. I have elaborated on this subject in Almagor (1978, Chs. IX and X).
11. For further details see *ibid.*, Chs. II, IV and VI.
12. The Dassanetch kinship system is in fact bilateral; it has a very shallow genealogical memory, and a man's cooperation with some of his cognates differs from one period in life to another and similar variation in cooperation is found among individuals.
13. The rate of divorce among the Dassanetch is very high, and divorcees usually marry elders. The issue is not immediately relevant here, and will be elaborated elsewhere. But for my present analysis I should only note that in most cases affinal ties persist even after a marriage has broken up.
14. For further details on bond partnerships see Almagor (1978, Ch. V), and Almagor, 'The Ethos of Equality among Dassanetch Age Peers' (forthcoming).
15. A somewhat comparable situation exists among the agriculturalist Taita, where an elder pays higher bridewealth; cf. Harris (1962: 70).
16. The 'gerontocratic index' suggested by Spencer (1965: 300), which is based on 'the extent to which polygyny is a privilege of old age', cannot be applied to the Dassanetch since it is not a privilege but a competition.

17. There are various uses of the term generation-set, generation group, or generation class, corresponding to the variety of systems; but their common denominator is that a man's offspring join the age-system according to a certain criterion that determines the interval between the sets of a father and his sons. These are sometimes adjacent groups as among the Karimojong, Kuria, and Jie (where two or three such sets usually co-exist); sometimes they are alternates, as among the Dassanetch; and sometimes there may be an interval of five sets between a father and his sons as in the Gada system. The use of the term 'generation' in the context of age-systems derives, it would seem, from a combination of the notion of genealogical generations (i.e., fathers, sons, grandsons, etc.) and the chronological sense of a generation (i.e., 'he is of my generation') which emphasizes the aspect of age.

18. All uncircumcised children and those born into a generation-set after the fourth circumcision ceremony are relegated to the alternate set to the one into which they were born. Thus, a situation can arise in which brothers belong to different generation-sets and a father and his sons can belong to the same one.

19. The Dassanetch age-system is divided into two alternations of 'fathers' and 'sons' as illustrated in the diagram; marriages are contained within alternations. This rule of marriage has little effect on the general argument pursued in this essay about the competition for women.

20. Other forms of dependency of young men on elders are described in Almagor, 'Raiders and Elders: A Confrontation of Generations Among the Dassanetch' (forthcoming).

21. Blau (1964: 141).

22. *Ibid.*, p. 121.

23. Cf. Hamer (1970: 69); Spencer (1965: Ch. 6), and Dyson-Hudson (1966: 179).

24. Mair (1974: 31); italics in the original.

25. Spencer (1975: 165).

26. Gulliver (1971: 249).

27. A comparable situation exists among the Ndembu, where 'old men who are not buttressed by authority or professional or supernatural skill, are thought of as weak and foolish'. Cf. Turner (1956: 125).

References

Almagor, U. (1978). Pastoral Partners — Affinity and Bond Partnership among the Dassanetch of Southwest Ethiopia. Manchester University Press, Manchester.

Almagor, U. (1978). The Ethos of Equality among Dassanetch Age Peers, *in* "Age, Generation and Time — Some Features of East African Age Organizations" (eds. P.T.W. Baxter and Uri Almagor), Ch. III. Hurst & Co., London (forthcoming).

Almagor, U. (1978). Raiders and Elders: A Confrontation of Generations among the Dassanetch, *in* "Warfare among East African Herders" (eds. K. Fukui and

D. Turton) (forthcoming).

Blau, P.M. (1964). Exchange and Power in Social Life. John Wiley and Sons, Inc., New York.

Dyson-Hudson, N. (1966). Karimojong Politics. Clarendon Press, Oxford.

Frazer, J.G. (1919). Folklore in the Old Testament, Vol. II. Macmillan & Co., London.

Gardner, P.M. (1968). Discussion *in* "Man the Hunter" (eds. R.B. Lee and I. DeVore). Aldine Publishing Company, Chicago.

Gulliver, P.H. (1971). Neighbours and Networks. University of California Press, Berkeley.

Hamer, J.H. (1970). Sidamo Generational Class Cycles: A Political Gerontocracy, *Africa*, **40**, 50–70.

Harris, G. (1962). Taita Bridewealth and Affinal Relationships, *in* "Marriage in Tribal Societies" (ed. M. Fortes), 55–87. Cambridge University Press, Cambridge.

Hart, C.W.M. and Pilling, A.R. (1960). The Tiwi of North Australia. Henry Holt and Company, New York.

Lee, R.B. and DeVore, I. (eds.). (1968). Man the Hunter. Aldine Publishing Company, Chicago.

Levine, R. and Keating, K. (n.d.). Rethinking Gerontocracy. Mimeograph. Department of Anthropology, Northwestern University.

Mair, L. (1974). African Societies. Cambridge University Press, Cambridge.

Rivers, W.H.R. (1914). The History of Melanesian Society. Cambridge University Press, Cambridge.

Rose, F.G.G. (1968). Australian Marriage, Land-Owning Groups and Initiation, *in op. cit.* (eds. Lee and DeVore), 200–208.

Spencer, P. (1965). The Samburu. Routledge and Kegan Paul, London.

Spencer, P. (1975). Opposing Streams and the Gerontocratic Ladder: Two Models of Age Organization in East Africa, *Man* (n.s.), **11**, 153–175.

Turner, V.W. (1955). The Spatial Separation of Generations in Ndembu Village Structure, *Africa*, **25**, 121–137.

Weber, M. (1947). The Theory of Social and Economic Organization. Oxford University Press, Oxford.

Woodburn, J. (1968). Discussion *in* "Man the Hunter" (eds. Lee and De Vore).

OBSERVATIONS ABOUT GENERATIONS*

P.T.W. BAXTER AND U. ALMAGOR

Grading by relative age, even between siblings, the grouping of
approximate coevals and distinguishing between generations are
probably basic modes of social categorisation, like distinctions by
sex. Distinctions of age and generation are integral to the etiquette of
daily intercourse, to kinship terminology, as Radcliffe-Brown instructed us and as Needham has recently reminded us, and to myth
and story. Every culture distinguishes successive stages of the life-
cycle from mewling and puking infancy to second childishness. Verbal
deference to grey hairs and protests about riotous youth have
probably been common to all cultures. Elders everywhere must have
echoed the Shepherd in *The Winters Tale*:
　'I would there were no age between ten and three-and-twenty, or
　that youth would sleep out the rest; for there is nothing in the
　between but getting wenches with child, wronging the ancientry,
　stealing, fighting.'
Likewise many youngsters must have complained about their fuddy-
duddy elders; even younger anthropologists have been known to
mutter against their elders.
　Age-grading, whether formally marked by a rite of passage or
merely tacitly recognised, is probably universal, and gives the process
of ageing a social impression. But age-setting or generation-setting,
that is the grouping of persons who are either close in age or of the
same generation into a structure of hierarchically ordered sets, which
are vested with a diffuse range of social and ritual responsibilities, is
an unwieldy, almost bizarre, mode of social organisation. Age-grading
is likely to be incorporated into, or to run in alignment with, age-
setting where setting occurs, and to be used as a means of regulating
relationships between old and young. As descent groups, where they

*This article forms part of the introduction to P.T.W. Baxter and Uri Almagor (editors),
Age, Generation and Time: Some Features of East Africa Age Organisations (London:
C. Hurst, forthcoming), and is published in this volume by permission.

occur, need to be compatible, or at least not grossly incompatible, with the kinship system and are likely to use the terminology of kinship, age-sets are likely to be compatible with age-grades and use age-grade terminology. It is crucial that, whereas age-grading does not require setting, setting requires age-grading.

Much of the work on age-systems has concentrated on elucidating the rules which regulate the recruitment to sets and the movement of sets within the system, with particular attention to the way in which political offices and authority are vested in sets in acephalous societies. This has frequently led to an emphasis in analyses: (i) on age-systems as political organisations, (ii) on historical explanations for the current organisational forms sets take (iii) on age-systems as systems of rules. By contrast, in descriptions of age-organisations in societies with centralised political systems, such as Swazi or Zulu, the special terminology which has grown up in the discussion of age-sets has been less used and age-groupings have been set firmly in a military context. Hilda Kuper, for example, writes of 'regimental age-classes' (1963: 62). Oddly where groups of coevals appears to have had what were apparently quite clear military, policing or work tasks they seem to have been less remarked about and less discussed than when their tasks have remained vague, diffuse and concerned with ritual; as if to kill people made more immediate and obvious sense than to meet in order to pray and offer sacrifices. This bias in observers in part springs from colonial obsessions with primitive unruliness and the supposed propensity to raiding and warfare of many African peoples, especially pastoral ones, which propensity was then used to justify their colonisation and, at times, their isolation in reservations.

Sets mostly occur in, or at any rate are most conspicuous in, non-centralised political systems and therefore have political tasks attributed to them by anthropologists. When these tasks are discovered to be unperformed, or casually performed, then the set systems are invariably described as less effective organisations than they were in some past time. Analysts have been tempted to suggest that, in the past, sets were more organised and more active politically, ritually and militarily than they were when the analysts were in the field. Following from this ascription of diffuse political, ritual and military authority to sets and their officers in the past, observers have then used that reconstruction to explain the current set activities which they have observed. Age-sets are thereby constantly represented as having fallen away from an earlier, more active and effective, mode of organisation.[1] Age-set obligations, like those of kinship (and sometimes with about as much truth), are reported as having been eroded by change; and their marital values, which stressed both individual valour and fortitude and intense group bonding, withered by schooling and wages.

Sets are often considered to be mechanisms for the socialisation of young men and socially therapeutic channels for their aggressive activities. The existence of sets makes them obvious choices for such purposes, but it does not mean that such activities are then necessary functions of sets. A regular gathering of approximate coevals does not make an age-set system, whether the get-together is to raid for cattle or to smash up rivals in football stadia. Keiser's study *The Vice-Lords* brings this out clearly and, we suggest, shows most succinctly that many of the traits and socialisation functions frequently attributed to age-sets are performed among poor urban blacks in Chicago by gangs. Keiser's 'warriors of the streets' form named groups, each with a territory, such as the particular gang the Vice-Lords, which are sub-divided by age and activities into Seniors, Juniors, Midgets and down to juvenile Pee-Wees. Expression of loyalty in the face of violence and danger to their sub-group and the maintenance of aggressive encounters with like neighbouring gangs are, according to the rhetoric of members, the primary purposes of gangs. Members flaunt common insignia, such as rings and capes. A gang attempts 'to monopolise girls', has officers with flamboyant honorific titles, maintains strict etiquette between members and even pours libations of wine and, above all, explicitly inculcates warrior values and values of mutual help into members. Also, like Maasai or Samburu moran,[2] gang members aim to pass out of warriorhood, as one informant put it: 'we are not going to be young savages all our life' (1969: 71). But when Vice-Lords move back into mainstream society, or a branch of it, they do so as individuals, not as a set where members jointly undergo a change of status. They are, in that respect at any rate, more like Boy Scouts than moran. The cultural comparisons with Samburu, Maasai, Karimojong or Boran junior age-sets are remarkable, but Vice-Lords, and other gangs, are not a unit in a sequence of similar units and are not an age-set in an age-system. The Vice-Lord traits which are similar to those of moran are of a very general kind, and related to the wide-spread processes of age-grading rather than to age-setting. Gangs are voluntary associations which at best are condoned, but sets are part of the formal social order blessed by tradition and membership and is usually ascribed and obligatory.[3]

The unravelling and systematising of the rule complexities which each age-system has evolved has its own fascination, as the recent works of Stewart (1972 and 1977) and Legesse (1973), for example, brilliantly show. Clearly if the rules which regulate an age-system have constraining force or influence they must be made explicit in any analysis of it. The rules of age-sets and generation-sets, because they attempt to regulate for the idiosyncracies of human behaviour, have to allow for variation and therefore to be complex. But, too narrow a concern with the study of rules has the danger that the intellectual effect involved can come to provide its own justification. Too intense concentration on the rules runs two other risks. On the one hand their very complexity and the possibility for almost infinite variation can result in the analyst playing a sort of mental game equivalent to the old kinship algebra. On the other, he can come to argue that any particular system should have worked in a particular way, because that is what the rules say, so if it does not work in that way it must be because some extraneous event, such as colonial rule, or drought, or labour migration, has interrupted the proper working of the system. What results is an intellectualist view of age-systems. What a rules approach tends to ignore is the actual behaviour of set-members to each other and to members of other sets, and the ways in which the members of an age-system are enmeshed in other social, economic and ritual relationships. To underweight these last is hazardous. On the one hand, if the rules themselves become the centre of the analysis, as if they were an isolated compelling force on the actors, the analyst can be led to doubt the statements of informants as recorded by ethnographers of proven reliability. Even as sensitive a commentator as Stewart,[4] for example, suggests that Gulliver's informants 'must certainly have misinformed him' (1972: 57) or that 'there is the question of whether to believe Jensen's informants' (1972: 80). To do this runs counter to one of the primary rules of analysis which is that, if the data provided by informants seems to contradict one's own assumptions, it is the time to question those assumptions. On the other hand, the explanatory power of the rules, as told by informants, is overweighted if the analyst ignores the distinction (so clearly pointed out by Levi-Strauss, 1953) between conscious models and those unconscious models which, though shrouded, may subtly and firmly constrain behaviour and, indeed, may inhere in those rules.

Age-systems attempt to create cognitive and structural order within and for a population by creating categories based on age and generation. They assume demographic regularity and long-run social stability within that population. An age-system implies continuity and replacement of personnel in an orderly and predictable manner through the replacement by birth of new members to replace those who die. Similarly, generation implies begetting, replacement and continuity. When a man's placement within a system is determined by that of his father's, an underlying assumption is that fathers will beget sons within a limited time span, and that therefore there will be approximate accord between age and generation. In social reality this assumption is false, so that a continuing dilemma in all such systems is the reconciliation of age, generation, and the steady flow of time. The biological facts of birth and death must slide out of alignment with the social order with which they should conform. Age-systems which are based on measured units of time are un-successful attempts to tame time by chopping it up intô manageable slices. So it should be useful, when examining a particular system, to attempt to examine this gap between the cognitive order and the social reality. One is bound to be at least a little out of kilter with the other and to result in 'a degree of built-in malfunctioning' (Dyson-Hudson 1966: 202).

Divisions by age and by generation then must have an arbitrary quality; as in an examination grading system, the persons on the neighbouring edges of two classes are likely to be more similar to each other than they are to members of their own class at its other extreme. Physical, mental, sexual and social ages do not necessarily correspond, as any teacher of a class recruited strictly by age can testify.

In societies in which 'age' is determined by social and/or biological maturation late or early developers are not anomalous and do not create difficulties. But where 'age' is determined by the calendar or some other arbitrary device, such as the periodic flowering of the *setiot* tree, age and maturity are bound sometimes not to coincide. We commonly speak of persons being 'old' or 'young' for their age and being typical, or untypical, of their generation.

Similar difficulties over defining boundaries which coincide with life-stages occur with generation. Many people have aunts and uncles, that is members of the generation genealogically senior to them, who are their coevals. In societies in which polygyny is favoured and old men may continue to father children on young wives, the likelihood of such anomalous relationships increases with each succeeding generation. If men can father children for a span of fifty years the differences in ages between their grandsons can be greater than the possible life-span of one of those grandsons. There is then a simple difference between a genealogical generation and what might be called a shifting social generation, that is persons who cluster in age and share similar social attributes, such as the likelihood of becoming grandfathers, fathers, etc. at about the same time. Generation in this social sense, in which similar social behaviour is expected of people who are similar in age measured in years, is the basis of all age-grading systems. When genealogical generation and social generation are out of alignment anomalies occur. Not surprisingly, therefore, we find that most age-systems and generation systems and especially systems which mix both principles, have secondary rules which regulate the legitimate procreation of their members, in an endeavour to control the birth of anomalous persons. These are usually rules which regulate marriage, but they may, as among the Oromo (see Baxter and Almagor, in press) also concern fostering or infanticide. Such rules follow from the logic of the particular systems and, though expressed in the vocabulary of kinship with appropriate moral overtones, they have nothing to do with incest prohibitions which are based on degrees of kinship or affinity.

In any discussion of age and generation systems it is essential to be clear whether what is being discussed is a distinct genealogical generation or a shifting social generation. A genealogical generation is one which consists of men who share the same genealogical level, that is, one which consists of men who are all of the generation of fathers and uncles and are followed by their sons and nephews who form the succeeding generation. An uncle and nephew cannot ever be of the same *genealogical* generation. A shifting *social* generation consists of men who are grouped, in effect, into clusters of similar age, status, etc. Uncles and nephews may be members of the same shifting social generation. In our own culture social generations are supposedly separated by a 'gap'. In many generation-systems the larger groupings are genealogical generations and the age-groups into which they are internally segmented are narrow span shifting social generations.

Rites of passage serve, as Van Gennep pointed out, to mark the passage of time and passing through of boundaries. They remove men from one category (or generation or set, or grade or stage in the life-cycle), pass them through a period of transition, and incorporate them into a new category. Sets seek to diminish differences between members by stressing their equality and by endeavouring to keep the social development of members in line by exaggerating the differences between sets. Age-systems thereby seek to arrest time for a period – so that it moves forward in jerks. The period between sets (or generations or grades) which are marked by transition rites, are periods of liminality, or moments out of time, which allow time to catch up with events or events with time. In extreme instances, such as Boran in the condition of *raaba*, during which men are not allowed to keep their offspring,[5] men are suspended in that one sense out of social life and time altogether. The hands of the clock which had been held back are moved forward again when they leave that condition. Van Gennep's comment on sacredness applies to time also: it 'is not absolute; it is brought into play by the nature of particular situations' (1960: p12).

Sometimes the sorts of discrepancies we have indicated above confuse the rules so that sub-rules are created to cope with them; at other times they merely cause uneasy anomalies which are dealt with by the use of social tact or simply endured as, for example, among the Nandi (Huntingford 1953: 73). But not only may men be born out of the time sequence of the system, as it were, which is usually called under-ageing or over-ageing, but their other social positions within the family or sibling group, or as affines, or as property holders, or as managers may conflict with their age or generation status. In brief, it is an example of the standard conflict between biological and sociological categories, or nature and culture. Age-systems which posit regularity must adapt their rules deliberatively, or develop secondary rules which can regulate for anomalies in terms of the system itself, or adapt the rules through an accumulation of ad hoc decisions taken to deal with anomalies as they appear. If they do not cultural rules will be burst by rampant nature. Indeed, some peoples, such as the Boran and Guji (Baxter and Almagor in press) in practise and over time, combine the three modes of dealing with the problem.

It is reasonable, therefore, to anticipate a discrepancy between expressed rules, which are based on idealised past experience, and contemporary practise. Any system of rules assumes an underlying set of general principles embedded in a system of thought, but men frequently endeavour to interpret, even to manipulate, rules and principles to their own advantage. Because men are members of society and not only members of an age-system, in order to understand the rules of any age-system it is necessary to examine the rules in action, as it were; that is in situations in which men are having to reconcile their age-set relationships with a range of other social relationships. Apparent breaches of, or contradictions or discrepancies in, the rules may then become explicable.

Ranks, titles, insignia and privileges are frequently accorded to members of sets by virtue of their membership. Similarly privileges and rights, such as permission to drink beer, or the right to carry arms, frequently mark the progress of sets and distinguish set from set. The right to marry and procreate though is often much more than such a privilege, in that it includes the hope and possibility of producing sons who will, in turn, become members of a later set or later sets. Marriage therefore is an act which may have consequences for the continuance and mechanics of the age-organisation itself so, almost invariably, set systems have rules which attempt to regulate the procreation of legitimate children. Quite specific political, military, legal and ritual responsibilities are often vested in sets on behalf of the community as, for example, those of Samburu fire-stick elders. But a striking feature of sets is that, though they may influence the use of resources and flow of labour, they neither own nor control stock nor any other means of material production. They do not even have the vestigial or residual rights sometimes said to reside ultimately in clans or lineages. At the most, sets, as sets, only own things which economically are trivia, such as smoking pipes, songs, drums or rights in club houses or meeting places.

   Social relationships which are neither embedded in property relationships, nor run contiguously with them need very, very strong sentiment indeed to maintain them. One of the few generalisations we can make about pastoral societies is that social relationships run close to stock-relationships and that stock have the quality of creating and transmitting social relationships. Relationships which require durability and resilience require rein-forcement by property sharing or property exchanging. Among the pastoral peoples of East Africa tools and stock are owned by individuals or families; improved water is usually owned by extended families or some group intermediate between family and tribe (only rarely and recently, as in parts of Somalia, by individuals); and grazing and unimproved water (both of which are God's) are open to responsible exploitation by all members of the largest political unit. Rights of ownership in, and access to, cultivable land vary, but we can think of no instance in which they are vested in sets,[6] though (as among Dassanetch) shared set membership may be used by one individual as sentimental or moral reinforcement of a claim he makes through another individual. Reports of incidents in which young men have had to filch stock from stock-owners in order to fulfil an obligation to entertain members of their set abound in the literature. So, also, do reports of elders who withold stock from juniors who wish to entertain their age-mates. But these appeals for stock are made, for example, by a son to his father and not by a member of a junior set to a member of a senior set. Set rituals often require the slaughter of many animals, indeed set ceremonies may be a major occasion of slaughter, as among Boran and Dassanetch, but the animals are contributed by family herds and their donation requires family approval.

Rights in herds rest in families; sets do not own herds. Even the stock which warrior-sets may acquire on raids, with the exception of the few used for immediate celebratory feasting, are distributed to individuals and absorbed into the family herds of individual members. Among the Boran a warrior who distinguishes himself and brings honour to his age-set (*hariiya*) by cutting off the testicles of an enemy, can only earn acclaim from his age-mates similar to that which is accorded to him by all men and women. For material reward he must go to the cow pen of his mother's brother and claim a heifer by attaching the trophy like a pendant to the beast's horns. This dependence on kin rather than sets or age-mates for gifts of stock seems to apply in mixed farming economies and in centralised states also. Age-regiments, for example, may even be mobilised to labour for the chief or their own support when they are not needed militarily, but for cattle to marry with they must look for family help or chiefly patronage. In Rwanda, for example, the chief distributed cattle captured by age-companies (*i-torero*) to members as his clients or stored them in the army herd which, in the end, also made clients for him (Maquet 1954: 130–7). Opinion and community action may be mobilised by sets and sets may have a moral power, but sets cannot help a man with marriage cattle nor in building up his herd. Family elders control the flow of stock and hence the marriages of their juniors.

Everything combines against sets having control, even in marginal ways, over such a crucial resource as stock. When a set is junior and its members are young and active their very youth, and hence irresponsibility, rules them out and, as they mature, their domestic and familial obligations and commitments demand all their energies. The ritual authority of elders waxes as their domestic and economic statuses are enlarged and their family and herd both increase. The extremely old who have relinquished, or been deprived of, the control of economic resources, that is stock, may be listened to but their words pass in through one ear and out the other. The Samburu age-system serves 'to retain power in the hands of the older men' (Spencer 1967: 140) because the old men control the stock, however dependent they may be on moran labour. Moran own nothing and are dependent on their family seniors for everything from their daily milk to the chance of, in time, becoming elders with homesteads of their own; just as they were harangued by their fathers they will need to harangue, in their turn, their own disgruntled sons.

Carefree bachelors can share what milk they can milk in the bush for themselves or what food they can scrounge from their mothers. Most food is controlled by women. Married men are fed by their wives and in that respect are dependent on them. Men may 'own' all the stock but women control the milking and the milk pots. Men may 'own' the fields but once grain is in the granary then it is controlled by the woman whose granary it is. Men do not help themselves out of their wives' milk pots or granaries. Once food has passed into a woman's care it is socialised and domesticated: it ceases to be either a natural product or one of which men dispose. (Meat is subject to different rules – only men slaughter or sacrifice, hence the stress in set-ritual on meat feasts.) A man can ask his wife to pour milk or cook porridge for his age-mates, but he cannot make her do so, nor can he control her demeanour nor make her appear to be truly welcoming. If a wife wants to keep back the food for her family, or even if she just begrudges it to her husband's age-mates, she can make them feel uncomfortable so that they do not call again to share food as age-mates should. (A wife can deal similarly, if she wishes, with her husband's age-mates who presume too far on the wife-sharing of age-mates.) Once a man is married he perforce relinquishes those considerable parts of set activity which are only suitable for bachelors. These same parts, however, as we noted of the Vice-Lords, can be features of gangs or informal youth groups or clubs as much as they can be of sets.

Indeed, we suggest, that it is because women are entangled in domestic cares much earlier and from the start much more tightly than are men, because they are usually married around puberty, that there are no age-systems for women. The transitions from girl, to betrothable maiden, to wife, to mother and to post-menarche old woman may, or may not, be much more dramatically marked than the equivalent stages are for men,[7] but the ceremonies mark individual status changes, of which a number for convenience occur together, rather than group changes (Paulme 1960 and 1971). There are groupings of women in which social age is a recruitment factor, such as the Dassanetch group of local girls *kob* or the Arssi *atete* which is a localised congregation of matrons (Baxter 1976); but, sets of women as part of a system of such sets, do not occur. Women are usually affiliated to the sets of their brothers' or husbands' for the regulation of marriage, placement of their children, etc.

Moreover the efficient management of a herd requires the

assistance of a wife and children. By the cultural definition of the division of labour a man cannot manage a herd on his own and any-one who attempted to do so would become a laughing stock. This paradox that a man must be a husband before he is a full man and must depend on a wife to be independent is, of course, very general and not specific to pastoral societies or those with age-sets. But, that dependence conflicts with the mutual dependence of male on male, which is central to setting, and directs men's practical energies to those on whom they depend for food and care and their posterity. As Monica Wilson noted in her classic study, even among the Nyakyusa who reside in villages of age-mates, 'the cultivation of fields requires the co-operation of a wife. Bachelors continue to eat their meals at their parents' village' (1951: 44). Sets may influence the direction in which a spouse is sought, they may limit choices and may delay marriage, but they cannot provide bridewealth, nor food, nor a herd which is the source of life, enduring relationships and a man's proper pride.

What is striking about age-systems is that men continue to be members of sets despite their increasing involvement in other social ties which must pull against set ties. Members may not be very en-thusiastic and active but they remain members and cannot, like members of a rural Welsh youth group, drop out 'inconspicuously' when they marry or sink into confirmed bachelorhood (Rees 1961 and Peters 1972: 110).[8] What varies greatly are: (i) the length of time for which a set continues to exist after its inception; (ii) the amount of activity which sets maintain over time; (iii) the degree of constraint they continue to maintain over members; (iv) the extent to which set activities are held at exclusive sites or are held in home-steads and villages. If activities are held in homesteads and villages and do not exclude families and neighbours, which frequently happens as sets advance through time and their members age, then sets are, in part at least, brought into the domestic and neighbourly domains. Separation from the homely village may be appropriate for bachelor warriors but not for elders whose main social roles and activities lie in the family and neighbourhood.

Because sets and age-grading need to be compatible, and sets become manifest agents of age-grades it follows, and is also stated by the folk, that members of a set should progress in step through the life-cycle, ensuring thereby that the passage of time and ageing are harmonised. Indeed a common folk explanation for the presence of sets is that they ensure that men of similar age and/or generation move through life in time together, which is rather like saying that the rules of incest exist to prevent men copulating with their mothers. Nevertheless, though the name of a set of Maasai or Samburu moran or of Boran age-mates continues to endure a set just seems to fade away as an active body; as they assume the cards thrust on them by their families, active members ooze away. (This characteristic, of course, they share with many gangs, sports clubs, etc..) Family exigencies, we suggest, overcome age-set loyalties.[9] If his senior agnates die a man has stock responsibilities thrust on him early, and needs must settle down to social elderhood and become a homestead head, even if by age, temperament and age-set rules he should be living it up as a member of a bachelor set. Of course most men do stock work appropriate to their age and status and hence work which is appropriate to their set. So men in junior sets are likely to be found in the wild performing the roughest herding and most onerous watering whereas herd management, which is considered suitable work for elders, is likely to be carried out by men in senior sets. But a careful reading of the literature shows that these associations hold only in so far as age-suitability for the task, age-grading and set rules fit in with the labour requirements of the family herd and the need to fill essential familial roles. Family bonds and loyalties, even for the enthusiastic initiates in the most recently formed set, override set bonds and loyalties. Members of a family should help each other without strictly reckoning cost even more than age-mates should, and a family feels dishonour and shame brought on it by a member even more than does a set. Baxter saw a Rendille youth have an epileptic fit as the knife of circumcision was about to nick him. His age-mates, who had just proudly endured the cutting, were outraged and carried the afflicted youth out of the ring and belaboured him while, from a distance, the women jeered. The age-mates returned and carried on, they could brazen out the incident, but the family of the youth crept away ashamedly and hid themselves.

A family will usually put up with a deal of inconvenience and expense to enable one of its members to enjoy set activities and celebrations; but, when there is a conflict, vital family needs must override set-rules and obligations. Just as an age-system must bend to accommodate men who are born out of sequence with their generation-set, or with the age-set to which they have been allocated by the alternate generation rule, it must also accommodate to family needs by having secondary rules or ignoring or glossing over breaches of rules. Indeed, as we have suggested, it is the control that elders have over stock, wives and management decisions which underlie the gerontocratic control which has been remarked

as a feature of so many East African pastoral societies.[10] It is
gerontocracy which encourages age-setting, rather than age-setting
which encourages gerontocracy: age-set rituals provide a platform
from which the gerontocrats (however young in years) can exercise
their power and harangue the youngsters (however old in years)
who are encapsulated in a junior set. They must act thus, not just
because they are older, or of a senior set, or have accumulated
mystical powers which makes their curse feared, but because they
are 'the bulls', 'the father of herds', that is the owners of the
primary resource.

That sets do not control vital productive resources does not, of
course, mean that sets may not constrain the behaviour of members
across an extensive range of activities; though many of the constraints may derive from an individual's stage in the life-cycle as
much as from his set membership. Most obviously where sets are
the basis of recruitment to military units, set membership may
affect an individual's chances of life and death. Also, in summary
an individual's position in a set, and the position of his set in a
system of sets, may influence his access to one or several of the
following; social privileges, marginal economic resources, choice
of wife and hence affines, political office and authority, ritual
office and general access to ritual benefits (especially blessings)
which can affect his whole well-being. Further, and what can be
extremely important, a man's age-mates may be not only a source
of congenial sociability and moral support, a sort of combination
of claque and club, but also, as among the Arusha, a body of
practical backers in dispute cases (Gulliver 1963).

Certain consequences follow from the simple fact that relationships between members of sets are not mediated by shared rights in
property, nor by property transactions of value made between them.
(Gifts such as bracelets or stock bells, such as young herders exchange, may have emotional significance for the givers but they are
insubstantial, like the beads young lovers exchange compared with
the bridewealth their elders negotiate.)[11] A man who seeks to
extend a set tie into an enduring and useful relationship is likely to
convert it into a stock associateship or affinity, because it is
difficult for relationships to flourish if men cannot extend them by
passing property along them.

Secondly, though men belong to a set throughout their lives,
moral compulsions and strong emotional bonding are associated with
initiation and with youth, as they were among the Vice-Lords, and
fade with maturity. Particularly, if they have shared harsh experiences

together at initiation, set members stress fraternity and mutual
obligation, even as far as allowing sexual access to each others wives.
Age-mates share responsibility for each others behaviour, and
should discipline their own backsliders. Disputes between age-mates
should be settled within the set. These injunctions are usually expressed most vociferously about and between members of junior
sets; that is, in those sets which are made up of young men who
have relatively few rights in stock, are likely to be bachelors, and
who are not responsible for managing the family herds. Sharing is
urged by and on those who are equal in their juniority and limited
access to those resources which differentiate men and who, in practise, have little to share but hardships and danger. This slight social
responsibility accords both with the casual bravery expected of
junior sets when they are called on to act militarily, and with the
common association of sets of recently initiated youngsters with the
bush and its wild beasts. As men mature they become patently less
equal in wealth, wives, influence, office and power; the responsibility
property brings divides as it socialises. The ideal of fraternity may
remain but it is eroded by cares and responsibilities. Spencer's
statement that it is a 'deep rooted Samburu ideal that each man
should have his own herd and ultimately be able to manage independently' (1965: 12), could be said of all pastoralists. Both a man's
interests in his family herd and his individual ambitions are opposed
to, and stronger than, the ideal of sharing all with age-mates. Young
Boran age-mates, for example, boast of their solidarity and prepared-
ness to stand together in battle, etc., but elders who are celebrating
Gaadamoji boast against each other about the martial exploits of
their youth and of the herds which, in their social maturity, so clearly
differentiate them. Fraternity becomes more a matter of 'words', and
less a matter of actions, as men and their sets are passed by time and
as the interests of members of senior sets merge.[12] We can recollect
no instances in the literature in which elders, representing the family
interests of their dependents, subordinate those interests to the ideal
of age-set equality and solidarity.

Thirdly, it is the limited rights in property and hence social
responsibilities of sets which, makes it permitted and even expected
that they will, as sets and not just as a gaggle of lads, act wildly to
the edge of delinquency at recognised times and in institutionalised
ways. Boran, for example, anticipate that newly inducted age-sets
and men in a generation-set who are in the condition of *raaba* will
act like wild bush animals, even if individual members do not
want to act so and look and feel silly while they do so. Samburu

moran are presumed to require constant harangues, and Karimojong juniors to need the threat of the elders' curse, to keep them in order.[13] This wildness seems to contrast with their parallel 'predisposition to obedience' to the will of the elders (Dyson-Hudson 1966: 188); but the role expected wildness and role expected obedience are different sides of the same coin. Members of junior sets, like undergraduates, are maintained in a state of suspended childhood, subdued by the hope that, so long as they only rampage in the ways expected by their elders, that they will, in due course and in turn, move into elderhood and responsibility themselves. It is very rare for elders to curse junior sets. Juniors may play up their seniors, but, in the end, they must be obedient because the elders have temporal control over all the productive assets and are backed by mystical sanctions such as curses.

Fourthly, the only general societal responsibilities usually entrusted to sets, other than ritual ones, are military or similar responsibilities such as, in states, collecting dues for the king. Even these are not restricted to sets in that when a settlement is attacked by surprise everyone turns out, even the women. Indeed, stories about demure old ladies who have turned into viragos to confront night raiders are commonplace. But martial activities generally, and stock-raiding in particular, are associated with sets and especially junior sets. This association with junior sets is appropriate because the members of junior sets have little to contribute but their lives and little to lose but those very lives which are not of much social value.

Since the tribal societies were colonised, control of force has passed out of local hands and into those of the colonial or post-colonial national governments. Traditionally, age-sets were often the formations which delivered the force and the age-system was 'the framework for the military organisation'. Among the Kipsigis the offensive military organisation was based on regiments which were organised provincially and the active part of which were 'members of the age-set in the grade of warriors'. The age system was a prominent structural feature and had military functions among all the Nandi-speaking peoples. (Evans-Pritchard: 1940a 69 and 75; Peristiany: 1939). But the association between age-sets and military organisation is not invariable: among the Turkana, for example, the age-set system 'provided the core of the primitive military organisation', whereas among the neighbouring Jie 'age-sets are not connected with military or political organisation' (Gulliver 1955: 11, 12). Where the age-system is involved in military activities sets operate as agents of force, not as the controllers of force. Sets as wielders of the force of society do so, in the last resort and even if rebelliously, as agents of the wider society. In states age-sets were likely to be converted into age-regiments and then, as among the Zulu, they 'belonged to the king alone' and did his bidding as his strong arm (Gluckman 1940: 31). Fifthly, then, age-systems could be the agents of force but, because they had no base in the property of their society nor control over its productive relationships, they could not be the disposers of that force. Even where, as among the Maasai, the voice of the elders seemed to speak through the senior set this was so; the age-system could only appear to be the political system, i.e. the controller of force, when there was national consensus. An example is the Maasai rebellion of 1918, when the Purko moran attacked a KAR camp to demonstrate their opposition to government schooling and the threat of conscription. The elders 'counselled the futility of resistance' to the government, but were ignored and the moran acted in conjunction with a *laibon* who emerged as a national charismatic leader.

A frequently reported custom which merits comment here is the one which permits access to (rather than sharing of) the wife of one member of a set by another; or, as it is perhaps more appropriately put, a rule which disallows adultery actions and payments between set members. Members of a set also protect its wives, that is its members' wives, from members of other sets. Such customs or rules clearly have benefits for sets as military formations. Cameraderie is essential between men who may depend on each other in battle. The maintenance of group morale and solidarity is important and quarrels over sexual rivalries are very likely between young men, so any custom which undervalues exclusive individual rights over a woman's sexuality and stresses group rights can have value for that group's solidarity. Such customs are not restricted to sets not to licentious soldiery, but outbreaks of practices such as gang rape are apposite to both (Huntingford 1953: 75 and innumerable war novels).

Such rules or customs seem to be stressed much more in respect of junior sets than of senior sets. That this should be so is appropriate for a number of reasons; all members of senior sets are likely to be married and may be polygamously so; promiscuity is not considered appropriate for members of senior sets; seniors sets are unlikely to be occupied in raiding, etc. As a set advances in seniority its members are more likely to be married, but while still only a few are married those few are anomalous in that they cease to be equal with their age-mates by the very fact of having a wife. This inequality is partially evened out by permitting sexual access to wives. When the majority of a set is married, then the anomaly ceases and the pressure is transferred to the bachelors to get a wife. A consequence is that age-mates prefer to keep their marriages in step. A man who marries too early, usually because his position in his family requires it, (if, for example, his own father is dead) may be providing sexual services for his age-mates for which they can claim no reciprocal satisfaction. Just because sexual access should be free to age-mates does not mean that fond young husbands enjoy honouring the rule. Baxter spent one depressing evening with a very dispirited new Boran husband whose wife was being properly hospitable to an age-mate.

The sixth point follows from the fifth; as age-systems do not control the use of force, sets are not formally constituted assemblies to which political powers are delegated. Sets do not compose rudimentary parliaments. Indeed sets seldom meet as a whole and, if they do, it is to perform rituals and not perform executive, administrative or legislative tasks.[14] We are not arguing that sets perform no political tasks, merely that if they do so, those tasks are ancillary. Sets are seized on, as it were, to perform the task simply because they are there. For example, among the Karimojong sets have a more than usual political importance, but Dyson-Hudson reports that, though the demonstrable *instrument* of political authority is the obedient membership of a sub-senior set', (1966: 155) the age-system is not the *source* of authority. Essentially the 'unity of an age-set is a conceptual unity in the minds of the Karimojong, not the observable unity of, say, a company on a drill square' (p. 174). Or, as Evans-Pritchard noted long ago, Nuer sets: 'have no administrative, juridical, or other specific political functions and the country is not handed over to their care . . . the age-set system ought not to be described as a military organisation' (Evans-Pritchard 1940b: 253). Again, he wrote: 'sets never act corporately' (1940: 259); that is they have no corporate structure, property or power, and: 'it is easy to conceive of the political system existing without an age-set organisation'. Gulliver has suggested that because there 'is no continuously operating system of public administration outside the ritual sphere' (1968: 130), age-systems have had an appearance of political effectiveness thrust on to them. The evidence we have from Oromo makes it clear that where age-systems have endured it is where they have been the vehicles of ritual which the actors have continued to regard as important; as Southall has indicated, age organisations are 'particularly compatible with elaborate symbolic identifications' (1970: 32).

Age systems, nevertheless, continue to have major political functions attributed to them in analysis, however ill-designed they are to perform them and because they lack corporate resources, however inappropriate political activities would be for them. Where age-systems occur in societies with non-centralised political systems they are especially likely to have political functions ascribed to them. This is the more likely when those societies also lack strong, localised descent groups, as they frequently do, because a strong descent group organisation and a strong age-group organisation tend to be incompatible. Age-systems, as it were, get political functions attributed to them just because they are conspicuous and other suitable institutions are not apparent. I would suggest that formal and informal general assemblies rather than sets perform such few political tasks as require performing. A residual ethnocentricity still makes it difficult, even for professional observers, to recognise that a society may rub along happily enough without institutions which are obviously political. Yet, everyone has got used to not finding obvious economic institutions. Even Evans-Pritchard felt bound to stress that Nuer age-sets did not have political tasks however hard you looked for them: as if that was a bit odd. We labour this point because, it seems to us, that the over attribution of political tasks to age-systems, as the primary institutions on which the maintenance of social order depends, has been a barrier to our understanding of them.

The key to the understanding of age-systems lies not so much in what practical societal functions they fulfil but in what benefit their ritual is perceived as conferring on individuals, groups and society. Age-systems create figurative representations of time and, to paraphrase Durkheim and Mauss, 'the classification of time reproduces the classification of men' (1963: 11). Just as the modes of animal classification used in each culture have an internal logical consistency but the modes vary from culture to culture so do classifications of time.

Age-systems give ageing a cultural stamp. In so far as age-systems allocate status to named segments of the population who share the same, culturally defined, segment of time, and that status incremented through time, age-systems are a device to make the cruel descent through life to decay appear as if it were an ascent to a superior, because senior, condition. They are a means of holding time past in a steady relation to time present and time future; a sign of the enduring past which endures through the present and into the future.

Footnotes

1. Most peoples also assume that in the past things were better; it is reported of the Ibo that 'deviations from the ideal are attributed to the actions of the Government' or similar extraneous agencies (Jones: 1962: 194).

2. Moran is a Maasai word which refers to younger unmarried men, up to the ages of thirty to thirty-five, who are in the warrior age-grade. The word has become part of the vocabulary of anthropology and therefore will not be italicised.

3. Set titles and offices or movement within a set cannot be 'bought' as in West African title societies. Societies such as Poro, though in effect obligatory, concerned with age-grading and involved in mystical and political activities are not internally age-setted.

4. Stewart 1972. Unfortunately Stewart's book (1977) was not available in time for reference to be made to it here.

5. See my essay in *Age, Generation and Time*. According to the logic of the rules of the Boran generation system *raaba* should be infant girls and hence incapable of becoming fathers. Their condition is marked by devices such as wearing their hair in the girls' style. In practise they may marry, but any children their wives bear are so anomalous and dangerous that, it is said, they must be thrown on a dung hill for the hyenas. In fact, the discarded infants are collected and brought up by the *waarta*, a caste-like group of hunters and smiths. *Raaba* are on the very forward time edge of their set, as it were, so that if they were allowed to rear up their children those children would be right out of time with their generation and their grand children would be even more so. The rule of 'infanticide' limits the misalignment between age and generation in that it prevents children being reared whose existence would imperil the generation system. Because, in folk theory they could not have been born they are treated as if they had not been. It follows that the rule keeps down the numbers of men who have to be in this onerous condition. *Raaba* may remain infants into their middle years and then move directly into elderhood, thereby missing out youth and young manhood altogether.

6. At first glance this does not seem to apply to the Nyakyusa who lived in age-villages on land allocated to them by members of the age-village of their fathers. But, as Monica Wilson makes clear (1951), the system only worked as long as land was plentiful. As soon as land became scarce, or took on economic value, the system collapsed. Moreover, the 'most valuable land of all ... that in old craters', was never redistributed, but was 'retained by an individual until his death and inherited by kinsmen' (174). 'The primary economic units in Nyakyusa society are the kinship groups – the elementary family, the cattle-owning lineage, and the group of cognates who co-operate in production and exchange many gifts, and among whom

cattle circulate' (44).

7. For example, Richards does not mention sets in her immaculately full analysis of puberty and nubility rites in *Chisungu* (1956) nor in her survey of socialisation and contemporary British anthropology (1967). Philip Mayer's stricture, in his Introduction to the A.S.A. survey of socialisation ((1967) that anthropologists have ignored age-systems in their role as 'the people's educational system', has some justice; but, sets are only sometimes, and secondarily and never exclusively, educational institutions.

    Similarly women do not have best-friends in the formal sense that men have, as the Bohannans noted of Tiv (1968: 73). Wives are too immersed in family responsibilities and have little time or property to invest in such relationships. As our folk saying has it 'men have friends, women have kin'.

8. Peters notes that: 'A cardinal feature of the youth group is that most of its members are not youths in terms of physical age' (115). Indeed the range of youths in the Llan group and that which covers moran seems to be much the same. Youths attach themselves to the group in latish adolescence and drop out between thirty and thirty-five, by which time have either married or given up hope of marriage. (From adolescence to as old as thirty-five seems a frequent age-clustering as, for example, in Wolof 'Companies' (*kompins*).) Llan youths like moran, are not trusted with 'the burdensome responsibilities of (farm) management'; the small sums of money they have they 'fritter away . . . on mineral waters and sweets' which they share. Vice-Lords fritter their money on wine which they share from the same bottle. Youths, moran and Vice-Lords all depend for their primary subsistence on their seniors and prefer to consume their titbits and extras in or by the shop, in the bush or in the street, i.e. they all prefer to meet in neutral places not domestic places. Peters argues that the youth group 'can function success-fully only if they have the backing of the adult population' (115). This generalisation also applies to junior sets; indeed in Samburu or Boran, for example, they need the specific blessings of their seniors; but a youth group or a gang is not a set. Gangs may be condoned by their elders and youth group may even be praised but, unlike sets, they are not institutionalised and approved (though aspects of members' behaviour may not be) and membership is not obligatory.

    Gulliver (1963: 40) points out that the large majority of Arusha *murran* were married and pre-occupied with consolidating their households. They had adopted the role of junior elders in daily life.

9. Eisenstadt's broad hypothesis B) does not appear to tally precisely. He writes: 'Age-homogenous groups . . . tend to arise in societies in which the family or kinship unit cannot ensure, or even impedes, the attainment of full social status by its members' (1956: 54). We suggest rather that while family and set may seem to be in conflict, as do contiguous generations in the family, sets do not foster an individual's social development in spite of the family.

10. Bonte (1974) starts from an analysis of productive relationships and, as far as we can understand it, his argument on the power of elders does not

controvert our own.

11. Such exchanges do not require an age-system. Jean Buxton noted that the Mandari had very recently started 'bead-sets-*rem*-groups of boys who were initiates together wear waist bands of coloured beads . . . bead-sets are related to courtship and have no political significance.' Buxton 1958.

12. Cf. L. Bohannan's comments on Tiv sets: 'The age-sets of very old men merge together, but such old men seldom have reason to turn to the age-set' (1958: 52 fn) and P. Bohannan writes 'After its members reach the age of about fifty, their age-set becomes very little more than a sentimental association'. (1965: 536).

13. Dyson-Hudson (1966: 183). On the same page the author notes he has never witnessed such a cursing; we can recollect no-one who has reported one.

14. Even among the Arusha, whom Mair takes as the best described example of a society in which age-sets are important, 'An age-set never acts as a unit except in promotion rituals' (1974: 140). Ruel writes similarly that Kuria generation classes 'act as clearly defined social groups' only 'on ritual occasions' (1962—28).

References

Baxter, P.T.W. (1976). An Arssi Women's Neighbourhood Festival: *Atete*. Paper presented to the First World Congress on Cushitic Languages and Cultures. Paris. In press.

Baxter, P.T.W. and Almagor, U. (eds.). Age, Generation and Time: some features of East African Age Organisation. C. Hurst, London. In press.

Bohannan, Laura. (1958). Political Aspects of Tiv Social Organisation, *in* "Tribes without Rulers" (eds. John Middleton and David Tait). Routledge and Kegan Paul, London.

Bohannan, Paul. (1965). The Tiv of Nigeria, *in* "Peoples of Africa" (ed. J.L. Gibbs). Holt, Rinehart and Winston, New York.

Bohannan, Paul and Laura. (1968). Tiv Economy. Longmans, London.

Bonte, Pierre. (1974). Etudes sur les Societes de Pasteurs Nomades II. Organisation economique et sociale des pasteurs d'afrique Orientale. Centre d'Etudes et de Recherches Marxistes, Paris.

Bonte, Pierre. (1975). Cattle for God: An Attempt at a Marxist Analysis of the Religion of East African Herdsmen. *Social Compass*, **XXII**, 3–4, 381–396.

Buxton, Jean. (1958). The Mandari of the Southern Sudan, *in* "Tribes without Rulers" (eds. John Middleton and David Tait). Routledge and Kegan Paul, London.

Durkheim, E. and Mauss, M. (1963). Primitive Classification. Cohen and West, London.

Dyson-Hudson, Neville. (1966). Karimojong Politics. Clarendon Press, Oxford.

Eisenstadt, S.N. (1956). From Generation to Generation: Age Groups and Social Structure. Routledge and Kegan Paul, London.

Evans-Pritchard, E.E. (1940a). Political Structure of Nandi-Speaking Peoples of Kenya, *Africa* (1940b). Reprinted 1965 *in* "The Position of Women in

Primitive Societies and other Essays in Social Anthropology" (ed. E.E. Evans-Pritchard). Faber and Faber, London.

Evans-Pritchard, E.E. (1940b). The Nuer. Clarendon Press, Oxford.

Gennep, Arnold van. (1960). Les Rites de Passage, Emil Nourry, Paris (1909). Translated by Monika B. Vixedom and Gabrielle L. Caffee as Rites of Passage, Routledge and Kegan Paul, London.

Gluckman, Max. (1940). The Kingdom of the Zulu of South Africa, *in* "African Political Systems" (eds. M. Fortes and E.E. Evans-Pritchard). O.U.P. for I.A.I., London.

Gulliver, P.H. (1955). The Family Herds. Routledge and Kegan Paul, London.

Gulliver, P.H. (1958). The Turkana age organisation, *American Anthropologist*, **60**, 900–922.

Gulliver, P.H. (1963). Social Control in an African Society: A Study of the Arusha, Agricultural Masai of northern Tanganyika. Routledge and Kegan Paul, London.

Gulliver, P.H. (1968). Age Differentiation, *in* "International Encyclopedia of the Social Sciences", Vol. I, 157–162. Macmillan and Free Press, New York.

Huntingford, G.W.B. (1953). The Nandi of Kenya. Routledge and Kegan Paul, London.

Jones. G.I. (1962). The Age Organisation, with Special Reference to the Cross River and north-eastern Ibo, *Journal of the Royal Anthropological Institute*, **92**, 191–211.

Keiser, R. Lincoln. (1969). The Vice Lords: Warriors of the Streets. Holt, Rinehart and Winston, New York.

Kuper, Hilda. (1963). The Swazi: A South African Kingdom, Rinehart and Winston, New York.

Legesse, Asmaron. (1973). Gada: Three Approaches to the Study of African Society. Free Press, New York; Collier-Macmillan, London.

Levi-Strauss, Claud. (1953). Social Structure Chapter XV, 277–323 of his "Structural Anthropology". Basic Books, New York and London. Reprinted with some modifications from "Anthropology Today" (ed. A.L. Kroeber). Chicago.

Mair, Lucy. (1974). African Societies. Cambridge University Press, Cambridge.

Maquet, Jacques J. (1954). Le Systeme des Relations sociales dans le Ruanda Ancien. Musee Royal du Congo Belge, Tervuren, 1954. Translated as The Premise of Inequality in Ruanda. O.U.P. for I.A.I., London.

Mayer, Philip. (1967). Introduction to "Socialisation: The Approach from Anthropology" (ed. Philip Mayer). Tavistock, London.

Paulme, Denise (ed.). (1960). Femmes d'Afrique Noire. Mouton, Paris and The Hague. (See especially the essays: 'Situation de·la Femme dans une societe Pastorale' by Marguerite Dupire and 'Le Role de la Femme dans l'organisation Politique des societes Africaines' by Annie Lebeuf.)

Paulme, Denise (1971). Classes et associations d'age en Afrique de Ouest. Plon, Paris.

Peristiany, J.G. (1939). The Social Institutions of the Kipsigis. Routledge, London.

Peters, E. Lloyd. (1972). Aspects of the control of moral ambiguities: a

comparative analysis of two culturally disparate modes of social control, *in*
"The Allocation of Responsibility" (ed. Max Gluckman). M.U.P., Manchester.

Rees, A. (1961). Life in a Welsh Countryside. University of Wales Press,
Cardiff.

Richards, A.I. (1956). Chisungu. Faber and Faber, London.

Richards, A.I. (1967). Socialisation and Contemporary British Anthropology, *in*
"Socialisation: The Approach from Anthropology" (ed. Philip Mayer).
Tavistock, London.

Ruel, M.J. (1962). Kuria Generation Classes, *Africa*, **XXXII**, 14–37.

Spencer, Paul. (1965). The Samburu. Routledge and Kegan Paul, London.

Spencer, Paul. (1967). The Function of Ritual in the Socialisation of Samburu
Moran, *in* "Socialisation the Approach from Anthropology" (ed. Philip
Mayer). A.S.A. Monographs 8. Tavistock Publications, London.

Stewart, Frank H. (1972). Fundamentals of Age Set Systems. Unpublished
D. Phil. thesis, University of Oxford.

Stewart, Frank H. (1977). Fundamentals of Age Group Systems. Academic Press,
London.

Southall, Aidan. (1970). Rank and Stratification among the Alur and other
Nilotic Peoples, *in* "Social Stratification in Africa" (ed. Tuden, A. and
Piotnicov, L.). Free Press, New York.

Wilson, Monica. (1951). Good Company: A Study of Nyakyusa Age-Villages.
O.U.P. for I.A.I., London.

NOTES ON CONTRIBUTORS

Abrahams, R.G. Born 1934, England. Educated: Cambridge, B.A. then Ph.D. 1962.
Junior Research Fellow, East African Institute of Social Research, 1957–60; University College London, Research Assistant, 1961–62; University of Cambridge, Assistant Lecturer, 1963–67; Lecturer, 1967.
Chief Publications: 'Succession to the chiefship in Northern Unyamwezi' in *Succession to High Office* (ed. J. Goody) 1966. *The Political Organisation of Unyamwezi* 1967 and various papers on the Nyamwezi and Labwor of Uganda.

Almagor, U. Born 1934, Israel. Educated: The Hebrew University, B.A. and M.A.; Manchester University, Ph.D. 1972; Simon Research Fellow, Manchester University, 1974–75; Lecturer, Hebrew University of Jerusalem, 1971–1977; Senior Lecturer, 1977–
Chief Publications: *Pastoral Partners: Affinity and Bond Partnerships among the Dassanetch of S.W. Ethiopia*, Manchester University Press, 1978. ed. with P. Baxter *Age, Generation and Time*; Hurst forthcoming.

Baxter, P.T.W. Born 1925, England. Educated: Cambridge, B.A.; Oxford, B.Litt. 1951, D.Phil. 1954.
Senior Research Fellow, East African Institute of Social Research, 1954–56 University of Ghana, Lecturer, 1956–62; University College Swansea, Lecturer in Social Administration, 1962–64; University of Manchester, Lecturer, 1964–
Chief Publications: *The Azande and Related Peoples*, Ethnographic Survey of Africa 1953; *Social Organisation of the Boran of N. Kenya*; ed. with U. Almagor: *Age, Generation and Time*. Hurst forthcoming; various papers on the Oromo-speaking peoples.

Harris, O. Born 1948, England. Educated: Oxford University, B.A.; now candidate for the Ph.D. London School of Economics.
Part-time Lecturer, University of Sussex, 1975–76; temporary Lecturer in Social Anthropology, University of Kent, 1977–
Chief Publications: co-author, 'Conceptualising Women' in *Critique of Anthropology*, 1977; "Parentesco y la economia vertical en al ayllu laymi" in

Avances, revista de estudios socio-historicos   La Paz, 1978.

Hugh-Jones, C. Born 1943, England. Educated: London School of Economics, B.Sc.; Cambridge, Ph.D. 1978.
Visiting Lecturer, Institute of Social Anthropology, Oxford, 1978; Research Fellow, New Hall, Cambridge, 1978–

La Fontaine, J.S. Born 1931, Kenya. Educated: Cambridge, B.A. then Ph.D. 1958.
Part-time Lecturer, University of Durham (at Newcastle), 1960–61; Chargée de Cours Université de Lovanium, Kinshasa, Zaire, 1962–63; Lecturer, Birkbeck College, 1965–68; Reader, London School of Economics, 1968–78; Professor, 1978–
    Chief Publications: The Gisu of Uganda, Ethnographic Survey of Africa, 1959; *City Politics: Leopoldville 1962–3*, 1970; ed. *The Interpretation of Ritual* 1972 and various papers on the Gisu of Uganda and aspects of urban life in Zaire.

Sansom, B. Born 1938, South Africa. Educated: University of the Witwatersrand, B.A. 1961; Manchester University, Ph.D. 1973.
Lecturer in Social Anthropology, University of Manchester, 1965–75; Research Fellow, Australian Institute of Aboriginal Studies, 1975–77; Professor of Urban Anthropology, University of Western Australia, 1977–
    Chief Publications: 'A signal transaction and its currency' in *Transaction and Meaning* (ed. B. Kapferer) 1976; Words and Happenings (in press) and other papers.

Schildkrout, E. Born 1941, New York. Educated: Sarah Lawrence College, B.A.; Cambridge University, M.A., Ph.D.
Assistant Professor of Anthropology, University of Illinois, 1970–72; Visiting Assistant Professor, McGill University, 1972–73; Assistant Curator of African Ethnology, American Museum of Natural History, 1973–
    Chief Publications: 'Strangers and Local Government in Kumasi', *Journal of Modern African Studies* 1970; 'Government and Chiefs in Kumasi' in Crowder and Okime (eds.) *West African Chiefs: Their changing Role and Status under Colonial Rule and Independence.*

INDEX